What They're Saying About *Finding Our Way to God*

In *Finding Our Way to God*, Fr. Dennis Billy pragmatically reveals how to gauge spiritual growth and bridge the gap between how we live today and how to live the good life of Christ, the source of all goodness. This work of love is a delight and an elixir for the heart. Clergy, religious, spiritual directors, pastoral counselors and adult faith formation ministers will find a treasure map to this good life that abounds with the fruits and gifts of the Spirit.
   —**Deacon James E. Bogdan, MS**, St. Joseph Parish, Downingtown, PA

An important work for current times! Solidly anchored in Alphonsian spirituality and moral theology, Fr. Dennis Billy's book, like a triptych, unfolds to reveal how it is truly Catholic, yet easily adapted to embrace ecumenical and interfaith settings of spiritual direction. Through his comprehensive treatment of the scope and skills required for spiritual direction; overview of the moral life; review of virtues, gifts, and fruits of the Holy Spirit, *Finding Our Way to God* is an excellent renewal resource for veteran spiritual directors, and it's a handbook for beginning spiritual directors and those without formal training in direction whom the Holy Spirit has chosen to work with those in need. Readers will discover how the common tasks of spiritual direction and the moral life come into focus and merge.
   —**Bonnie Lemelle Abadie**, director-theological field education, Oblate School of Theology, San Antonio, TX

As a son of St. Alphonsus, Fr. Dennis Billy continues Alphonsus' mission to lead others to a deeper, more intimate relationship with God. Readers of *Finding Our Way to God* will find it informational, inspiring, practical, pastoral, and helpful, whether they are spiritual directors, people currently in spiritual direction, or those curious about what it involves and whether they might benefit from it.
   —**Fr. Kevin O'Neil, CSsR**, staff member at the San Alfonso Retreat Center, Long Branch, NJ; and coauthor of *The Essential Moral Handbook* and numerous books and articles.

Finding Our Way to God

Finding Our Way to God

SPIRITUAL DIRECTION *and the* MORAL LIFE

IN THE SPIRIT OF ST. ALPHONSUS DE LIGUORI

Dennis J. Billy, CSsR

Liguori

Imprimi Potest: Stephen T. Rehrauer, CSsR, Provincial
Denver Province, the Redemptorists

Published by Liguori Publications
Liguori, Missouri
Liguori.org

Copyright © 2018 Dennis J. Billy

Scripture citations are taken from the *New Revised Standard Version Bible*, copyright 1989, Division of Christian Education of the National Council of the Churches of Christ in the United States of America. Used by permission. All rights reserved.

Library of Congress Cataloging-in-Publication Data
Names: Billy, Dennis Joseph, author.
Title: Finding our way to God : spiritual direction and the moral life / Dennis J. Billy, CSsR.
Description: First Edition. | Liguori : Liguori Publications, 2018. | Includes bibliographical references.
Identifiers: LCCN 2018012611 | ISBN 9780764828034
Subjects: LCSH: Spiritual direction—Catholic Church. | Liguori, Alphonsus Maria de', Saint, 1696-1787. | Contemplation. | Christian ethics—Catholic authors.
Classification: LCC BX2350.7 .B43 2018 | DDC 253.5/3—dc23
LC record available at https://lccn.loc.gov/2018012611

All rights reserved. No part of this publication may be reproduced, stored in a retrieval system, or transmitted in any form or by any means—electronic, mechanical, photocopy, recording, or any other—except for brief quotations in printed reviews, without the prior permission of the publisher.

Liguori Publications, a nonprofit corporation, is an apostolate of the Redemptorists. To learn more about the Redemptorists, visit Redemptorists.com.

Cover and interior design: Wendy Barnes
Cover Image: Shutterstock

Printed in the United States of America
22 21 20 19 18 / 5 4 3 2 1
First Edition

*To the faculty, staff, alumni, and students
of the Alphonsian Academy in Rome*

*But the wisdom from above is first pure, then peaceable, gentle,
willing to yield, full of mercy and good fruits,
without a trace of partiality or hypocrisy.
And a harvest of righteousness is sown in peace
for those who make peace.*
JAMES 3:17–18

*My Jesus, my Jesus, I desire nothing of you but yourself.
Now that you have drawn me to your love, I leave all,
I renounce all, and I bind myself to you.
You alone are sufficient for me.*
ST. ALPHONSUS DE LIGUORI

Contents

FOREWORD	xiii
PREFACE	xvii
ACKNOWLEDGMENTS	xix

Introduction — 1

Part One
Moorings in Spiritual Direction — 7

CHAPTER ONE
Spiritual Direction — 9

CHAPTER TWO
Relationships — 13

CHAPTER THREE
Listening — 25

CHAPTER FOUR
Prayer — 33

Part Two
An Alphonsian Approach to Spiritual Direction — 41

CHAPTER FIVE
The Spiritual Legacy of St. Alphonsus de Liguori — 43

CHAPTER SIX
Interpreting St. Alphonsus Today — 53

CHAPTER SEVEN
An Alphonsian Model of Spiritual Direction — 61

CHAPTER EIGHT
The Qualities of an Alphonsian Director — 69

Part Three
Spiritual Direction and the Moral Life — 79

CHAPTER NINE
The Moral Dimensions of Prayer — 81

CHAPTER TEN
The Spiritual Journey — 91

CHAPTER ELEVEN
The Way of Virtue — 101

CHAPTER TWELVE
The Gifts of the Spirit — 115

CHAPTER THIRTEEN
Attending to the Virtues and Gifts in Spiritual Direction — 127

Part Four
Dialoguing With Other Traditions — 137

CHAPTER FOURTEEN
An Open View of Spirituality — 139

CHAPTER FIFTEEN
Natural Law and Interspirituality — 149

CHAPTER SIXTEEN
Embracing One's Tradition — 161

CHAPTER SEVENTEEN
A Suggested Template — 175

CHAPTER EIGHTEEN
Living in the Gap — 183

Conclusion — 193

Appendices and Resources — 195

APPENDIX A
Excerpts from the Writings of St. Alphonsus de Liguori — 197

APPENDIX B
Internet Resources on the Moral Life — 225

NOTES — 233

SUGGESTED READINGS — 249

Foreword

Saint Alphonsus de Liguori, the founder of the Redemptorist missionary congregation and an extended apostolic family, dedicated his life to the care of souls. Everything he did—from his heartfelt preaching and intense missionary activity to his balanced confessional practice and gentle direction of souls, from his vast theological writings and moving poetry to his inspirational music and engaging artwork, and, most especially, to his deep life of prayer and pious devotion—was done out of an intense desire to help people find their way to God. A man of his times, through his personal encounter with Jesus Christ, his beloved Redeemer, Alphonsus tapped into the perennial values of the gospel message and made them come alive for the people of his day.

ST. ALPHONSUS DE LIGUORI

Alphonsus' pastoral zeal and spiritual insight into the love of Jesus Christ led him to focus on one of Christianity's most basic principles: that we find our way to God by recognizing that God has anticipated our deepest yearnings and already found his way to us. We see this happening when we look at life through the eyes of faith and become serious about the life of prayer. Authentic prayer presupposes faith and helps us to find our way to God. "We walk by faith, not by sight," the Apostle Paul reminds us (2 Corinthians 5:7). Alphonsus referred to prayer as "the great means of salvation," precisely because it immersed us through faith in the great narrative of Christ's redemptive journey.

Crib. Cross. Sacrament. Mary. These four pillars of Alphonsus' gospel spirituality testify to God's impassioned, "crazy love" for humanity, which led him to enter our world, give himself completely, to the point of dying for us, become nourishment for us, and remain a lasting source of hope. The motto he gave to his missionary family, "*Copiosa apud eum redemptio*" ("With him is great power to redeem" Psalm 130:7), reminds us that the fullness of life comes in and through the person of Jesus Christ, who is "the way, and the truth, and the life" (John 14:6).

Saint John Paul II once called Alphonsus "a gigantic figure, not only in the history of the Church but for the whole of humanity as well." He also referred to him as "the teacher of the Catholic soul of the West" and claimed that he "did for Catholicism that which Augustine accomplished in ancient times." These words remind us of the great impact of Alphonsus' moral and spiritual writings on Catholic believers and that his missionary zeal and spiritual legacy continue to influence them to this day.

As with any historical figure, however, Alphonsus' insights into the Christian moral and spiritual life need to be broken open, chewed, digested, and interpreted in the light of the problems and circumstances facing today's believers. Otherwise, his thought, rooted as it is in the distant societal and cultural milieu of eighteenth-century Bourbon Naples, would be difficult to access and perhaps even seem irrelevant to the mindset and sensitivities of the world today. For this reason, we welcome Fr. Dennis Billy's creative and insightful adaptation of Alphonsus' approach to mental prayer to the dynamics of spiritual direction.

The ministry of spiritual direction has made great strides in the past fifty years, not the least of which is that it has involved the laity to a much greater degree than ever before and has become a concern not only for Catholics but also for members of other philosophical, religious, and ethical traditions. Fr. Billy has focused on a particular aspect of St. Alphonsus' thought (his approach to mental prayer) and shown how it can serve as a useful model for the care of souls. In doing so, he uses the Alphonsian tradition in a way that is both continuous with the past and relevant to the situations of those seeking spiritual guidance in the early decades of the third millennium.

In his own day, Alphonsus was someone who sought to take the vast treasures of the Church's spiritual tradition out of the rarified domain of privileged elites and bring them to everyday believers, especially the poor and marginalized. Using St. Alphonsus for his inspiration, Fr. Billy has given us an approach to spiritual direction that is simple, practical, heartfelt, easy to learn, and rooted in resolute action. He is also very modest in his claims, presenting this approach as only one of many tools to which spiritual directors can have recourse in conducting their ministries. I commend Fr. Billy for his hard work in this area and thank him for his translation of the Alphonsian tradition in a meaningful and relevant way for today's spiritual directors. I also thank the Templeton World Charity Foundation for the grant that has given him the time and support to make this work possible. May the fruit of his labors reap great benefits for many.

Michael Brehl, CSsR
Superior General
Congregation of the Most Holy Redeemer

Preface

I have been a member of the Congregation of the Most Holy Redeemer (the Redemptorists) for more than forty years and have tried my best to immerse myself in the writings of its founder, St. Alphonsus de Liguori (1696-1787). This was no easy task, especially since he was a prolific author, with more than 100 published works and thousands of letters penned by his hand. He was one of the most renowned moral and spiritual theologians of his day and widely read throughout the nineteenth century and well into the twentieth.

His influence continues to this day. Saint John Paul II called Alphonsus "…a saint who was a master of wisdom for his time, and who continues to enlighten the path of the people of God with the example of his life and teaching, as a light reflecting Christ, the light of the nations."[1] According to Pope Emeritus Benedict XVI: "To pastors of souls and to confessors, Alphonsus recommended faithfulness to Catholic moral doctrine, accompanied by a comprehensive and gentle attitude so that penitents could feel accompanied, supported, and encouraged in their journey of faith and Christian life."[2] Spiritual wisdom, enlightening the path of God's people, gentle and comprehensive accompaniment in the faith: these are some of the hallmarks of Alphonsus' approach to the care of souls. These same marks also have great relevance for the ministry of spiritual direction as it is practiced today.

This book is an attempt to highlight the relevance of Alphonsian spirituality for the ministry of spiritual direction and the moral life. It does so not by simply restating the thought of this great doctor of the Church but by adapting it to our present sensitivities. It focuses not on what Alphonsus himself taught about spiritual direction (his insights could well comprise a book in its own right) but instead uses his simple approach to mental prayer as the basis for understanding the underlying dynamics of the process of direction itself. In doing so, it takes to heart Jesus' words to his disciples: "…every scribe who has been trained for the kingdom of heaven is like the master of a household who brings out of his treasure what is new and what is old" (Matthew 13:52).

Interpreting Alphonsus in this way opens up many possibilities for the ministry of spiritual direction. For one thing, it offers a simple, easy-to-learn, and practical way of understanding the direction process—one that can be used in a variety of contexts to meet the spiritual and moral needs of today's world. For another, it draws a close connection between spirituality and morality, between the ministry of spiritual direction itself and the moral life, thus providing an integrated approach to life that sees an intimate relationship between holiness and wholeness, between spiritual experience and moral action in the world. It also offers a way of adapting the model to members of other religious, philosophical, and ethical traditions so they can benefit from this approach to direction without sacrificing the values embedded in their own traditions.

The patron saint of confessors and moral theologians, St. Alphonsus was also known as a great doctor of prayer. In his writings he embraced a balanced view of the moral and spiritual life that steered a delicate and hard-fought *via media* in the midst of controverted and heated extremes. A highly focused and practical author, he used whatever means he could find to bring others closer to Christ. Throughout his works he stressed the importance of the search for practical wisdom through careful reasoning, prudential judgment, and heartfelt prayer.

This book seeks to infuse one particular aspect of Alphonsus' thought—his approach to mental prayer—into the practice of spiritual direction today. This approach is a new and valuable tool that spiritual directors can use to help others become themselves in their faith. May it assist both directors and those they serve to navigate the turbulent waters of the moral and spiritual journey.

Dennis J. Billy, CSsR
Feast of St. Alphonsus de Liguori
August 1, 2018

Acknowledgments

Versions of material in this book have appeared elsewhere under the following titles: *What Is Spiritual Direction?* (Liguori, MO: Liguori Publications, 2010) [Chapter One]; "The Relations of Spiritual Direction," *Studia moralia* 36 (1998): 67-94 [Chapter Two]; "Spiritual Direction and the Art of Active Listening," *Seminary Journal* 19 (no. 1, 2013): 22-26 [Chapter Three]; "Spiritual Direction as 'Faith Seeking Understanding,'" *Seminary Journal* 19 (no. 1, 2013): 27-32 [Chapter Four]; "An Alphonsian Model of Spiritual Direction," *Studia moralia* 41 (2003): 47-72 [Chapters Five, Six, Seven]; "Fifteen Qualities of a Spiritual Director," *Pastoral Life* 39 (no. 10, 1990): 2-9 [Chapter Eight]; "The Silent Reader: Prayer as the Source of the Moral Life," *Studia moralia* 56 (2018): 103-21 [Chapter Nine]; "The Three Ways," *Lexicon of Redemptorist Spirituality*, eds. Sean Wales and Dennis Billy (Rome: General Secretariat for Redemptorist Spirituality, 2011): 279-81 [Chapter Ten]; "Gifted by the Spirit," *Pastoral Life* 43 (no. 9, 1994): 2-7 [Chapter Twelve]; "Growing in the Virtues and the Gifts: Spiritual Direction as a Practical Theological Locus for the Convergence of Spirituality and Morality," *Studia moralia* 39 (2001): 433-59 [Chapter Thirteen].

This book was made possible by a grant from the Templeton World Charity Foundation.

Special thanks to: Michael Bloom, president of Now You Know Media, and Sebastian Mahfood, president of En Route Books and Media, for their assistance in writing the grant proposal and their help in bringing the entire project to a fruitful conclusion. A word of thanks also goes to Fr. Byron Miller, CSsR, president and publisher of Liguori Publications, and his staff, for their help in editing, producing, marketing, and distributing the book.

Introduction

This book deals with the relationship between spiritual direction and the moral life. It comes out of the Catholic tradition, more specifically from the moral and spiritual mindset of St. Alphonsus de Liguori, doctor of the Church, patron saint of confessors and moral theologians, and the founder of the Congregation of the Most Holy Redeemer. It does not claim to be an exhaustive treatment of either spiritual direction or the moral life. Its purpose is to examine the relationship between the two and, in the spirit of Alphonsus, do so in a way that is simple, practical, pastoral, focused on the poor and marginalized, and easy to implement. It wishes to make sound spiritual direction accessible to as many people as possible and to offer it across boundaries that, more often than not, have kept people apart, rather than united. It is a practical primer for an approach to spiritual direction that looks to the future by reflecting on the past and learning how both impinge upon the decisions of the present.

A Biographical Sketch

Alphonsus de Liguori (1696-1787) was born into the lower nobility of the Kingdom of Naples, studied law at the University of Naples, and became a doctor of both civil and canon law (*doctor utriusque juris*) by the age of sixteen. He practiced law for roughly ten years before deciding to become a priest. He was ordained a priest of the Archdiocese of Naples in 1726 and soon gained a reputation for his preaching as a member of the Apostolic Missions and the Chinese College. Early on in his ministry he demonstrated a marked concern for the poor, as manifested in his work at the Hospital of the Incurabili and in organizing the outdoor evening chapels (*Cappelle Serotine*) conducted for the poor *lazzaroni* of the streets of Naples.

In 1732, Alphonsus founded the Congregation of the Most Holy Savior (later changed to Redeemer) in the town of Scala, situated along the Amalfi

Coast. The work of this new apostolic institute was to preach the gospel to the poor and marginalized of the rural, mountaintop villages of southern Italy. After years of mission preaching in these abandoned outskirts, he was consecrated bishop of St. Agatha of the Goths in 1762, an office he would rather have avoided and which he accepted only in obedience to Pope Clement XIII. For the next thirteen years he served the people of his diocese with great dedication, focusing specifically on the formation of priests, the reform of the clergy, and the spiritual renewal of the people. In 1775, he was permitted to retire from his episcopal duties for health reasons.

Alphonsus was an accomplished artist, author, composer, letter writer, poet, and theologian. During his illustrious career, he published a total of 111 works mainly in the areas of moral and ascetical theology. Although a man of his times, his literary corpus reveals an integrated vision of the moral and spiritual life that carries great weight and continues to inspire. His most popular works include *Visits to the Blessed Sacrament* (1745), the four large tomes of his *Moral Theology* (1748), *The Glories of Mary* (1750), and *The Practice of the Confessor* (1755), *The Way of Salvation* (1766), and *The Practice of the Love of Jesus Christ* (1768).[1] Having suffered from poor health for many years, made worse by a crippling form of arthritis, he died among his Redemptorist community in Pagani, Italy, at the age of ninety-one. He is remembered for his tremendous zeal for the salvation of souls and is known throughout the Catholic world as "The Most Zealous Doctor" (*Doctor Zelantissimus*).

Alphonsian Spirituality

Alphonsus was considered one of the great moral theologians and spiritual writers of his day. He immerses us in a spirituality that seeks to pattern the lives of all believers after the Gospel narrative of Jesus' Incarnation, passion, death, and resurrection. According to this narrative, Jesus entered our world in the mystery of the Incarnation, gave himself to us in his public ministry and the mystery in his passion and death, became nourishment for us in the mystery of the Eucharist, and remains a source of hope for us through the mystery of his resurrection. For Alphonsus, this narrative, once encountered, should evoke from us a similar response. Like Jesus, we are called to enter the world of those around us, give ourselves to them in a life of service, become nourishment for them, and a source of hope. Alphonsus summarized the movement of this Gospel narrative in four key words: crib, cross, sacrament, and Mary, who, according to Catholic belief, is the only person besides her Son who has experienced the fullness of the resurrected life.

Alphonsus' own spiritual journey reflects this basic Gospel narrative. At a decisive moment in his discernment to abandon his legal career and, with it, all hopes of worldly gain, he knelt in prayer at an altar dedicated to Mary, Mother of Mercy, drew his sword, and laid it at her feet as a symbol of his firm resolve to leave everything and follow her Son, the Lord Jesus Christ. This image of a two-edged sword evokes those famous words in the Letter to the Hebrews: "Indeed, the word of God, is living and active, sharper than any two-edged sword, piercing until it divides the soul from spirit, joints from marrow; it is able to judge the thoughts and intentions of the heart" (4:12).

For our purposes, this image provides us with a way of understanding Alphonsus' gospel spirituality. One edge of the sword represents a "spirituality of practice," which focuses on living out our faith with the fundamental values and attitudes of Jesus. The other edge of the sword may be likened to a "spirituality of heart," which focuses on lifting up one's mind and heart to God and revealing to him our deepest thoughts and feelings. These two edges come together at a single point in a "spirituality of mission," which focuses on spreading the good news of redemption to those around us. Alphonsus' spirituality, we might say, seeks to touch people's minds and hearts, bring about a radical conversion (*metanoia*) in their lives, and inspire them to share their experience with others.

For Alphonsus, spirituality and morality, contemplation and action, prayer and virtue have a single purpose: to immerse us in the values of the kingdom and, in doing so, facilitate its spread. His approach to mental prayer contains each of these elements of his understanding of the moral and spiritual life.

The Manner of Making Mental Prayer

Alphonsus simplified the manner of making mental prayer so that it could be easily learned and remembered. He believed it was meant not only for clergy and religious but for everyone. Among the three major types of prayer, it falls between vocal prayer (praying to God aloud either alone or with others) and contemplation (wordless prayer done in the silence of one's heart). It falls between these two categories for two reasons: Unlike contemplation, it actually uses words when talking to God; unlike vocal prayer, it does not express them aloud but articulates them in the quiet of one's heart. According to Alphonsus, mental prayer was morally necessary for salvation. He liked to say, "If you pray, you will be saved; if you don't pray, you will be damned."[2] Rephrasing it in a way that might be more palatable to our present sensitivities, the statement would read something like: "If you pray, then you will eventually find your way to God; if you do not pray, then you will spend eternity wandering about aimlessly trying to fill a giant hole in your soul that, in the end, can only be filled by God."

For Alphonsus, this saying applied first and foremost to mental prayer. Without it, he believed it would be very difficult to find one's way to God. If you pray, you will be saved; if you don't pray, you will end up wandering off the road that leads to God and be lost. The road to God is the moral life, the good life, the blessed life. Prayer, in other words, is the great means of salvation. It fosters our relationship with God, it makes us friends of God; and it empowers us through God's grace, to live the fundamental commandments of the moral life given us by Christ himself: the love of God and the love of neighbor (Mark 12:29–31).

A Fourfold Plan

The book is divided into four parts with two appendices and a list of suggested readings, all of which attempt to approach the relationship between spiritual direction and the moral life by adapting Alphonsus' simple approach to mental prayer to the dynamics of the direction process by focusing on virtue as the best way to integrate our spiritual and moral lives.

Part One, "Moorings in Spiritual Direction," consists of four chapters and focuses on some of the general features of the direction process itself. It treats many basic questions concerning the process of direction as a whole and seeks to provide a firm foundation for all that follows. Part Two, "An Alphonsian Approach to Spiritual Direction," covers another four chapters and demonstrates how Alphonsus' approach to mental prayer can be adapted to the dynamics of the spiritual direction. It shows that the same movements used in opening our hearts and minds to God can be integrated into the process of direction itself. Part Three, "Spiritual Direction and the Moral Life," offers five chapters on how the virtuous life and the gifts of the Spirit lie at the very heart of the direction process. It provides the theological basis for a further integration of spirituality, morality, and life in the Spirit. Part Four, "Dialoguing With Other Traditions," devotes five chapters to examining how the Alphonsian model of spiritual direction can be adapted to other religious, philosophical, and ethical traditions. It seeks to show that elements of the model can be used to help others become themselves in their faith. Appendix A provides various excerpts from St. Alphonsus' spiritual writings that can be used as material for meditation and as points of departure for spiritual direction. Appendix B offers a list of helpful Internet sources related to many relevant topics on spiritual direction and the moral life. The readings section has helpful resources for those wishing to further their study of the topics covered in the book.

Taken together, the four parts of this book and their related back matter show how the Alphonsian approach to spiritual direction can assist us in getting in touch with our deepest thoughts and feelings about the ultimate realities of life, bring them to the surface of our awareness, listen to them, share them with others, and resolve to do something about them. They also help us to recognize what people of varying backgrounds share in common and how they can use them to grow in respect and mutual understanding.

Conclusion

Some years ago, there was a debate about whether there was a single Christian spirituality or many.[3] Are the many so-called Christian spiritualities nothing more than variations on the theme of Christian discipleship, or is each of them distinct in its own right and worthy of a separate designation? In a certain sense, both answers are correct. Down through the centuries, the one spirituality lived by Jesus of Nazareth has been assimilated by his followers and adapted to changing historical circumstances.

Today we speak of Augustinian, Benedictine, Franciscan, Dominican, Carmelite, Ignatian, and Alphonsian spiritualities. We also speak of priestly, religious, and lay spiritualities, as well as separate spiritualities for men and women—and many others. All of these spiritualities are similar and dissimilar; distinct, yet also very much alike. They are all variations on the one gospel spirituality of Jesus Christ, who entered our world, gave himself completely to us, in order to become nourishment, and be a source of hope for us. The genius of Alphonsian spirituality is that it brings this underlying narrative to the fore and places it at the heart of the gospel proclamation.

Much the same can be said for spiritual direction. There are many models of spiritual direction: direct and indirect, sacramental and nonsacramental, Christian and non-Christian—to name but a few. The approach developed in these pages does not claim to be the only approach to spiritual direction, nor does it purport to be necessarily the best. It simply wishes to propose an alternative approach that is simple, easy to learn, practical, and pastorally based. It also seeks to present a model that focuses specifically on integrating morality and spirituality in the life of the believer. Although the model presented in these pages stems from the Catholic tradition and specifically from the approach to mental prayer of St. Alphonsus de Liguori, it has much to offer those of other religious, philosophical, and ethical traditions. The hope is that it will be valued as such and used as just one of many tools that directors can turn to in their attempt to help others become themselves in their faith.

PART ONE

Moorings in Spiritual Direction

Part one offers a general overview of spiritual direction. It focuses on what it is (chapter one); its primary relationships (chapter two); its use of active listening (chapter three); and its prayerful search for wisdom (chapter four). By examining the essentials necessary for helping people to navigate the turbulent waters of life and become themselves in the faith, it hopes to shed light on what will help those seeking guidance to have a safe, yet adventurous journey to distant shores that beckon them and for which they yearn. By examining the essentials of this important ministry, it also shows how spiritual direction can become a place where the moral and spiritual dimensions of the Christian tradition can come together and find a home.

CHAPTER ONE

Spiritual Direction

⇵

*Make me know your ways, O Lord; teach me your paths.
Lead me in your truth, and teach me, for you are the God
of my salvation; for you I wait all day long.*
PSALM 25:4–5

As we begin our discussion of spiritual direction and the moral life, it is important for us to start with a common understanding of what the ministry is all about. Although most of us have probably heard of spiritual direction, it is quite possible that some of us, even those with much experience in pastoral care, do not have a clear idea of what it is or exactly what to expect from it. In this brief opening chapter, we will present the bare bones of this important ministry and with an emphasis on its primary focus.

What Is Spiritual Direction?
Spiritual direction (spiritual guidance or accompaniment, as it is also called) is a helping relationship that focuses on growth in our relationship with God. A person may seek out spiritual direction for any number of reasons: not knowing how to deal with sinfulness; being stuck in efforts to grow in holiness; examining relationships in the light of one's faith; wanting to draw closer to God

through prayer; and discerning God's will in one's life, for example. Direction can be either *directive* or *nondirective* and normally involves a long-term relationship between the director and the person seeking guidance. In this relationship, the director looks upon himself or herself as a servant of the Holy Spirit, whom the Christian tradition consistently recognizes as the spiritual director par excellence.

When the director takes a prominent role in instructing us how to draw closer to God, spiritual direction is *directive*. The director, in such a scenario, *gives specific instructions* (directives) and uses the Scriptures and teachings of the great saints and spiritual masters of the Christian tradition as a kind of blueprint for growth in the Spirit. These directives can be general (pray more often, do more spiritual reading, be more charitable) or concrete (meditate every morning for thirty minutes, read *The Imitation of Christ*, volunteer a specific amount of time to a particular charity). Scrupulous people often need this kind of direction and actively seek it out.

When the director, by way of contrast, employs careful listening and honest personal feedback to help us *discover for ourselves* the next steps that we need to take on our journey, spiritual direction is *nondirective*. In this instance, the director seeks to be present to us and help us make sense of our relationship with God. In such a situation, he or she seems more like a spiritual friend or companion than a spiritual teacher or master. The director encourages us to open our hearts, look at what has been going on in our lives, and look for God in the dark places, as well as in the light. In time, we develop a relationship of trust with the director and gradually feel free to share with him or her our innermost secrets.

Over time, each spiritual director will develop a unique style of direction, sometimes incorporating elements of both the *directive* and *nondirective* approaches into something uniquely his or her own. It is worth noting that spiritual direction can also be adapted to a group setting. In such instances, the director becomes a kind of facilitator who pulls out common themes from a group discussion and encourages individual members to examine those themes in their lives.

The kind of direction employed in a given instance depends on any number of factors: the knowledge, skill, and availability of a competent director; the amount of time at his or her disposal; our own personality, needs, and temperament; and so forth. Directors should be acquainted with a variety of approaches to spiritual direction, as well as the wealth of insights on growth in the spiritual life from the Christian tradition.

Before entering into a relationship of spiritual direction, a director normally meets with the person seeking guidance in order to discuss expectations regarding the specific kind of direction being offered, frequency of meetings, the length of the individual sessions, confidentiality, qualifications, and, when appropriate, even payment. It may be helpful to distribute beforehand a small informational pamphlet such as *What Is Spiritual Direction?* to serve as a point of departure for the discussion.[1] Periodic reviews of how the relationship has taken shape are also expected, as is close oversight by trained supervisors, to ensure that the process is not in some way being compromised.

Primary Focus

The primary focus of spiritual direction is our relationship with God. We become ourselves in the faith by bringing our ties to God consciously to the fore and reflecting on them in their most intimate details. Spiritual direction provides a place where this quiet process is brought into focus and honestly examined in the presence of another human being. It gives us the opportunity to look at our lives through the eyes of faith, and encourages us to invite God into our daily lives. In the words of the Apostle Paul, "We walk by faith, not by sight" (2 Corinthians 5:7).

A number of factors should always be kept in mind during spiritual direction: our understanding of ourselves, how we act toward others and the world in which we live, our relationship to God, and the quality of our prayer. During direction, we are not looking for an abstract knowledge of these important dimensions of the spiritual life but an experiential awareness of them. We examine both our thoughts about God and our feelings toward him. We look at our feelings of intimacy with him, as well as our experiences of distance and perhaps even estrangement from him. From such practical, existential knowledge, a number of important questions will come to the fore at some point in the direction process: How do we treat ourselves? How do we act toward others? How do we live in the world? How do we behave toward God? How do we pray?

Such questions touch essential dimensions of our relationship with God and must be given due consideration in the ongoing course of direction, although not necessarily with the same degree of intensity at every session.

Although every relationship (indeed, every session) of spiritual direction is unique, a number of common threads are often woven into the relationship over time.

Spiritual direction involves a relationship of giving and receiving that focuses on enabling us to delve more deeply into the mystery of God and to understand more clearly the ramifications of that experience in the concrete circumstances of our daily lives. As a helping relationship, it offers us the possibility of a grace-filled response to a faithful and loving God, who promises to enter into the process and to accompany both helper and the helped at every stage of their journey in faith.

Conclusion

The process of spiritual direction involves taking an honest look at the way we relate to God and to ponder its effect on our relationship with ourselves, others, and the world around us. Doing so enables us to better understand the various strengths and weaknesses in the manner we address God. Direction gives us the opportunity to examine every level of our relationship with God. Taking place against a contemplative backdrop of silence, it focuses on the thoughts, feelings, needs, and practical steps needed for us to draw closer to God. It can also help us to arrive at a better understanding of what it means to converse with God intimately with an open heart and to live the gospel on a deep level of awareness. In the next chapter, we will look at the various relationships at work in the process of spiritual direction and the manner in which they interact. See chapter seven for a detailed overview of a spiritual direction session.

Reflection Questions

How would you describe what spiritual direction is and how it differs from other helping relationships, such as counseling and therapy?

What is the purpose of spiritual direction?

What is the job of the spiritual director?

In what sense is spiritual direction a process?

Why is silence so important in spiritual direction?

CHAPTER TWO

Relationships

The virtuous soul that is alone and without a master,
is like a lone burning coal;
it will grow colder rather than hotter.
ST. JOHN OF THE CROSS, SAYINGS OF LIGHT AND LOVE[1]

Simply knowing about spiritual direction should not be enough to satisfy us. We must take many other insights into account to have an honest assessment of its value today. Numbered among them are certain relations that touch the very heart of the direction process. For instance, a helping relationship seeking to draw people closer to God should take place within an atmosphere of mutual trust and privileged respect. If it does, then those seeking spiritual guidance will come to a deeper awareness of God in their lives. If it does not, then the quality of the direction will suffer, sometimes to the point of damaging their relationship with God and others. This chapter explores five important relationships involved in spiritual direction and offers pertinent observations about their significance for the Christian moral and spiritual life.

I. The Person Seeking Guidance and God
The primary focus of spiritual direction is the relationship between directees

and God. That is not to say the other relations involved in direction are unimportant. Nor does it mean these other relations are never to be thought of as having priority in other areas. It only means they do not have priority of purpose in the helping relationship known as spiritual direction. People become themselves in the faith by bringing their relationship with God consciously to the fore and reflecting upon its most intimate details.[2] Spiritual direction focuses on this quiet revelatory process and allows people to examine their lives honestly in the presence of another.

When going to direction, those seeking guidance must keep in mind three interrelated factors: their understanding of themselves, their understanding of God, and their understanding of prayer. The word *understanding* refers here not to an abstract conceptualization of these important dimensions of the spiritual life but to an experiential, action-oriented awareness. From such practical knowledge, certain key questions arise during the direction process. A person seeking guidance needs to ask: "How do I treat myself? How do I behave toward God? How do I pray?" These questions touch essential dimensions in a person's relationship with God. They must be given consideration in the ongoing course of direction, although not necessarily with the same intensity at every session.

These factors, however, only go so far when it comes to a person's relationship with God, because each of them must be turned on its head and directed to God. With helpful aids of the imagination we can accompany those seeking guidance along a series of encounters with the God of Christian revelation. We must be willing to ask questions such as: "Who is God for you? What image comes to mind when you say the word? How does God speak to you? What does God want of you? What do you want of God?" Using the same imaginative process with the person before us, God will also be asked about his own understanding of himself, the directee, and how he speaks to him or her. Such questions are extremely important, because they underscore the mutuality of the relationship between the human and divine. Directees, in other words, are encouraged to explore not only their point of view concerning their self-image, God, and prayer but also the viewpoint of God himself. If the whole point of spiritual direction is to enable those seeking guidance to grow in the friendship of God, then the marks of friendship—benevolence, reciprocity, and mutual indwelling—must somewhere be in evidence. In other words, God's action for the good of, his loving concern for, and his presence in the heart of those seeking help must also be taken into account.[3] If they are not (or rarely ever referred to), then spiritual direction becomes too one-sided in its contemplation of the individual's relationship to the divine.

II. The Director and God

In addition to the relationship between those seeking guidance and God, the one between director and God also comes into play. This relationship is not the primary focus of spiritual direction but it has an important effect on its success. The more we as directors nurture our relationship with God through appropriate means, the more will we be in a situation to help those seeking guidance. Such means would include: ongoing spiritual direction for ourselves; frequent recourse to the Church's liturgical and sacramental life; mature, solid friendships; and participation in the Christian community.

If we value spiritual direction so highly that we are willing to give it, we should also be willing to make the time and the effort to receive it. If we are not ourselves in the faith, how can we expect to help others to become so? Receiving spiritual direction should be an essential element of every director's life. In receiving it, we will be drawn more closely to God and be of more help to those seeking us for spiritual direction.

As directors, we should also have frequent recourse to the sacramental and liturgical life of the Church in order to deepen our relationship with God. Christ's redemption is mediated to us through these means. For this reason, the sacraments and the liturgy of the Church hold a primary place in nourishing the spiritual life of the believer. To neglect them is to close ourselves off to the primary areas in life where God enters our world and communes with us as "Emmanuel, which means, 'God is with us'" (Matthew 1:23).

As directors, we also need the support of intimate friends for our psychological well-being and for our own development as mature human beings. Such friends not only actively seek our good and share with us an experience of mutual indwelling but also help us to understand our own relationship with God. By having close friends who are a special manifestation of God in our lives, we receive a deeper experiential basis with which to understand our own intimate relationship with God. Such a unique relationship will enable us to facilitate a similar deepening of faith in others.

Finally, as directors we must foster our relationship with God in the context of the body of Christ. Participation in the life of the Christian community is an essential precondition of our personal relationship to the Lord. We are baptized into Christ's body, the Church, and called to live in service to the community to which we are called. This means keeping our primary community commitments (to family, to a religious congregation, to a parish) at the fore of our understanding of God's call.

By tending to our relationship with God through these appropriate means, we draw close to God in friendship and can thus be of service to those who come to us for direction. Directees are normally looking for someone with a personal knowledge of God who will be able to guide them in their journey toward God in friendship. This personal experience of God in our lives cannot be feigned. If we do not have it, then perhaps we should question our involvement in this important ministry.

III. Within God

The relations among the persons of the Trinity also must be taken into account in spiritual direction. Such an affirmation may at first seem rather bold for the likes of the ordinary, matter-of-fact dialogue that takes up much of the time spent in this important helping relationship. A closer look at the statement, however, reveals the extraordinary truth of the Christian faith: "God became man," Athanasius of Alexandria tells us, "so that man might become divine;"[4] God has visited the human race in Jesus Christ and through his Spirit continues to inspire it by taking an active role in the helping relationship of spiritual direction. For this reason, an understanding of the primary relationships within the Godhead will also be of great help to directors.

One of the greatest contributions of the doctrine of the Trinity to the history of ideas is that it places the concept of "relation" within the very nature of God. The ungenerated Father, the generated Son, and the proceeding Spirit are distinct from one another by virtue of their differences in relationship, making the Godhead relational in its very essence. But since essence and being are identical in God, the contrary conclusion must also be true: the divinity is distinct by virtue of its oneness of being and one by virtue of its distinctive relationships. Such is the incomprehensible mystery of the relational God of the Christian faith, expressed so eloquently in the tradition by the simple term *Trinitas*.

To speak of the Trinity as relational is to emphasize the social character of the Godhead. The Christian God is a community of love, one in being yet three in person: ungenerated in its Source (the Father), eternally generated in its

Otherness (the Son), eternally proceeding in its Oneness (the Spirit). The relations that differentiate the persons are united by virtue of the latter's oneness in being; the oneness in being that unites the persons is itself differentiated by virtue of the latter's relations. Unity and multiplicity, therefore, find their resolution in the metaphysical juxtaposition of being and relation in the mystery of God's eternal love.

IV. The Director and the Person Seeking Guidance

From what has been said so far, it follows that the director and those seeking guidance will be united by virtue of their own intimate bonds with the triune God. This bond is not unique to the spiritual direction relationship but flows from their common faith in the saving love of Christ. The more transparent we and our directees are in our personal relationships to God, the closer will we be drawn to one another in the community of the friends of God. Even if our personalities clash and we decide to discontinue the helping relationship, we will still be united in this common unifying bond of faith.

Besides relating in and through our faith in God, however, we and our directees also interact directly, on a person-to-person level. This concrete relationship touches the core of spiritual direction, should take place in an atmosphere of warmth and genuine concern, and is fostered when we, as directors, receive qualified supervision. The general movement of the spiritual direction relationship is Christological in tone. Just as Christ came in order to bring humanity closer to the Father, so also we are present to help those seeking guidance to deepen their relationship to God. In this context, we are following in the footsteps of Christ who entered our world, gave of himself completely, and became nourishment for us. As directors, we need to ask ourselves: "How have I entered this person's world? How have I given myself to and nourished this individual?"

As directors, we also seek to be a source of hope for directees. This means, first and foremost, that we will be a constant source of encouragement. It also means that, when necessary, we will be willing to confront them on those areas in need of improvement so they can deepen their relationship with God. We need to ask ourselves: "How have I encouraged this person? How have I challenged him? How have I been a source of hope for her?" Through spiritual direction, we have the unique privilege of witnessing the gradual transformation of a person's life in Christ. As Jesus entered our world and gave of himself completely to the point of becoming nourishment and a source of hope for others, so are we called to enter the various worlds of those we direct and to give of ourselves to the point of becoming nourishment for them and a source of life-giving hope. We accomplish this, not on our own but by our cooperating with Christ and, with the aid of sound supervision, using the appropriate and available means to help those seeking guidance interpret their religious experiences.

V. God and Those Involved in Direction

The final relationship to be referred to in spiritual direction is between the triune God and the relationship of spiritual direction itself. Our imitation of Christ in the fourfold movement discussed earlier evokes from directees a reciprocal response that at times has them entering into the world of, giving themselves to, becoming nourishment for, and even a source of hope for us. As directors, we know from experience the many benefits the ministry can bring to our lives. By being Christ for others, we encourage directees to respond in a reciprocal fashion. Within the strict bounds of the spiritual direction agreement, this complementary Christological relationship provides the condition for the possibility of the *transposition* of the trinitarian relations of the Godhead onto the level of spiritual direction itself. That is to say that the relationships of the Father as Ground, the Son as Other, and the Spirit as Bond become visible in the strong spiritual bond that gradually develops between us and those seeking guidance. In the context of spiritual direction, the word *transposition* simply means "the putting of the higher into the lower."[5] As our relationship with directees deepens, this movement of the higher to the lower takes place as the relations within the Trinity become manifest in the deep spiritual bond we share. God, who is love, becomes visible in the love made manifest in the spiritual friendship between us.

The transposition of the trinitarian relationships onto the lower level of the spiritual direction relationship results in a deep bond between the triune God and those involved in direction. This bond goes beyond whatever private relationship either person has with God and should be viewed in the context of the Body of Christ, the Church, which, filled with the Spirit, forever offers praise and thanksgiving through Christ to the Father. While the relationships are primarily analogous and therefore must not be given extreme interpretations (for example, directors identifying themselves with the Father or speaking in the name of the Holy Spirit), we must not overlook the relationship between directors and those seeking guidance as one that participates in the trinitarian relations of love. As one commentator said: "The deepest meaning of our Christian lives is the total transformation of our being into a new creation that comes through the transposition of the Holy Spirit into our human selves. 'God's love has flooded our inmost heart through the Holy Spirit he has given us'" (Romans 5:5).[6]

Since "transposition" is not "equivalence," care must be taken not simply to collapse the trinitarian relations into the spiritual direction relationship.[7] At the same time, the total absence of a transposition of the trinitarian relations onto the plane of the spiritual direction relationship would signal something has gone wrong in the direction process and that, if care is not taken to correct it, the relationship should be brought to a close. Inadequate training on the part of the director, poor listening skills, unresolved personality conflicts, lack of ongoing supervision, a lack of openness on the part of the person seeking guidance, and overcommitments are some of the common reasons for this lack of transposition. When the spiritual direction relationship does not reflect equality based on the distinction and harmony of persons involved in listening and responding to the innermost needs of the Spirit, then the situation warrants careful consideration. When direction does not tend toward an ever-deepening sense of trust but is, instead, marred by suspicion, lack of reserve, and at times even dishonesty, then God's role in the relationship has not been taken seriously and appropriate steps should be taken to make things right.[8]

Observations

Once the distinct relationships outlined in this chapter are considered in the context of their close interconnection, a number of important insights follow.

To a large degree, the art of spiritual direction consists in our ability as directors to discern which particular set of relations should be specifically referred to and brought to the fore at any particular moment. In this act of discernment, we must make a concerted effort to be present to directees, listen carefully to their concerns, and avoid imposing a personal agenda on the situation. To discern well in this regard, we must be conscious of the characteristics of the relations themselves and the various ways—positive and negative—in which they interact. We should also try to understand which relations have been ignored or, for whatever reason, left untended. Exactly when we should make personal observations about someone's relationship with God, the nature of the Godhead, our own relationship with God, the spiritual direction relationship itself, or God's presence in it, should come out of a concern to help those seeking guidance draw closer to God. In the process of spiritual direction this one relationship holds priority over the rest.

The interplay of these relations also helps to clarify the various ways in which God speaks to both persons in the context of direction. This can take place during a person's prayer to God, in our personal relationship with God as we consider our directees in prayer, or in a sudden realization that becomes strikingly clear in a specific direction session. It can also take place through the Church, which safeguards the teaching of the relations of the Trinity, or through the transposed relations of the Trinity in the concrete circumstances of their relationship. The variety of means through which the Lord manifests himself in direction should not lead us to confine the movements of the Spirit to any one of these avenues of revelation to the exclusion of the others. If in the past directors placed an exaggerated emphasis on the words of counsel God would give them during direction (with their corresponding emphasis on strict obedience to their spiritual directives), we sometimes go to the opposite extreme today in confining God's word exclusively to what those seeking guidance discern in prayer. As a result, we place little emphasis on any of the other relations, least of all our own judicious insights. Part of the art of spiritual direction involves being sensitive to the various ways in which the Lord speaks to those seeking guidance. This means being attuned to the various relations outlined above and taking the risk that God may be using any one or a combination of them to draw a person closer.

The interplay of relations outlined in this chapter also underscores the objective and subjective features of human experience. A relationship of spiritual direction cannot exist outside of the context of a deep, endearing faith that goes beyond mere intellectual assent to the doctrine of the Christian faith but which also embraces both a trusting and action-oriented affirmation of God's personal presence in the world of both believer and nonbeliever. Based on the insights of faith, people enter spiritual direction hoping we will help them discern the will of God. This implies an active effort on our part to help those seeking guidance to delve beneath the various motivational layers comprising their moral and spiritual life. It also implies a firm acceptance of God as an operative player in the direction process, as someone who has something to say to those seeking guidance and who says it through veiled (though not indiscernible) means that must be deeply reflected upon in order to uncover their true spiritual worth. Spiritual direction, in other words, involves not only our own subjective predispositions and those coming to us for guidance but also the active and discernible initiatives of God in the life of an individual. This twofold relational emphasis sets direction apart from both psychological counseling (with its strictly horizontal stress on human growth) and pastoral counseling (with its strong focus on problem-solving).

The interplay of these relations also brings out more clearly the relationship between spiritual direction and the sacrament of reconciliation. These two distinct but related Christian ministries approach personal conversion from two different perspectives: spiritual pilgrimage and repentance. While these two facets of conversion are themselves closely related and can be incorporated in varying degrees in either process, the contours of the ministries clearly focus on one's journey to God in spiritual direction and one's sorrow for sin in the sacrament of reconciliation. Considering that ordained and nonordained alike can be spiritual directors while only ordained priests can administer the sacrament of reconciliation, some of the major differences between these two important approaches to conversion involve the element of time normally given to each and the manner in which the relations developed in this chapter come to the fore. Spiritual direction, for example, normally takes place in sessions of forty-five minutes to one hour, where a relaxed atmosphere is fostered and where there is the possibility over time of referring to one or combinations of the relations outlined in this chapter. The sacrament of reconciliation, in contrast, often takes place during a shorter time, in uneasy, sometimes embarrassing contexts, where penitents humbly confess thoughts and deeds from the shadows of their personality. While all of these relations should be present in during sacramental reconciliation, circumstances usually do not permit them to be referred to in the same way as they would in the more relaxed atmosphere of direction. Rather than trying to incorporate either approach into the other, spiritual directors and confessors would do well to stay within the limits set for them in the context of each ministry and encourage those who come to them to make sufficient use of the opportunities available. In those situations where the two ministries occur during a single session, the confessor/director should keep the different processes distinct in his mind, being sure to preserve the integrity of the sacrament.

Finally, the interplay of these relations in spiritual direction should give both the director and the person seeking guidance deeper insights into the significance and abiding character of prayer for daily life. The relational nature of God, the relation between the director and God, between directees and God, between the director and the directees, and between God and the spiritual direction relationship all provide unique clues into the continuing conversation, known as prayer, between God and the person. "Rejoice always, pray without ceasing, give thanks in all circumstances; for this is the will of God in Christ Jesus for you" (1 Thessalonians 5:16–18). Prayer originates in God, who gives everyone enough grace to pray, and takes on different forms on different levels of our anthropological makeup (the bodily, emotional, intellectual, spiritual, and social). The relations outlined in this chapter exist on every level of our human makeup. The relationship of directees to God comprises bodily, mental, spiritual, and social aspects, as does their relationship with the director, and the director's relationship with God. The doctrine of the Incarnation introduces these same aspects into the trinitarian relations themselves. They are also at work as they are transposed into the relationship between directors and directees. The *sacredness* of these relationships (in the case of trinitarian relations) and their *growing sacredness* (in the case of the other four) provide a helpful way of understanding the abiding presence of God in the direction process and the great import it has for a person's relationship to the entire web of life.

Conclusion

The above observations reveal the depths direction can achieve when consideration is given to their ongoing interplay, demonstrating the complexity of human and divine dimensions we must take into account when we try to help others become themselves in the faith. It would be a mistake to think of these relations as isolated entities, as if they rarely interacted or entered into the direction process at separate intervals of a prearranged linear unfolding. As directors, we should be aware that the relations themselves interrelate and that the way they do so is what gives each helping relationship of direction its uniqueness. The mutual innateness of these relations gives the direction process a rich, multifaceted range of meaning that will never exhaust the efforts of those motivated to explore its hidden depths.

Spiritual direction involves a series of relationships of giving and receiving that focus on enabling people to delve more deeply into the mystery of God and to understand more clearly the ramifications of that experience in the circumstances of daily life. As a helping relationship, it offers the possibility of a grace-filled response to the relational God, who promises to enter into the process and accompany both helpers and those being helped at every stage of their faith journey. In the next chapter, we will explore how active listening can be a useful tool in helping everyone concerned remain centered on the direction process and focused on the one thing that matters.

Reflection Questions

What relationship does spiritual direction focus on most?

What other relationships are important?

How do these relationships contribute to the process of discernment?

How should they help you come to a better understanding of yourself?

How should they help you focus on your relationship with God?

CHAPTER THREE

Listening

Always remember...to retire at various times into the solitude of your own heart even while outwardly engaged in discussions or transactions with others. This mental solitude cannot be violated by the many people who surround you since they are not standing around your heart but only around your body. Your heart remains alone in the presence of God.
ST. FRANCIS DE SALES, *INTRODUCTION TO THE DEVOUT LIFE*[1]

Transformation in spiritual direction comes from a listening presence. To be effective as directors, we need a thorough understanding of the dynamics of active listening used in direction sessions and reflected upon during supervision. We use this important skill over time, making it an integral part of our ministry. This brief presentation of the elements of active listening can be a great help, especially to those of us just beginning our practice.

The Proper Backdrop

Before listing these characteristics, however, it's important to say something about the proper backdrop for active listening to take place. To a large extent, the background of an artist's painting determines how the various foreground elements will be perceived and evaluated. In the same way, the backdrop against which listening takes place in spiritual direction will determine both the content and quality of what is heard.

Humans are blessed with the power of self-awareness: we are conscious not only of the world around us but also of ourselves. This ability to look upon ourselves as both object and subject manifests itself in the very structure of human thought. When we think, we have an internal dialogue with ourselves. This dialogue is both intuitive and reasoned. It can be clinically detached or charged with emotion. It goes on within each of us at varying rates and intensities. It is capable of following specific rules of inquiry or, when left unbridled, proceeds by way of free association.

At one time or another, we have all likely found ourselves quietly talking to ourselves in our minds. The conversation can be about almost anything and often represents a hodgepodge of thoughts, feelings, and reflections: "What do I need to accomplish this day? What are my priorities? Who do I need to call? Why do I feel stuck? How do others perceive me? What should I wear? What should I have for breakfast?" This internal dialogue of overlapping thoughts and feelings is normal and forms the backdrop against which everything else in our lives takes place. Although it will never go away, its level and intensity can be disciplined so other relevant features of our character can come forward. For this reason, it is important, when directing people, that directors be conscious of the types of conversations going on inside them. It is also important that we take appropriate steps to quiet this inner dialogue so an atmosphere of silence (and not incessant thinking) will form the primary backdrop for what will occur during the direction process.

The best way for this to happen is for directors to make an ongoing effort to foster a contemplative attitude toward life.[2] With such a disposition firmly rooted in our daily outlook, we should be able to make adequate adjustments when the need arises so that the level and intensity of the dialogue within us does not get in the way of the direction process. A period of preparatory prayer or inner stillness before the session may also be helpful. We become still by immersing ourselves in the surrounding silence, casting out all thoughts as best we can, and centering ourselves on a simple word, such as *Jesus*, *Love*, or *Mercy*. Whenever it surfaces, this internal conversation should be concerned with making appropriate judgments about the direction process. Otherwise, it should move to the background so the contemplative dimension of our lives may be the primary point of encounter between us and those seeking guidance.

The Elements of Active Listening

When the inner dialogue is calm and there is a backdrop of contemplative silence, we are ready to employ the art of active listening. When describing this important skill, seven characteristics come to mind.

1. Inner Awareness. To begin, we need to be aware of the continuing (though diminished) presence of the ongoing dialogue inside of us. Although we will never be totally free of the quiet conversation in our heads, we must discipline ourselves to minimize its impact and focus on the person before us. We do so by noticing its intensity from time to time and measuring its appropriateness for our current level of listening. People can sense when we are not really being present to them. When we catch ourselves drifting into space, we must quietly say to ourselves, "There you go again!" and refocus our attention on the person before us. Failure to do so may cause unnecessary distractions to enter our minds, thus compromising the attention we seek to give to directees. We should also remember that, just because we began the direction process with internal calm, there is no guarantee we will stay that way throughout the session. For this reason, it is important for us to check on our internal conversation from time to time so the content and level of intensity remain appropriate to what is going on during a session. On the flip side of the coin, we should also occasionally return to the backdrop of silence against which the direction process is taking place. Doing so will help to ensure a contemplative context for our dialogue with directees and form the basis for an experience of communion with them. Whatever the reason, the need for such internal monitoring should remain on the periphery of our awareness and not interfere with the focused attention those before us deserve.

2. Emptying of Self. As important as it may be for the overall good of the direction process, our awareness of the intensity of our internal dialogue needs to be complemented by an active process of *kenosis* or "self-emptying." This process represents a movement from "self-centeredness" to "otherness" and involves a threefold activity of awareness, detachment, and renewed focus. In the first place, we need to identify those elements of our internal dialogue (distracting thoughts, daydreaming, unruly emotions) that are out of place and do not belong in the direction session. Second, we need to detach ourselves from this unnecessary and often obtrusive interference. Third, we need to fill the intervening void by refocusing our energies on the dialogue we are engaging in with those before us. This threefold action of identification, detachment, and refocusing helps us to empty ourselves of any unnecessary distractions that may be getting in the way of our attempts at listening. It moves us out of ourselves and orients us toward those seeking direction. This process of self-emptying may need to be repeated numerous times during the direction session. Those having perfected it will perform it regularly, while not needing to consciously think about it.

3. Disciplined Attention. Once we are solidly oriented toward those seeking direction, we then enter into a process of disciplined attention. This kind of regard is highly focused. We try to experience those who come to us in the light of the various dimensions of their human makeup: the physical, emotional, intellectual, spiritual, social, and environmental. In doing so, we seek to relate the various segments of their lives to the whole—and vice versa. We want to listen to and engage the whole person, trying to take in all that they are saying to us. We ask them appropriate questions such as: "What is the feeling behind the thoughts you just shared? What would your friends think about what you just shared? What would God have to say about it?" Doing so gives them a valuable filter through which the direction conversation passes. This filter will also include numerous "self-constituting" narratives we have agreed upon beforehand (either implicitly or explicitly) which serve as a touchstone for the various moral and spiritual values that need to be instilled in the direction process. For Catholics, the Gospel narratives, the liturgy, and the living tradition of the Church (and especially the teachings of the Second Vatican Council) provide an important narrative basis for the dialogical process of self-reflection that takes place during the direction process. It is important we be aware of the underlying narratives we are using to help directees to interpret their experience. Otherwise, various kinds of stereotyping and other latent prejudices can enter into the direction process. It is also important that we not impose these narratives on those before us but help them to engage in an ongoing process of correlation that will help them discover relevant themes that resonate with their experience.

4. Passive Reception. Only after we have given directees this highly focused attention can we go to the heart of the listening process and engage in what is typically referred to as "passive reception." For this to happen, we must do our best to empty ourselves so we can welcome the thoughts, words, and feelings of those seeking guidance with unconditional positive regard. We receive these insights with respect and are careful not to make judgments that would get in the way with the process of self-revelation. Passive reception is an ascetical practice that requires openness to others and a willingness to *simply be* in another's presence. It requires patience, the kind that is willing to suffer the tediousness of the present moment for the sake of a higher good. Here, "being" takes precedence over "acting." We listen to our clients not in a superficial way but from the heart. We receive everything said and not said into ourselves and allow it to penetrate the very core of our being. Although the process of passive reception is highly focused and disciplined, it appears to the external observer as nothing more than a quiet, attentive gaze. At this stage of the listening process, we undergo a silent suffering that receives the experience of those before us into ourselves and renders the possibility of it being transformed.

5. Simple Understanding. The listening process continues by moving from reception to synthesis. After we have allowed directees to enter within themselves and penetrate their hearts, we must give ourselves time to gather the various elements of what has been shared into a coherent whole. This part of the process is more intuitive than reasoned. It requires quiet, attentive listening to what has been shared from one's heart and an attempt to grasp it from the perspective of the other's experience. This understanding is simple because it does not seek to analyze what was said but merely to hold it and relish it as an authentic expression of another's self. It is silent because it seeks to understand what has been shared in an atmosphere of quiet contemplation. It is a simple silence that speaks volumes, one that tells the other person that you are truly listening and not simply waiting for a pause in the conversation so that you can add your own thoughts. It seeks to assimilate what we have heard and carry it in our hearts as a cherished offering from another. A genuine expression of self is a gift from one person to another. Simple understanding results from an authentic reception of that gift. It is a turning inward of the listening process where we hold what we have received in our heart. Once understood, what was shared must be allowed to rest in the heart and dwell in the home it has found. Only when it has rested in another person's heart can something ever really be understood and appreciated.

6. Open Acknowledgment. An understanding heart, however, is not enough. If it is to bear fruit, the process of listening must lead us to acknowledge what we have heard. We can do this by simply reflecting back what we have heard with phrases like "What I am hearing is…" or "Is this what you mean…?" In fact, directees will only be able to affirm whether we've understood them when we've clearly stated our intuition of the whole. In our first attempts to express our newfound understanding, we should move from the general to the specific in small, incremental steps. We should be hesitant in reaching conclusions (so as not to impose our preconceptions upon our clients) and ask for frequent feedback through questions such as "Am I on target here?" or "Have I left anything out?" In giving directees the opportunity to amend or correct what they are saying, we help them take charge of their experiences and refine them in such a way so each of us can come to a mutual understanding of what has been shared. This process can at times be arduous. For directors, it also requires great humility. When acknowledging our version of what has been shared, we risk being misunderstood ourselves by the very people we are trying to help. For this reason, we need to be flexible in acknowledging what will always be a limited, revisable presentation of our understanding. We must be willing to present one draft of their experience after another—until we get it right. When what we say has been received and accepted by directees, then we can we be confident to have understood them correctly.

7. Humble Recognition. When met with our genuine attempt to understand their experience, directees find it easier to discern the truth about themselves. They may not like what we have reflected back to them and, at the outset, may react against it by telling us that we have gotten it all wrong or that we have left out an important piece of the puzzle. If they are faithful to the direction process, however, and if they have sincerely listened with their hearts, they will recognize the truth of what has been said and be willing to take steps that may be required of them. At this point, we have done all we can to help directees get in touch with, examine, and own their experiences. It is now up to them to bring the listening process to an end by affirming what has taken place and humbly recognizing and accepting the truth of what has been said. That truth may be challenging, comforting, or both. It may move them to action or perhaps to deeper reflection on their experience. It may also confirm for directees the value of the listening process for self-understanding. As the listening process draws to a close, those seeking guidance have also been helped to internalize its various movements for themselves. In being listened to, they themselves have learned to listen. It the future, they will have the opportunity to refine this skill and use it in their relations with others.

Conclusion

Even the best directors can learn something more about their ministry. These seven characteristics of the listening process demonstrate the deep spiritual moorings of the skill and why good listeners are so difficult to come by. The nature of a skill, however, is something that becomes increasingly easier through practice. As our experience increases, we should be able to regulate the intensity of our interior dialogue and become increasingly better listeners. If not, then something has probably gone awry in our understanding and implementation of the direction process.

For this reason, it is important that we belong to a peer group like Spiritual Directors International, where a free exchange of ideas can take place and where we may have access to appropriate supervision for our ministry through their membership directory.[3] From time to time, these groups focus on the various listening skills involved in the direction process. The best way to do that is to have sessions with a trained supervisor where the actual manner of giving direction is closely scrutinized. In this way, others might be able to identify lapses in the listening process that have been previously neglected or ignored.

Finally, as directors, we should remember that listening is a natural human skill that is quickened by the movement of the Spirit in our lives. A fervent and dedicated life of prayer will help us deepen our contact with the promptings of the Spirit and enable us to listen more and more as Christ listened to the God he called "Abba, Father" (Mark 14:36). Contemplative prayer, in particular, should help us acquire the necessary requisites of a listening heart. Prayerfulness transforms our natural listening skills and enables us to hear with a depth of mind and heart we never knew we had. This transformation manifests itself in the deep understanding we attain, and in the way we are able to correlate what we have heard to Christian traditions, then articulate it in a simple, understandable manner. These skills for active listening deepen our prayer life and help us grow in wisdom and love.[4] In the next chapter, we will look at how prayer and a deepening awareness of the divine hold a prominent place in our search for wisdom during the direction process.

Reflection Questions

How do you listen to someone who does not want to be listened to?

How do you slow a person down so that silence may penetrate the ceaseless flow of thought that holds him or her captive?

What does active listening mean when the person before you cannot separate from the daily events that victimize him or her?

How can you gradually wean someone from the chaotic flow of external events and help the person construct a meaningful life narrative?

As difficult as it may be, could active listening be the key to this person's spiritual growth?

CHAPTER FOUR

Prayer

Just as soul and body combine to produce a human being, so practice of the virtues and contemplation together constitute a unique spiritual wisdom, and the Old and New Testaments together form a single mystery.
MAXIMUS THE CONFESSOR, "FOUR HUNDRED TEXTS ON LOVE"[1]

A listening presence leads us to yet another important mooring for spiritual direction—the need for prayer. "If you are a theologian, you will pray truly; and if you pray truly, you are a theologian."[2] These words of Evagrius Ponticus (AD 345-399) remind us of the intimate connection between *conversing with* and *understanding* the mystery of the divine. A true knowledge of God involves an experience of the divine mystery, not simply knowledge of it. Such experiential knowledge comes not through rational analysis but from a living relationship with God nourished by prayer. This understanding of theology emphasizes the importance of knowing God by participating in the intimate community of divine love. It emphasizes the living reality of God over our theological constructions of him. That reality is closer to us than we are to ourselves. We tap into it by being present to it and allowing it to be present to us. In this chapter, we will see how spiritual direction helps us to get in touch with this deeper spiritual reality.

Praying in Truth

The theologian, for Evagrius, is one who knows how "to pray in truth." To do so, we must strip off the old self and put on the new. Only then, by being renewed in the image of our Creator, will we gradually progress toward true knowledge of the divine (see Colossians 3:9–10). "To pray in truth" is to pray in Christ, the way, the truth, and the life (see John 14:6). Praying in truth has to do with opening our hearts and revealing ourselves to God as we really are. It means having the courage to look inside ourselves and confront the various masks and self-deceptions we find. It means being willing to risk baring our souls to God so God might bare his soul to us. Intimacy with the divine first requires intimacy with self. We cannot communicate with God in truth if we are unwilling to know the truth about ourselves. We need to take a good, hard look at ourselves in the mirror of our souls.

Coming to an intimate knowledge of ourselves is no easy task. Most of us cannot go it alone and are in dire need of help. We find facing our inner wants and insecurities much too threatening. Left to our own resources, many of us would end up rationalizing away our fears and discounting our deepest hopes about who we are and want to become. We are afraid to examine our deepest thoughts and feelings out of fear of what we might find, so we put off until tomorrow what needs to be done today. Spiritual direction seeks to remedy this. It provides the help we need to confront ourselves and open our hearts to God. It does so by gently helping us recognize and then listen to the voice of the Spirit manifested in the nitty-gritty circumstances of our lives. More often than not, that voice, as the experience of the prophet Elijah reminds us, is found not in the tumultuous whirlwinds, earthquakes, and fires about us but in the small whispering sound that can only be heard in the solitude of our hearts (see 1 Kings 19:11–13).

Spiritual direction seeks to settle our hearts so we can rest in this solitude and become ourselves in our faith. As a helping relationship between two people, it focuses on both conscious and unconscious interactions with the divine. It helps us to sift through the conflicting, often troublesome personal narratives vying for our attention so we can make responsible judgments about where we have come from and where we are being called. It pays special heed to our life of prayer, helping us to discern the true self from the false and authentic prayer from its paltry imitation.

The ultimate goal of spiritual direction is to help us pray in truth. To do so, it seeks to empower us to confront ourselves so we can eventually discover our authentic voice. That voice alone will lead us to intimacy with the divine. To find it, however, we must be patient, still, and ever so silent. We must listen to our heart and not be afraid to hear what it has to say. When we speak from the heart, we soon discover the gentle voice of the Spirit yearning within us and crying out "Abba! Father" (see Romans 8:15). To pray in truth is to pray in the Spirit, the re-creative presence of God that hovers over and revives the primal forces within us. We know we are praying in the Spirit when our lives manifest its various gifts and fruits (see Isaiah 11:2–3 and Galatians 5:22–23). Spiritual direction helps us to identify these spiritual riches and allow them to do their quiet work within us. That work concerns an ongoing, gradual process of divinization that draws us into a deeper participation in the eternal celebration of love within the Godhead.

Solitude of Heart

The primary means by which the Spirit accomplishes its task is by nurturing within us a deep desire and yearning for solitude. By helping us empty our hearts of unnecessary attachments, it enables us to make room for the divine indwelling. Solitude of heart is the precondition for our experience of the fullness of life. "The glory of God," says Irenaeus of Lyons, "is man fully alive."[3] We who are created in the image and likeness of God become ourselves only by allowing God to become himself in us. Spiritual direction seeks to help people open their hearts to the heart of God. It does so by helping them foster a contemplative attitude toward life that enables them to see all that happens in the light of God's providential plan.

Spiritual directors play an essential role in this process. By offering directees the hospitality of a listening heart, we set the tone for all that happens during the session. Being silently present to them with our full attention affirms the seriousness of what is taking place, which often develops into a lasting bond of friendship. This bond springs from our reflective gaze upon the person's unfolding experience and results in a shared experience of solitude. Three persons share in this solitude of heart: the director, the person seeking guidance, and the Holy Spirit. One of the goals of the direction process is for the director and directee to gradually turn their attention to the presence of this silent third partner in their midst.

They do so by discerning the signs of the Spirit in the narrative of life that directees share with their director. The Spirit leaves behind traces of its presence in the fabric of a person's life. When we look at our lives with prayerful reflection, these hidden vestiges gradually rise from obscurity and find their way into our conscious awareness. Once seen, the task is to interpret what these signs are saying so that the person seeking guidance can respond to them appropriately.

One of these signs is peace. After his resurrection, Jesus comforted his disciples with a reassuring message of peace that stemmed from his immediate and unquestioning trust in the Father's love (see Luke 24:36 and John 20:19, 21). Today this same message comes to us through the yearning of the Spirit in our hearts who intercedes for us to the Lord with unutterable groaning (see Romans 8:26). As directors, we need to help those seeking guidance to recognize those factors in their lives contributing to the further establishment of peace. Such peace comes not from the world but by giving oneself wholeheartedly to the one thing that ultimately matters—the love of God dwelling in the human heart. "The paradise of God," said Alphonsus de Liguori, "is the heart of man."[4] The peace of Christ works its way outward from within. Rooted in the love of the Lord, it eventually finds outward expression in our striving to form right relationships with others on every level of human society (family, country, the community of nations). Peace, or the "tranquility of order," as Augustine of Hippo referred to it, possesses personal, communal, and transcendent dimensions.[5] Solitude of heart is a necessary prerequisite for its discovery in our lives. Spiritual direction, in turn, is an important instrument given to us by God for allowing that discovery to take place.

Faith Seeking Understanding

If the theologian is the person who prays in truth, then spiritual direction concerns the process that allows such prayer to take shape in a person's life. Theology, as the learned editors of *The Philokalia* tell us "denotes…far more than the learning about God and religious doctrine acquired through academic study. It signifies active and conscious participation in or perception of the realities of the divine world—in other words, the realization of spiritual knowledge."[6] To be more specific, theology has to do with our attempt to reflect upon our experience of the indwelling of the Trinity in our hearts. When seen in this light, the classical Western understanding of theology as "faith seeking understanding" developed by Anselm of Canterbury under the influence of the Latin

Vulgate and Augustine of Hippo needs to be rescued from the overrationalized interpretation it had been subjected to in later centuries and examined within the broader framework of the acquisition of Christian wisdom.[7] When understood as a sapiential (as opposed to a narrowly defined rational) enterprise, theology's true task comes to the fore.

All of us are called to reflect upon the meaning of our lives in the light of the gospel message. To accomplish this task well we must reflect upon the experience of God within our hearts and try to ascertain what is being asked of us. When understood wisely, theology as "faith seeking understanding" tries to discern the movement of the Spirit in our lives so we can better understand how to live out our call to discipleship maturely and responsibly. The ministry of spiritual direction is an important arena where this acquisition of spiritual wisdom occurs. With a goal to help us to become ourselves in our faith, it helps us talk to God, listen to him, and engage in a process of discernment that ultimately leads to deeper intimacy with him.

Spiritual direction achieves this goal through an honest, sharing relationship between two persons. The dynamics of this relationship, while complex, are primarily focused on the relationship between those seeking guidance and God. Within this framework, our role as directors is to help directees come to a better understanding of themselves and their interaction with and ongoing response to the divine. We seek to enable them to draw closer to God, and we do so in a way that is both challenging and consoling. As directors, we need to challenge those coming to us to be honest with themselves and to identify significant areas of future growth. We also need to comfort them in times of discouragement and loss. Knowing when to exercise this dual role of challenge and comfort comprises one of the primary skills necessary for the formation of competent directors.

In the final analysis, the process of "faith seeking understanding" in spiritual direction requires flexibility, strength, adaptability, and the capacity to withstand adverse challenges. The fruits of the process stand for themselves: the belief that as one searches for meaning in life, it leads to a deeper understanding of one's situation and ultimately to one's relationship with oneself, others, and with God. Spiritual direction, in its many shapes, seeks to empower us to affirm our faith so we can become ourselves more fully in the process.

Becoming Holy

Becoming ourselves in our faith is but another way of speaking about our desire for holiness. Spiritual direction is not simply a matter of helping us gain greater insight into our relationship with God. It has very much to do with turning those insights into concrete practices that will help us walk further along the path of conversion.

These practices (personal prayer, fasting, spiritual reading, acts of charity, frequenting the sacraments) must not be imposed from without but arise from within. They must be based on a realistic assessment of our needs seen in the light of the insights gained during the direction process. A truly wise person is also a holy person—and vice versa. According to Thomas Aquinas, wisdom is the gift of the Spirit that corresponds to and is guided by the perfection of charity.[8] The wisdom derived from spiritual direction leads us eventually from knowing God to loving and serving him. When seen in terms of "faith seeking understanding," the work of spiritual direction is not only to help us see more clearly into the nature of our relationship with the divine but also to incorporate those insights concretely into our daily lives.

This close relationship between "being" and "action" is an important theme for the sapiential function of spiritual direction and the way it manifests itself in the direction process. Virtuous actions are performed by people striving to be virtuous, and they contribute to making them even more virtuous. When the question "What should I do?" arises during the direction session, the directee is ultimately asking about what kind of person he or she wishes to become. When properly exercised, spiritual direction helps us to see this important connection and encourages us to make communion with God the underlying motivating force of all of our actions. Living in communion with God is another way of talking about becoming holy. It is a primary concern of the direction process and its ongoing goal of helping people become themselves in their faith.

When seen as an ongoing process of "faith seeking understanding," spiritual direction tries to help us not only to discern but also to act. By far, the most important action any of us can do is to pray. Prayer is often termed "the great means of salvation."[9] Our manner of prayer—its frequency, form, and composition—should always remain a vital subject in the direction process. During direction, we need to ask if the prayer forms we are using address the various dimension of our human makeup: the physical, emotional, intellectual, social, and spiritual. With the help of our director, we should try to identify in prayer which dimensions we are neglecting and take appropriate steps to achieve a proper balance in our lives. The way we pray says a great deal about our own self-understanding and how we relate to God. By examining our prayer with care and looking for ways to improve it, we demonstrate our love for God and longing for holiness.

Conclusion

Spiritual direction helps us to understand and practice the nature of true prayer. It points the way to self-knowledge and invites us to deeper intimacy with God. This experiential knowledge transcends the conceptual world of the professional theologian. It grants us a participation in the divine love and endows us with an intuitive sense of the divine mind.

By helping us "to pray in truth," spiritual direction aids us in our faith-filled search for understanding and enables us to become ourselves in our faith. The goal of spiritual direction is to draw us closer to God so we can share in the full benefits of what it means to live in the Spirit. One of the primary benefits of this process is the reception and exercise of the gift of wisdom, an intimate knowledge of God that comes to us through the ongoing perfection of charity in our lives. By teaching us to listen to the movement of the Spirit in our hearts and to respond accordingly, spiritual direction initiates us into the ways of wisdom. It does so by helping us to view the world around us with eyes of compassion and with a sense of God's intense longing to dwell in our hearts. Saint Alphonsus de Liguori viewed the world in this way. In the next part of this book, we will propose an approach to spiritual direction rooted in his moral and spiritual vision.

Reflection Questions

Is it possible to direct someone who may be further along the path of holiness than you?

What are some of the dangers to expect when directing someone who has advanced far in his or her relationship with God?

What negative signs should you look for that would indicate that something has gone awry?

What can you do to make sure this person continues along the path of holiness?

Would there ever come a time when you might suggest that he or she see another director?

PART TWO

An Alphonsian Approach to Spiritual Direction

Part two flows out of the general overview of spiritual direction in the preceding chapters and develops a model of direction based on Alphonsus' manner of mental prayer. It offers a brief presentation of Alphonsian spirituality (chapter five), discusses how Alphonsus should be interpreted today (chapter six), presents the dynamics of the Alphonsian model of direction (chapter seven), and looks at the various qualities of an Alphonsian director (chapter eight). It presents the basic elements of the model so that directors can study them and adapt them to their particular needs and circumstances. The goal is to provide directors with a simple, easy-to-learn, and practical tool they can use to help directees become themselves in their faith. Those interested in expanding their reading on this subject can turn to my book *With Open Heart: Spiritual Direction in the Alphonsian Tradition*.[1]

CHAPTER FIVE

The Spiritual Legacy of St. Alphonsus de Liguori

⇵

O robber of hearts, the strength of your love has broken the exceeding hardness of our hearts! You have inflamed the whole world with your love. O most loving Lord, inebriate our hearts with this wine, consume them with this fire, pierce them with this dart of your love.

ALPHONSUS DE LIGUORI,

THE PRACTICE OF THE LOVE OF JESUS CHRIST, INTRODUCTION[1]

After our overview of the fundamentals of spiritual direction, we now need to ask ourselves if the spiritual doctrine of Alphonsus de Liguori—founder of the Redemptorists, doctor of prayer, and patron saint of confessors and moral theologians—has anything to offer today's spiritual directors as they seek deeper insights into the nature of their ministry. Can his teachings offer directors anything that will enable them to practice their craft with more competence and heightened pastoral concern? Can they provide directors with insights into how they can help others to listen and respond to the gentle movements of the Spirit deep within their hearts? Answering such questions is more difficult than many of us might first admit. The spiritual landscape of eighteenth-century Naples and its environs was very different from our own.² Some of the most basic presuppositions of Alphonsus' approach to spiritual direction (for example, its highly directive nature, its close link with sacramental reconciliation) are questioned by many involved in the ministry today, if not outrightly opposed.³

A Shift in Focus

What is more, today's spiritual directors are likely to be men and women from all walks of life, a stark contrast to the predominantly clerical influence upon the ministry prominent in Alphonsus' day. In many circles, moreover, the phrase "spiritual direction" has itself given way to more nondirective expressions such as "spiritual friendship," "spiritual guidance," and "spiritual accompaniment."⁴ Such changes give witness to the radical shift in the approach taken towards spiritual direction over the past fifty years. Today the ministry is much more interdisciplinary and ecumenical than it was in eighteenth century, so much so that one may wonder if Alphonsus has anything to offer spiritual directors whose approach to ministry is so different from his own.⁵

When dealing with the life and works of Alphonsus de Liguori, we cannot expect to find precise, ready-made solutions for how the practice of spiritual direction should be conducted today. It would be equally unrealistic, however, to think that he has nothing to offer our current understanding of the ministry. Although Alphonsus was limited by the general spiritual outlook of his day, he was also at times both probing and creative enough to surpass it—and often with great benefit to the people he served.⁶ In understanding Alphonsus' relevance for spiritual direction today, much will depend on how we approach his thoughts and which aspects we choose to emphasize. In this chapter, we will examine the basis of his reputation as a "spiritual master" and identify those elements that can be helpful to those interested in using the Alphonsian perspective as a touchstone for their practice of spiritual direction.

A Gospel Spirituality

At the outset, it is important for us to recognize Alphonsus' deep missionary fervor. The major projects of his life—his mission preaching, his writing, the work of founding the Redemptorist Congregation, his life of prayer—were all motivated by his profound desire to share the good news of plentiful redemption in Christ with others, especially the poor and abandoned. Alphonsian spirituality is, first and foremost, a gospel spirituality, one rooted in the person of Jesus Christ and which takes seriously the Lord's injunction to his apostles "to make disciples of all nations" (Matthew 28:19).[7] In the context of eighteenth-century Naples, Alphonsus interpreted this calling and personalized it in a very specific way. Rather than looking to the foreign missions, he focused on those areas in his own back yard, where people did not have easy access to the ordinary means provided by the Church for spiritual growth.[8]

This emphasis on the poor and willingness to go where others refused to travel led Alphonsus and his small band of followers to the hilltops and small mountain villages on the back roads of the kingdom of Naples. Their evangelizing efforts for the poor, illiterate, peasant stock they found in the forgotten hamlets of Campania, Puglia, Basilicata, and Calabria helped change the spiritual landscape of southern Italy. These early Redemptorist missioners reminded those they served that God had not forgotten them but was very much with them in their thirst for spiritual growth. To make sure that such growth would continue, Alphonsus and his followers set up flexible structures of devotional practice (for example, confraternities, eucharistic devotions, pious spiritual exercises) that would help to foster a life of prayer and devotion in these fledgling faith communities after they had left.[9]

Alphonsus' particular brand of gospel spirituality helps us to appreciate even more the various nuances in the old debate about whether there is a single Christian spirituality—or many.[10] To the extent that every expression of it must be rooted in the person of Christ, Christian spirituality is fundamentally one. At various times in Church history, however, certain individuals and groups have been called to root their following of Christ in a particular work, spiritual practice, or style of living. The great number of religious congregations, secular institutes, and lay movements that have appeared in the history of the Church point to the almost infinite number of expressions that can be given to following Christ. In this sense, there are many Christian spiritualities—and many still to come. For our purposes, Alphonsus' own way of practicing the love of Jesus Christ can be thought of as being both different from and united to all other authentic Christian spiritualities. Because of its flexibility and popular diffusion, moreover, his particular brand of gospel spirituality reminds us that the term "spirituality" itself allows for various nuances and can be treated on a number of levels.[11]

A Man of Prayer

Throughout his life, Alphonsus' overriding purpose was to do all he could to draw others closer to Christ. He believed that everyone could share an intimate relationship with Jesus, and that the key to developing such a relationship was to be persistent and dedicated in the life of prayer. "He who prays is certainly saved. He who prays not is certainly damned."[12] These words of Alphonsus indicate the strong emphasis that he placed on the role of prayer in fostering a mature relationship with God.

Prayer, for Alphonsus, was "the great means of salvation."[13] Everyone, he believed, received sufficient grace to pray. *Meditatio*, or mental prayer was particularly important for turning one's whole heart and mind to the Lord.[14] Alphonsus, in fact, would develop a very simple formula of mental prayer that could be easily taught to the simple rustics of the Italian hill country. He simplified this "prayer form" for them and thus introduced them to one of the great riches of the Church's spiritual tradition. In doing so, he was heavily criticized by a number of diocesan and religious clerics for "casting pearls to swine" and thereby desecrating the Church's treasures by sharing them with people who could not possibly appreciate them, let alone put them into practice.[15]

Alphonsus, however, had little time for such judgmental remarks (or for those who made them). Throughout his life, he pursued a consistent policy of popularizing the Church's teaching on prayer in a simple, easily understandable style. He met people where they were and helped them, little by little, to pray to God as intimate friends speak to one another. Prayer, for Alphonsus, was the means par excellence for fostering friendship with God and bringing about an intimate communion of hearts. He never tired of emphasizing the centrality of prayer in the spiritual life: "There may be some who, after the perusal of my spiritual works, will accuse me of tediousness in so often recommending the importance and necessity of having continual recourse to God in prayer. But I seem to myself to have said not too much but far too little."[16] Not only did he emphasize this central theme in his own writings but he also encouraged others to do the same: "…I say, and repeat, and will keep on repeating as long as I live, that our whole salvation depends on prayer; and therefore, that all writers in their books, all preachers in their sermons, all confessors in their instructions to their penitents, should not inculcate anything more strongly than continual prayer."[17] It is no small coincidence that Alphonsus is often referred to as the Doctor of Prayer.[18] Prayer was the centerpiece of his spiritual doctrine. For him, we can get nowhere in the spiritual life without it. With it, we have access to the copious redemption made possible for us through the passion, death, and resurrection of Jesus Christ. (Alphonsus' more particular teaching on mental prayer will be examined in detail in chapter six.)

On Leading Others to God

Leading others to Christ was what Alphonsus' missionary vocation was all about. When understood under the general heading of the "care for and cure of souls," spiritual direction encompasses virtually every aspect of the Church's pastoral ministry. Preaching, teaching, celebrating the sacraments, visiting the sick—*any* activity whose ultimate goal is to help people draw closer to Christ can be thought of as a type of spiritual guidance or accompaniment. When taken in the more specific sense, however, of "a helping relationship focusing on a person's growth in the spiritual life," it displays unique characteristics in its own right and emerges as a highly specialized ministry.[19]

Such an assessment would be doubly true for someone like Alphonsus, who labored assiduously through his preaching, writing, direction of souls, and general pastoral care to do all he could to lead others to a deeper, more intimate relationship with God. When taken in this general sense, everything Alphonsus did can be considered a kind of spiritual direction. Even activities that did not directly touch the lives of those he served (for example, his prayer, spiritual reading, and private devotions) had an underlying missionary dimension to them. For Alphonsus, prayer and action are two sides of the same apostolic coin. To separate them or to give undue precedence to one could run the risk of doing grave damage to both the missionary and the people he has been called upon to serve.[20]

When taken in the more specific sense of "a helping relationship focusing on a person's spiritual growth," Alphonsus' approach to spiritual direction is generally directive in nature and closely tied to his confessional practice.[21] That is not to say that he did not, at times, resort to spiritual direction through correspondence or that he never conducted a session of spiritual direction outside of the confessional.[22] On the contrary, his prudent temperament and practical use of the Church's spiritual tradition led him to take extenuating circumstances into account and to adapt his pastoral practice to the cases at hand. In general, however, Alphonsus saw a close connection between spiritual direction and sacramental confession. While he was aware of the distinction between the two, he was very firm in his insistence that the confessor be someone who not only forgives sins but who helped form the penitent's conscience and thus lead him or her further along the path of sanctity.[23]

Alphonsus' strong penchant for uniting the two appear most clearly in his *Praxis confessarii*, where he delineates in descending hierarchy the four offices of the confessor to be those of father, doctor, teacher, and judge.[24] For Alphonsus, every confessor had the responsibility of guiding souls to sanctity. This was because all the faithful (not just a select few) were called to the perfection of Christian living. The term *spiritual director*, in other words, was not meant simply for those who guided people through the rarified states of mystical experience but for all confessors who helped people from various states of life within the Church to walk the path of holiness. When seen in this light, Alphonsus went a long way to demystify the role of spiritual director in the Christian tradition. His strong popularizing efforts brought the riches of the spiritual life to the person in the pew. This meat-and-potatoes approach to the spiritual life was a benchmark of Redemptorist practice and characterized the Alphonsian approach to direction for years to come.

More specifically, Emilio Lage identifies the principal characteristics of the Alphonsian confessor-director as:

1. An attitude of being more of a father and doctor than a judge. This attitude manifests itself in the charity, goodness, and mildness with which the confessor welcomes and treats the penitent and in the task of disposing him or her to penitence so that the confessor would not feel obligated to defer or to deny absolution.

2. An attitude of kindness in giving penance, seeking more that which would heal the soul than the punishment or satisfaction for the fault committed.

3. A marked preference for the poorest and most ignorant social class.

4. A concern for giving the penitent not only the means of perseverance for preventing a relapse into sin but also the means for advancing in the way of holiness.

5. Recognizing the relationship between preaching and confession: preaching prepares the way for confession and continues the work undertaken by it.[25]

These characteristics of the Alphonsian confessor-director demonstrate the practical orientation of Alphonsus' mission. He sought to preach the good news of plentiful redemption to as many people as possible. In this capacity, he saw the wisdom of treating the confessional not as a tribunal but as a means for educating the faithful in the ways of holiness. The intrinsic connections he saw between preaching and confession also reveal that he himself understood the direction process as something that extended to the ordinary care of souls.

For Alphonsus' approach to direction outside the confessional, we can turn to his letters to women religious. Joseph Oppitz summarizes his approach:

> *The first step*: The person must be made aware of God's unsurpassable love for him or her. To this end, all the Gospel texts that point to the Father's loving, salvific plan, carried out in Christ and his sacraments, must be marshaled forth and passionately proclaimed. In a word, the authentic image of God as a God of love must be accepted, internalized, and then responded to in the following ways.
>
> *The second step*: There then follows a firm decision and deep resolve to take all the positive moves and accept the negative denials that are necessary in a sincere striving for an ever more intimate love relationship with the Father and his loving will. This is the sacrificial and self-denial aspect of love.
>
> *The third step*: The will must be set on fire with ardent desires, a real yearning for an efficacious union of wills, and this involves a constant discerning as to what is God's will. Alphonsus often uses the phrase "to give him pleasure" to express the effect of love's yearning.
>
> *The fourth step*: There must be a continual refocusing of the heart on the final goal of total union in heaven. For this purpose Liguori insists upon daily mental prayer with special emphasis on what he called "the eternal truths," namely the ultimate meaning of human existence as seen in the loving, salvific will of God, the basic options, and so on.[26]

Whether inside or outside the confessional, Alphonsus' primary objective in spiritual direction was to help a person draw closer to God. He encouraged those who came to him to take concrete, practical steps that would move them in that direction. For him, the ultimate goal of spiritual direction was to help a person turn his or her whole heart and mind over to God. This ardent desire to bring about a radical conversion (*metanoia*) in a person's life lay at the very heart of his apostolic message.

Conclusion

Alphonsus de Liguori was revered in his day as an outstanding moralist. The focus of his spirituality was to help others draw closer to Christ and instill in them a deep awareness of God's love for them so that they might respond in turn. Typical for its day, his approach to spiritual direction was directive and closely tied to the formation of conscience and the Church's confessional practice. At the same time, it was imbued with a love for freedom under the law, a concern for balance and prudential judgment, and an emphasis on fatherly kindness.

Alphonsus' missionary spirituality was entirely focused on leading others to God. He was deeply aware of humanity's sinful condition yet firmly believed that God's love for us as manifested in the life of Jesus of Nazareth could cast out all darkness from our hearts and lead us along the way of holiness. Alphonsus continued Christ's missionary efforts through his preaching, the promotion of the Church's sacramental life (especially confession), and his numerous writings. Even his prayer life was oriented toward the conversion of souls. After all, how could he expect others to walk the way of holiness if he himself did not take his own spiritual life seriously and forge a path ahead for them?

As we shall see in the following chapters, Alphonsus' moral and spiritual outlook has much to offer us today. Although a connection between spiritual direction and sacramental confession still exists today, in recent decades it has become more common to separate the two. This is due in large part to the growing number of laity who have become spiritual directors and, not being priests, cannot administer the sacrament. If such be the case, we maintain that spiritual directors in the Alphonsian tradition should, at the very least, maintain a healthy respect for the sacrament and be able to help directees discern when they need to take advantage of the sacrament. Alphonsus' spiritual legacy has much to offer today's spiritual directors, especially if, as outlined in the next chapter, they focus on his approach to mental prayer and adapt it to the dynamics of the direction process.

Reflection Questions

How would you describe Alphonsian spirituality?

What role does the heart play in Alphonsian spirituality?

What role does prayer play in Alphonsian spirituality?

What did Alphonsus understand by "mental prayer"?

How did Alphonsus understand the relationship between the moral and spiritual lives?

CHAPTER SIX

Interpreting St. Alphonsus Today

*Accustom yourself to speak to God, one to one,
in a familiar manner as to the dearest friend you have
and who loves you best of all.*
ALPHONSUS DE LIGUORI, *THE WAY TO CONVERSE ALWAYS
AND FAMILIARLY WITH GOD*[1]

Alphonsus' understanding of mental prayer has much to contribute to the process of spiritual direction. As stated earlier, Alphonsus' reputation as a spiritual master has led many to refer to him as the Doctor of Prayer. His renown as a spiritual director comes from his creative, pragmatic use of the traditions that preceded him. As an interpreter of these traditions, he focused on the one thing that, in his judgment, ultimately mattered in life: to enter into an intimate relationship with Jesus, the Redeemer.[2] Prayer, for him, was the primary means to accomplish this end. Spiritual direction, in his mind, was both general and particular. It could take place in many contexts but primarily had to do with the confessor's task of helping a person grow in holiness.

Spiritual Direction and the Confessional

While Alphonsus saw a distinction between the confessional and spiritual direction, his pragmatic orientation, zeal for souls, and deep popularizing sensitivities brought him to the conclusion that the people of God could best be served by drawing a close bond between the two. Sacramental confession, after all, was an application of Christ's redemptive love to the life of the penitent. Since redemption was plentiful for Alphonsus, it followed that the experience of sacramental reconciliation should include not only the forgiveness of sin but also concrete guidance that would enable the penitent to grow in holiness.[3] He believed spiritual direction was for the masses—not a select few—and for people of all walks of life. The close bond he saw between preaching and the confession-spiritual direction experience also points to the organic (even circular) relationship between the general and particular elements of the direction process.

These considerations have great importance for those who are trying to understand the relevance of Alphonsus' moral and spiritual doctrine today. His walk with the Lord was both similar to and different from our own. Walking in his footsteps today cannot possibly mean following his teachings to the letter. Such an approach would overlook the prudent nature of Alphonsus' own pastoral decisions and fail to take into account the pressing concerns and different pastoral needs of our own historical circumstances.

On the contrary, following Alphonsus today means being willing to make a creative and pragmatic use of the spiritual traditions that have preceded us—especially that of Alphonsus himself. It means sifting through the various teachings and practices that he considered beneficial for the people of his day and trying to find appropriate practical parallels for our times.[4] For our purposes, it means trying to develop an approach to spiritual direction that will give people easy access to the liberating message of the plentiful redemption of Christ and helping to foster an ongoing conversation with God in the deepest recesses of their hearts. Spiritual direction in the Alphonsian tradition today should not pretend or even try to be an exact replica of what it was during Alphonsus' lifetime. It should resonate with his teaching, however, and be clearly seen as something that flows from his zealous missionary spirit and his deep desire to lead as many people as possible into a deep, intimate friendship with the Lord.

The chapters to follow will attempt to make this important historical correlation by applying the dynamics of Alphonsus' approach to mental prayer to the process of spiritual direction. I will argue that the manner of making mental prayer promoted by Alphonsus has great relevance for the way his followers should understand and implement their approach to the ministry of spiritual direction today. Here is a look at his approach to mental prayer.

The "How" of Mental Prayer

In implementing his pastoral aims, Alphonsus was a great popularizer and synthesizer. His doctrine of prayer is actually very simple. "Everyone receives sufficient grace to pray."[5] "He who prays is certainly saved. He who prays not is certainly damned."[6] "God wishes us to speak to him with confidence and familiarity."[7] "Mental prayer is morally necessary for salvation."[8] These simple phrases represent the hallmark of his teaching and could be easily remembered by those who came to him. They also point to the main characteristics of his spiritual doctrine. Alphonsian prayer is honest, humble, passionate, practical, spontaneous, continual, popular, devotional, and petitionary. Above all, it is simple and childlike.[9] In Alphonsus' mind, everyone might not experience the heights of mystical prayer, at least in this life. All, however, are called to a life a prayer, one that will provide them with the means of salvation and which will enable them to talk to God as one friend to another. For him, mental prayer is the form of prayer that best fosters this type of relationship in the lives of the faithful. It is meant for everyone, not a select few, and for this reason is the centerpiece of his teaching on prayer.[10]

Alphonsus lived at a time when there already existed a great variety of mental prayer methods to choose from, including those of Ignatius of Loyola, Teresa of Ávila, Francis de Sales, John Baptist de La Salle, and the priests of St. Sulpice.[11] Those methods employed a variety of techniques for helping a person to foster in his or her life an intimate conversation with God. They were similar in that each contained: (1) an element of reflection on a divine truth, (2) the application of the insights gained from this reflection to one's life, and (3) making a decision to do something about it.[12] Alphonsus used these same basic ingredients in his own approach to mental prayer. What set him apart was his creative and practical use of these other methods in order to "custom build" an approach to mental prayer that was especially suited to his particular pastoral concerns.

Alphonsus treated the topic of mental prayer a number of times in his literary corpus, an indication of the important place it held in his overall pastoral strategy.[13] Even though he believed that everyone received sufficient grace to pray, he was utterly convinced that people needed instruction in the basics of how to carry on a close, intimate conversation with God. Mental prayer, in his mind, was the simplest and most expedient way of doing so. Without it, a person would be unable to pray as he or she ought. With it, that person was sure to enjoy a vital relationship with Christ. It was for this reason that Alphonsus considered mental prayer morally necessary for salvation. He developed his approach in order to reach as many people as possible. When compared to some of the other methods available at the time, it was simple, straightforward, and relatively easy to learn.[14]

Alphonsus, we should note, preferred to speak of "the manner" or "way" (*il modo*) rather than "the method" (*il metodo*) of making mental prayer.[15] He understood that the relationship between the human and the divine fostered in mental prayer could suffer from too much structure. To approach God with a ready-made, step-by-step recipe for intimacy could be a sign of disrespect and perhaps even a subtle form of manipulation. His method was really nothing more than a series of flexible guidelines that he had found from his own experience to be valuable tools in nurturing one's relationship with God. Taken together, the various elements of his manner of making mental prayer involved a person's body, emotions, intellect, will, spirit and, when done in common as he strongly suggested, even community. During mental prayer, these important dimensions of human existence were opened up to God and laid bare. By expressing oneself in this way, a person concretely manifested his or her dependence on God. Recognizing one's need for God was the necessary first step in developing a vital, intimate relationship with the divine.[16]

Alphonsus firmly believed that God wanted everyone to be saved and that teaching people the manner of making mental prayer was the best means at his disposal for insuring that they were headed in the right direction. In developing his approach, he was especially indebted to Teresa of Ávila for the close connection she saw between prayer and love and to Francis de Sales for a simple model that would eventually become even simpler. Alphonsus, one might say, followed the spirit of Teresa and simplified the model of Francis de Sales to meet his particular pastoral concerns.[17] The result was an approach to mental prayer that could be taught to anyone, especially the poor, unlearned peasants whom he encountered on the back roads and in the forgotten villages of the southern Italian hill country.

"Mental prayer," for Alphonsus, "...is nothing more than a converse between the soul and God; the soul pours forth to him its affections, its desires, its fears, its requests, and God speaks to the heart, causing it to know its goodness, and the love which he bears it, and what it must do to please him."[18] He considers it essential for growth in the spiritual life: it enlightens our minds; it disposes us to practice the virtues; and it helps us to pray as we should. For these reasons, it is an indispensable part of our walk to holiness and can be considered morally necessary for salvation.

Mental prayer, according to Alphonsus, is not just for the select few. Anyone can do it, and everyone is called to it. It is also relatively easy to learn. It has a clearly defined beginning, middle, and end—what Alphonsus calls the preparation, the meditation itself, and the conclusion. In the *preparation*, the person praying affirms his or her faith in God's presence, makes an act of humble contrition, and requests enlightenment during the upcoming exercise. The *meditation* involves four movements: (1) reflecting on some aspect of the life of faith by using a passage from Scripture or a devotional work as a point of departure, (2) raising one's heart and affections to God by naming our current feelings and sharing them with the Lord, (3) asking God for help in meeting our needs, both large and small, and (4) making resolutions to improve one's walk with the Lord by coming up with a practical, concrete course of action. The *conclusion* consists of thanking God for the enlightenment received, affirming one's decision to carry out the resolution, and asking God for the grace of fidelity. At the end of each session, Alphonsus also encourages the one meditating to pray for others, especially the deceased and those hardened by sin.[19]

At the heart of Alphonsus' approach lies the need to retreat to the solitude of one's heart to get in touch with one's deepest yearnings and express them to God.[20] Asking God for help is a central feature of this manner of mental prayer. When making these petitions, we are not telling God something he does not already know but simply getting in touch with our dependence on him for all things. Our recognition of this dependency puts us in touch with our ongoing need for conversion. Integral to this process is our need to make concrete resolutions of a practical order that will improve our relationship with ourselves, others, and God.[21]

Alphonsus' approach to mental prayer has great relevance today. In it, he offers an easy, uncomplicated way of probing our hearts and expressing what we find there to God. Although certain adaptations to his approach would have to be made in order to respond to our present sensitivities, the substance of his teaching remains a valuable point of departure for those interested in nurturing their relationship with the divine. Alphonsus believed that God's offer of plentiful redemption extended to everyone. His manner of making mental prayer provides us with a way of tapping into God's bountiful love for us so that even today that same love can become an integral, vital part of our daily lives.[22]

When properly carried out, this manner of making mental prayer can help a person foster an intimate relationship with the divine. It makes possible a dynamic encounter with God that involves an ongoing process of self-discovery, revelation of heart, request, and resolution. Interestingly enough, all of these elements are directly applicable to the ministry of spiritual direction in the Church today.

Conclusion

Alphonsus simplified the approach to mental prayer and made it accessible to everyone, not simply clergy and religious. He simplified it because he believed it was morally necessary for salvation and that even those who were illiterate and uneducated should be able to practice it.

One way of remembering his approach is by connecting its beginning, middle, and end with the number 343. The preparation involves three parts: an act of faith ("Lord, I believe in you."), and act of contrition ("Have mercy on me."), and a request for enlightenment ("Give me light."). The body, or middle part, contains four parts: a meditation on a mystery of the faith and its relevance for our lives ("Reflection"), expressing our feelings and affections to God ("Affections"), bringing our needs to God ("Petitions"), and making a practical decision to take the next step forward in the walk of faith ("Resolution"). The conclusion, in turn, has three parts: showing gratitude to God for the light we have received ("Thanksgiving"), asking God for the grace to carry out our resolution ("Seeking Grace"), and asking God for the grace of perseverance ("Asking for Perseverance"). From beginning to end, the whole process unfolds against a backdrop of silence: solitude of heart is necessary for any genuine dialogue with God (or anyone, for that matter) to occur.

We believe that Alphonsus' simple approach to mental prayer can be adapted to the dynamics of spiritual direction and seen as a basic model or template for directors wishing to meet people where they are and help them uncover the next steps they should take in their spiritual journey. The next chapter will draw out this connection and show how Alphonsus' teaching on prayer can reveal a great deal about how it relates in a vibrant way to today's more nondirective approach to the ministry.

Reflection Questions

How did Alphonsus understand the relationship between spiritual direction and the confessional?

How should that relationship be understood today?

What is solitude of heart?

What are the various steps in the Alphonsian approach to mental prayer?

Why is it important to bring our needs to God?

CHAPTER SEVEN

An Alphonsian Model of Spiritual Direction

All saints become saints by mental prayer. Mental prayer is the blessed furnace in which souls are inflamed with divine love.
ALPHONSUS DE LIGUORI, *MENTAL PRAYER AND THE EXERCISES OF A RETREAT*[1]

Alphonsus' guidelines for mental prayer can be taken as a metaphor for the spiritual direction process itself.[2] Before drawing out the various parallels involved, note that projecting Alphonsus' manner of mental prayer onto spiritual direction may contribute to the rediscovery of this important prayer form among Redemptorists and those they serve. Incorporating them into the dynamics of spiritual direction will help us draw important links between this facet of our spiritual heritage and our practice of this specialized ministry in the life of the Church. It will also offer hope to those who, for lack of guidance or misunderstandings about its purpose and scope, have had difficulties practicing Alphonsus' approach with regularity and conviction.

The "How" of Spiritual Direction

When receiving spiritual direction according to the upcoming proposed model, a person's appreciation of Alphonsus' approach to mental prayer should deepen considerably.

1. The Preparation. The spiritual direction session itself should always be preceded by a period of preparation. To a large extent, the quality of the session will be a function of the serious personal preparation that each of us has brought to it. Although the time allotted for this private preparation will vary from person to person, a minimum of fifteen to twenty minutes for an examination of consciousness should be set aside at some point prior to each session. During this time we look back on our lives and try to identify those encounters, events, and circumstances that have affected us most deeply and that we would like to explore during the direction session. This remote preparation will make the more immediate preparation at the outset of the session even more poignant and meaningful.

In addition to whatever the director and directee do privately, a session of direction should begin with them sitting together in silence. A minimum of one to three minutes should be set aside for this. As they do so, they bow their heads, assume a comfortable posture of prayer, and simply rest in the divine presence. When they have become sufficiently recollected, they should make brief acts of faith in God's presence, humility and contrition of heart, and a request for guidance. These acts can be done either silently or aloud. If the latter, they should occur at the end of the period of silence, just before the time for sharing begins. We can adapt Alphonsus' words to the direction process in this manner: "Lord, we believe that you are present with us during this period of direction" (Act of Faith in God's Presence). "Lord, we are sorry for our sins from the bottom of our hearts; have mercy on us" (Act of Humility and Contrition). "Dear Lord, give us light during this period of direction, that we may draw fruit from it" (Request for Guidance).[3] However they are expressed, making these prayers at the start of the direction session helps both the director and the directee to recognize the sacredness of what is about to take place. It helps them to place God at the center of the process and to see that, without his help, they can do nothing. By acknowledging the presence of the Lord in this way, they prepare to engage in a dialogue that is not a mere exchange of ideas but an encounter of holy listening where one discerning heart speaks to another. When the appropriate moment comes, they end the silence by praying together the doxology to the Lord's Prayer: "For the kingdom, the power and the glory are yours, now and forever. Amen."[4]

This opening period of silence is an essential part of the direction process: it provides a quiet starting point and lingers on in the conversation that follows. It also gives us an opportunity to center ourselves and to place our relationship before God. Sitting before one another, we can sense the sacredness of what is about to take place and allow the silent, existential backdrop of our lives to come to the fore. It also gives us time to settle down in each other's presence so that the spiritual direction process can begin to unfold. During this time, both of us adopt an attitude of active listening.[5] We open our spirits to the Spirit and ask it to dwell within us and in our midst. In doing so, we acknowledge the presence of the Lord and prepare to engage in a dialogue that is not a mere exchange of ideas but an encounter of holy listening where one discerning heart speaks to another.

2. *Spiritual Direction Process.* After the period of preparatory silence, the director and directee enter into the actual direction process. Following Alphonsus' guidelines for mental prayer, this process would include four distinct periods: meditation (what we will call reflection), affections, petitions, and resolutions. We will now demonstrate what each of these would look like in the context of spiritual direction.

a. *The Reflection.* Moving from silence into the direction period itself, the director invites the directee to engage in a process of reflection over the events since their last meeting. If the directee does not know where to begin, the director should reassure him that one place is as good as any other. When describing the manner of making mental prayer, Alphonsus encourages the meditative use of a book to get one going and to keep from being distracted. One is to stop reading, however, when one finds oneself touched or inwardly moved.[6] In spiritual direction, the directee should be encouraged to go over the book of his life and ask questions such as: "What has been going on in my life? What have been my triumphs? What have been my troubles? What are my deepest concerns? How have I been physically, emotionally, psychologically, and spiritually? How have my relationships and friendships been going? Where is God in all that has been happening to me? What is God asking of me at this point in my life?"

Recounting these events helps a person to gain perspective on them and receive deeper insights into their meaning. When the directee is moved by a particular event, he should be encouraged to look into the experience more deeply. The director should help the directee to reflect on the significance of the event through attentive listening, by finding connections with other things that have been shared, and by inviting the directee to look for God in the midst of these circumstances. During this time, the directee is more or less "unpacking" his life before the director and should be given the freedom to do so as he sees fit. The director, in turn, needs to listen carefully to what is being said, taking in the words and the intricate combination of bodily gestures, feelings, ideas, and silences that contribute to making the directee's statements a unique revelation of self.

b. *The Affections.* After an appropriate period of reflection, the directee should be helped to focus on the feelings about what has been shared. Until now, a significant effort has been made to unravel these events and to reflect upon their significance; it is now time to process them on an emotional level. In his guidelines for making mental prayer, Alphonsus encourages the meditating person to raise the heart to God with pious sentiments and acts of love.[7] To do so authentically, however, a person must first be in touch with feelings and recognize them for what they are. Many people cannot bring their emotions to prayer because they are terribly out of touch with them. At this stage of the direction process, the director needs to help the directee to identify and express the various nuances of her experience. This would include one's reactions toward particular situations, as well as one's emotional stance toward oneself, others, and God. During this time, the director should help the directee to probe his or her feelings—both positive and negative—about the various issues that have been raised thus far during the direction session. This can be done through sensitive, nonthreatening questions that invite the directee to delve into and to try to understand the emotional side of his or her life. If the directee finds this difficult, the director might be able to help by suggesting possible emotional responses and then asking the directee to identify which comes closest to her experience. When the directee's feelings have been sufficiently examined, the director can say something like: "You have expressed these feelings and emotions to me but have you ever expressed them to God?" (Wait for a response) "Do you think you can?" (Wait for a response) "Are you willing to try?" (Wait for a response). In most cases, the directee will say that she will try to bring these feelings to God in prayer. Once this happens, the directee should be able to express the genuine affections of love to God indicated by Alphonsus.

c. The Petitions. As the process of spiritual direction continues, we are called to get in touch with our feelings and our needs. In his guidelines for mental prayer, Alphonsus emphasizes the importance of bringing our needs to the Lord and asking for his help.[8] It is difficult to bring our needs to God, however, if we do not know what they are. At this point in the direction process, we are called to delve beneath our thoughts and feelings and to concentrate on what we need. When doing so, most of us will first focus on externals (for example, passing an exam, a problem at work, a raise in salary). While these are to be affirmed, the director should also encourage the directee to identify his interior needs as well, such as patience, gentleness, compassion. On the deepest level, the directee should, in time, surface his or her need for God. The goal is to be as honest with oneself and with one's director as possible. All of one's needs should be identified and taken possession of, regardless of how minor or insignificant they may seem. The director can help the directee in the identification process by mentioning the various anthropological dimensions of human existence—the physical, the emotional, the intellectual, the spiritual, and the social—and by reminding him that it is quite normal for us to have needs of various kinds. Once ample time has been given to discovering and taking possession of one's needs, the director should help the directee to recognize the even deeper need of expressing them to God. Scripture will be particularly helpful in this regard, especially those passages dealing with the importance of relying on God at all times and bringing our needs to him (see Matthew 7:7–11, Matthew 11:28–30, and John 15:1–8).

d. The Resolutions. Once the directee has been helped to probe his or her thoughts, emotions, and needs and to express them to God in prayer, the direction begins to wind down. In his guidelines for mental prayer, Alphonsus stresses the importance of making some practical resolutions which, through repeated effort, will help a person grow in virtue and holiness.[9] In a similar way, the director should encourage the directee to look back over the discussion that has taken place during the past hour and identify some concrete practices that will help draw the person closer to God. The goal is for the directee to take an honest look at his capabilities and to make a realistic decision about what steps should be taken next. The resolutions, in any case, must not be something imposed from without but discovered and embraced from within. The process of spiritual direction focuses on the directee's unique relationship with God. As such, it should eventually lead him or her to an awareness of what concrete steps can be taken to strengthen that bond. The director's role here should be to help the directee to be as realistic as possible in forming appropriate resolutions. Care should be taken to avoid broad, sweeping generalizations such as "spending more time with the Lord" or "deepening one's prayer life." If the directee seems too vague or abstract in forming these resolutions, questions should be asked like, "Practically speaking, what does this mean for you?" or, "How will this change your life?" Care must also be taken that the directee does not make a concrete resolution that is so demanding that he or she will have little hope of ever putting it into practice. It is much more desirable to make resolutions that lead to small incremental ways of deepening one's relationship with God, rather than formulate grandiose schemes that will never be implemented. The goal should be to help the directee ask honest questions about what he is capable of doing in trying to foster a deeper, more intimate relationship with the divine. In this way, the director will foster in the directee a deep sense of the importance of the continuity between belief and action. This "spirituality of practice" will gently lead the directee along the way of conversion and, in time, enable him or her to orient every dimension of life to the Lord.

3. *The Conclusion.* After the resolutions are made, the direction session should draw to a close, preferably through another period of silence. During this time, the director and directee gather into themselves all that has happened during their time together and thank the Lord for being with them. In the silence of the word, they recognize the limitations of their feeble attempts to articulate their experience and appreciate the importance of listening to life's experiences with attentive care. In his guidelines for mental prayer, Alphonsus suggests that the meditation period conclude with three acts of prayer: (1) thanksgiving for the enlightenment received, (2) asking for help to fulfill one's resolutions, and (3) petitioning Jesus and Mary for the grace of perseverance.[10] In a similar way, the director and directee should use the silence at the end of the direction process to thank the Lord for the guidance received, to seek help in implementing the practical steps decided upon, and to ask for perseverance in the walk of discipleship. These prayers can also be verbalized at the end of the period of silence with the simple words, "Thank you, Lord for guiding us during this hour. Enable us to put what we have learned into practice. Help us always to remain faithful." Spoken or unspoken, such prayers allow the director and directee to affirm the Lord's involvement in their search for discernment. As they sit together in silence, they gain a stronger sense of the Lord's deep, attentive listening to their concerns. So deep is this listening that it contains within itself the unspoken beginnings of an articulated response. God's word speaks to them in silence and sustains them in their struggle to make sense out of their lives. It follows them wherever they go and penetrates their experience from one moment to the next. When it is time to leave, they lift up their grateful hearts and repeat the same words with which they began the direction session: "For Thine is the kingdom, the power, and the glory, forever and ever. Amen!"

Conclusion

The Alphonsian tradition has much to offer today's spiritual directors as they seek to help others "to become themselves in their faith."[11] The model presented in this chapter understands that the dynamics of prayer fostered in a person's relationship with God can be transposed onto the process of direction itself and used to give that person deeper insights into the inner workings of his or her own spiritual life. When seen in this light, this new approach to spiritual direction is nothing but an extrapolation onto the plane of spiritual direction of some of Alphonsus' finest insights about the nature of prayer.

Using St. Alphonsus' guidelines for the manner of making mental prayer as the basis for a model of spiritual direction has many advantages. For one thing, it presents a viable approach to the ministry of spiritual direction in the Church today, one that is practical, easy to remember, and potentially beneficial to a great many people. It also offers a distinctive approach to this important ministry that is both highly creative and deeply rooted in the Alphonsian tradition. When the appropriate lines of confidentiality are drawn, the approach can also be used as a model in supervision sessions to help directors reflect on their experience and improve their own participation in the process. This correlation between the dynamics of mental prayer and spiritual direction also makes a great deal of sense.

It is appropriate that this practical, meat-and-potatoes approach to spiritual direction should have direct parallels with a prayer form so zealously promulgated by Alphonsus. The whole purpose of spiritual direction, after all, is not unlike the goal of mental prayer itself: to help a person draw closer to God.[12] This approach to spiritual direction should strengthen rather than diminish interest in this particular approach to prayer. Each of these practices, moreover, reflects different (albeit related) spheres of the spiritual life: one focuses specifically on conversing with the Lord; the other, on examining one's relationship with the Lord in a prayerful manner. Because of their close structural resemblance, the practice of one should reinforce the practice of the other—and vice versa.

This model of spiritual direction will matter very little, however, if directors do not take the time to ponder it, take ownership of it, and implement it in their ministry. To do so, they need to maintain an ongoing dialogue with the past so that helpful parallels can continue to be discovered between their rich spiritual tradition and the pressing needs of their ministry.

Directors have much to be grateful for in the heritage bequeathed to us by St. Alphonsus. In many respects, the process of transforming his insights into practical and relevant structures for today's ministry has only just begun. As this process continues, we need to be creative, yet watchful. The next chapter will focus specifically on the helping role assumed by Alphonsian directors and the qualities they should exhibit in the practice of this important ministry.

Reflection Questions

How would you describe the Alphonsian model of spiritual direction?

What are its various steps?

Are some of these steps more important than others?

How does this model parallel Alphonsus' approach to mental prayer?

What are the strengths and weaknesses of this model?

CHAPTER EIGHT

The Qualities of an Alphonsian Director

⤓⤒

Saint Paul gives us the marks of true charity and at the same time teaches us the practice of those virtues which are the daughters of charity; and he goes on to say: "Charity is patient, is kind; charity envies not, deals not perversely, is not puffed up, is not ambitious; seeks not her own, is not provoked to anger, thinks no evil; rejoices not in iniquity but rejoices with the truth; bears all things, believes all things, hopes all things, endures all things"
(1 Corinthians 13:4–7).

ALPHONSUS DE LIGUORI,
THE PRACTICE OF THE LOVE OF JESUS CHRIST[1]

What qualities should we look for in a spiritual director? Although more and more of today's faithful would like to receive the benefits of sound spiritual direction, many feel frustrated by what they perceive as an increasing lack of qualified personnel. The difficulty in finding a good spiritual director is a common complaint among those interested in their own self-knowledge and spiritual growth. It is often compounded by a tendency among many involved in pastoral ministry to leave this growing demand in the hands of qualified experts. While such an attitude is understandable in light of the current movement in the Church toward theological and pastoral specialization, it nevertheless overlooks the great amount of good that can be done in this area by less specially trained pastoral ministers, such as local pastors, deacons, and lay associates. The Alphonsian model of direction is particularly suited to such ministers, since it is sound, practical, user-friendly, and easy to implement.

Although not everyone in ministry should be engaged in the practice of spiritual direction, not everyone needs a long list of credentials in the field. More likely than not, the interested and conscientious pastoral minister can be a good director with a minimal amount of training and a sensible awareness of his limitations. Most cases of spiritual direction, in fact, do not require the opinion of experts. The relationship between a spiritual director and a directee can be fruitful even when the director devotes only a few days a month to developing the art. That is not to say that certain qualities are not required of every good spiritual director. Based on the premise that quality direction can be offered with a minimum of time and without a relaxation of standards, the following list of helpful hints seeks to inspire those capable pastoral ministers who may be interested in taking up the practice but, for whatever reason, are reluctant to do so.

Setting the Outer Limits

At the outset, it is important for directors to pinpoint the precise level of commitment they are willing to make to their initial training, ongoing reading and supervision, frequency of sessions, number of directees, and, most importantly, level of directional competency. Such a commitment should entail a clear idea of the time per month they are willing to devote to spiritual direction and to the number of persons they are willing to counsel. Overcommitted directors can easily hinder the spiritual growth of those they are ostensibly trying to help. This level of commitment should be reviewed periodically with the help of a qualified supervisor, perhaps in the context of a support group of spiritual directors that meets regularly to compare notes and to discuss specific cases from verbatims, case studies, and such.[2] Before taking on directees, directors should have completed at least three courses in the practice of spiritual direction from a qualified institute: one involving the various models of direction; the second, on the Alphonsian model itself; and the third, a supervised practicum. They should also be aware of the various types of direction possible; have access to a comprehensive bibliography on direction methods; and have themselves received extended, regular direction from a certified director.[3]

It is also advisable that directors have an extended support and referral network which includes: (1) a supervised support group, (2) a more experienced mentor willing to help with difficult cases, (3) a counselor or therapist who has worked in the field of spiritual direction, (4) a medical doctor, and (5) lawyers in both civil and canon law.[4] The purpose of such a network would be to ensure easy access to competent help in the event of extreme or complicated cases. Such a system would be of little benefit if directors never used it. Sensitive to their own inexperience, directors should not be afraid to have frequent recourse to such professionals. An appropriate knowledge of one's own level of competency—such as when and when not to refer—normally comes only after a system of support and referral has been tried and comfortably set in place. Since it is precisely through such a system that even expert directors have come to know their strengths and weaknesses, the sooner it is set in place for directors, the more adept they will be in discerning the quiet presence of God in the many spheres of human experience.

Setting the Inner Limits

Directors should also have a clear idea about what goes on in spiritual direction. These inner limits should define the nature of the relationship between the director and directee, and include a reflective consciousness of the various preconceptions being made about God, society, the person, Scripture, tradition, suffering, and more. Directors, in other words, should be concerned with enabling their directees to confront the various anthropological, philosophical, and theological presuppositions they make about human existence. The limits should also include a clear understanding of the particular model of spiritual direction being undertaken (direct, indirect, or various combinations of the two) and be flexible enough to change with the developing needs and expectations of their directees.

During spiritual direction sessions, the discussion should focus specifically on the correlation between the directee's daily life and prayer life. Directors should ask questions that enable their directees to see how their actual experiences of life are integrated with their consciously expressed spirituality. The aim in all of this is to help the directees discern the hidden patterns of grace in their lives, to come to a deeper awareness of the presence of God and a clearer understanding of what God is calling them to be and do. During this time, directors should take special care to preserve the dignity of the persons under their care by refusing to impose a particular interpretation of the spiritual life that does not resonate within the heart and mind of the directee. In this respect, their task is only to elicit and to suggest a spectrum of possible interpretations and to allow their directees to discover for themselves the particular insights which ring true. Directors should challenge their directees only when they are convinced that the latter's expressed discernment runs counter to the patterns of grace that God has already revealed through the process of spiritual direction. They should also be particularly sensitive to when the direction relationship should end. The ultimate goal of spiritual direction is to enable directees to become themselves in their faith and more self-directed. In this respect, the directors' role in the relationship of spiritual direction should become increasingly less important as a growing independence evolves and takes effect. If such a dynamic does not eventually crystalize, directors should examine more closely the motives behind the continuing relationship and question both themselves and the directee about its appropriateness in their current circumstances.

The Qualities of the Alphonsian Director

As described above, the inner and outer limits of spiritual direction require directors to possess a number of specific qualities, many of which can be a natural part of a person's makeup and others that can be acquired and developed over time. Most of these qualities are important for any pastoral ministry; it is precisely for this reason that those involved in the various ministries of the Church should consider involving themselves to some degree in the practice of spiritual direction. While the following list of qualities is by no means exhaustive, it offers a description of the types of people spiritual directors in general, and Alphonsian directors in particular, are called to be.

Alphonsian directors are people of prayer. They are experienced in how prayer engages people on every level of their makeup (the physical, emotional, mental, spiritual, communal); knowledgeable of prayer forms in the tradition of the Church (vocal, mental, contemplative, communal); and able to discern the appropriateness of each for different types of individuals under different circumstances. Prayer is a central concern in their everyday life, a part of life where theory is actually put into practice. Most importantly, directors pray for the Spirit's guidance in the practice of spiritual direction and also bring the concerns of each directee before the Lord.

Alphonsian directors are open. People can approach them without feeling threatened and can open up to them without the fear of being judged or demeaned. To be such persons, directors look back to those individuals in their own lives whom they have found to be most receptive to their own problems and difficulties. In doing so, they reflect upon and seek out ways in which they themselves can be more open and approachable for those in need.

Alphonsian directors are reflective. They listen to those under their care and reflect back in an organized and orderly manner the various ideas and emotions which they hear. Sometimes the only thing a directee needs is someone who is willing to listen and understand. Sometimes this alone is all that is necessary for directees to find God in their lives. Once understood, directees often take whatever steps are needed without further pastoral assistance.

Alphonsian directors are loving. They seek to follow in the footsteps of Christ, who showed his love for us by entering our world (in his Incarnation), giving of himself completely (in his passion and death), becoming nourishment for us (in the Eucharist), and a source of hope (in his resurrection). With the help of God, directors seek to emulate this fourfold movement of love by entering the worlds of those they serve, giving of themselves completely to them, with the view towards becoming nourishment and a source of hope. Such a loving attitude must be authentic, kind, and heartfelt. Directees can usually sense when the effort is contrived or insincere.

Alphonsian directors are discreet. It goes without saying that the relationship of spiritual direction is confidential. It will be successful only if directors create an atmosphere of mutual trust with their directees. That is to say that the directees must be made to feel they can tell their directors absolutely everything that pertains to their spiritual life: the good, the bad, and the ugly. Directors should step outside the bounds of confidentiality only in those rare cases when harm may be done to those under their care or to someone else. In these cases, directors must be willing to use their system of referrals quickly and decisively. When, on occasion, direction takes place in the context of sacramental confession (and for the reasons just expressed it is advisable to keep the two separate), the sacramental seal should be preserved at all costs.

Alphonsian directors are focused. They have a clear idea of what the relationship of spiritual direction is about and know how to bring the central issues of each session to the fore. To do so, they have an aptitude for both analysis and synthesis. They present to those under their care a wide range of possible interpretations of the material laid out before them at each session, and also a clear summary of the where their directees stand in their relationship with the Lord at a particular moment. Only in this way are the directees able to discern the patterns of God's grace in their lives over an extended time.

Alphonsian directors are believing Christians, preferably from the same tradition as their directees. Spiritual understanding cannot take place outside of the context of a particular faith tradition. Both directors and directees enter into a joint venture of "faith seeking understanding."[5] While it is certainly possible for the directors and directees to come from different faith traditions, the more usual arrangement would be for them to share the same community-shaped values of language, doctrine, and morals. While care must be taken that the mutual preconceptions of directors and directees are not merely taken for granted, the benefits gained from the sharing of a faith tradition usually outweigh the liabilities. The reason for this is that spiritual growth and development can only take place within the context of a particular tradition. People simply do not grow in isolation or as outside observers in a plurality of competing traditions. For this reason, both directors and directees are normally committed believers and followers of a particular Christian tradition.

Alphonsian directors are people of the Scriptures. They hold Holy Writ in high regard, not merely because of its privileged status in the Christian tradition as the revelation of God's plan for humankind or because it preserves the record of God's acts on behalf of his people but because it presents the reader with countless tales of human conversion from sin to new life in the Spirit. Directors immerse themselves in these tales of conversion so that they will see their appropriate application in the experiences of those who are under their care. Relating the directee's life experiences to the Scriptures is the most basic tool that directors have at their disposal for correlating a person's life with his prayer experiences. This great reverence and love for the experience of God in the Scriptures normally spawns a similar sense in the lives of those for whom they care.

Alphonsian directors are compassionate. The art of direction takes place on all of the anthropological levels of human existence—the physical, emotional, mental, spiritual, and the social. On each of these levels (often on many levels at the same time), directors seek to identify with the experience of their directees. Direction, therefore, is *not* a mere intellectual analysis of how one's prayer is going. It involves entire human beings on every level of their experience. The more that directors experience these various levels with their directees, the better able they will be to understand their particular difficulties and the better able they will be to help them interpret the particular signs of God's life in the midst of those circumstances.

Alphonsian directors challenge those under their care. They will be of little help to their directees if they simply reinforce and affirm every thought that surfaces during direction. Directors must help their directees to prioritize the insights gained from their spiritual journey and then to try to implement them. During this time, directors may find themselves in the position where certain presuppositions about the spiritual life must be torn down before any further progress can take place in their directees' lives. In this respect, directors must walk a fine balance between directive and nondirective approaches to spiritual direction. Some directees will have more of a need for one over the other. It is the task of directors to strike the proper balance between the two. At all times, the individual's personality, needs, and growth potential must be in the forefront of the director's mind.

Alphonsian directors are hopeful. They encourage their directees in prayer, especially during those dark moments when they feel lost and without purpose or direction. In the midst of such uncertainty, directors try to be a source of inspiration, helping their directees to find meaning in difficult circumstances, and trying to ward off the forces of depression when people are vulnerable. At all costs, directors try to prevent directees from self-absorption and self-pity. They do so by seeking to raise the spirits of their directees and by reaffirming them in their belief that the Lord is with them even during moments of defeat.

Alphonsian directors bring perspective. They help their directees to not take themselves too seriously. While directors are careful not to be overly light when the situation demands serious attention, they firmly believe that the ability to laugh at oneself and at one's triumphs and shortcomings is a true sign of spiritual health. To the extent to which directors can do so depends on the personality and temperament of those under their care. At the very least, directors are cheerful in their dealings with their directees, and careful not to bring their own personal agendas into relationships.

Alphonsian directors admit mistakes. When these occur, as they inevitably do (and usually at the outset of one's tenure as a director) they must be faced squarely, dealt with appropriately on both a professional and a personal basis, learned from, and grown out of. The worst thing for directors to do is to try and cover up mistakes in direction, be they in supervision, in a support group, or worse yet, before the directees themselves. Spiritual direction is to be pursued by directors and directees alike in truth and honesty. If either of these are lacking in either party, then one should question if spiritual direction is really going on at all.

Alphonsian directors are prudent. They help their directees find sound ways of arriving at the long- and short-term goals they have set for themselves. Ends are one thing; the means of achieving them are quite another. Spiritual directors first help their directees clarify their goals and then attain them. Strictly speaking, the concerns of prudence fall into the latter sphere. Once the directees understand where they are moving in the spiritual life, the job of their directors is not over: The directees still have to reach their goals. Their directors provide them with some of the resources for doing so.

Alphonsian directors are realistic. They understand that spiritual direction plays a small but important part in a person's life. Not every story will have a happy ending: Some will refuse to grow; others will not want to be healed. With so many variables at work, directors realize they do not have the final say. It is directees who take ultimate responsibility for their spiritual growth (or lack thereof). For this very reason, directors have expectations that are high but attainable. Progress in the spiritual life, as in any journey, comes but a single step at a time. Often the first steps are the most difficult in a person's spiritual journey; directors keep their directees aware of this sobering fact.

Conclusion

The above list seeks only to give a general description of the qualities important for a spiritual director in the Alphonsian tradition. Without pretending to be complete, even it may initially overwhelm those genuinely interested in taking up the practice. Who but an expert could possibly possess all of these qualities? Who else could use them at the correct moment and for just the right individual? Who else could strike the proper balance?

Such responses are understandable and, to an extent, even to be expected. At the same time, the qualities listed above are *not* the extraordinary domain of experts but the normal stuff of which many ordinary Christians in all walks of life, and particularly many involved in the pastoral ministry, are made. The most basic requirements of all good spiritual directors is that they value their faith, have a solid knowledge of it as it relates to the spiritual life, and know how to listen. During one's sojourn through life, no one is ever expected to possess each of these qualities to the fullest—not even the so-called experts. Like their directees, even they have not yet reached their final destination. In most cases, they just happen to be a little further along the way.

Perhaps some pastoral ministers have never taken the time to sit down, list, and reflect upon the various personal qualities necessary for the successful performance of their own pastoral responsibilities. If they did so, it would be surprising if, during the process, they did *not* encounter many of the above qualities. The point of this chapter is that they, of all people, should carefully consider offering their services in the field of spiritual direction. With the above guidelines, they can be of great help to the people of God who are hungry for such services and who would be appreciative of any help. To put a slight twist on a familiar Gospel adage: "The harvest is plentiful but the laborers are few—and need be resourceful" (see Matthew 9:37). The next part of this book will examine the close connection between the moral life and the spiritual journey, with particular attention to how this relationship affects the direction process.

Reflection Questions

Is spiritual direction a job or a vocation?

How would you know if you are being called to this ministry?

Is the possibility of becoming a director a topic to bring to spiritual direction itself?

Which of these qualities listed above do you possess? Which do you lack?

What would your strengths and weaknesses be as a director?

PART THREE

Spiritual Direction and the Moral Life

Part three addresses a particular concern of the Alphonsian model: how spirituality and morality come together in the direction process. It considers the moral dimensions of prayer (chapter nine), examines the various components of the spiritual journey (chapter ten), looks at the main virtues involved in the moral life (chapter eleven), treats the corresponding gifts of the Spirit necessary for completing the journey (chapter twelve), and discusses why growth in the virtues and gifts lie at the heart of the direction process (chapter thirteen). It presents the moral life as an integral part of the spiritual journey and life in the Spirit as its ultimate goal.

CHAPTER NINE

The Moral Dimensions of Prayer

⇵

Where does prayer come from? Whether prayer is expressed in words or gestures, it is the whole man who prays. But in naming the source of prayer, Scripture speaks sometimes of the soul or the spirit, but most often of the heart (more than a thousand times). According to Scripture, it is the heart that prays. If our heart is far from God, the words of prayer are in vain.
CATECHISM OF THE CATHOLIC CHURCH, 2562

The beginning of our discussion of the moral life begins with prayer. The moral life concerns our knowledge and pursuit of doing good and avoiding evil. Prayer helps us in this effort because it enlightens the mind, moves the heart, and incites us to action. It connects who we are, as believers, with what we think, say, and do. It comes from the heart of God and ultimately returns to it but not before passing through that weak, hungry, and solitary vessel of the human heart. Prayer helps us make sense of life. Through prayer, we give glory and honor to God. From it, God opens the eyes of our hearts and leads us along the way of the good life, the blessed life. For this reason, it is intimately related to the moral life. For this same reason, it is an important focus in the relationship of spiritual direction.

The Gift of Words

Prayer often involves words. To achieve their purpose, words must be both given and received. When we pray, our words are specifically directed to God or to one of God's friends, that is, a saint, someone close to him such as the Blessed Virgin Mary, St. Joseph, St. Francis of Assisi, St. Teresa of Ávila, St. Alphonsus de Liguori—to name a few. Our prayers can be spoken as in *oratio*, or vocal prayer (as when we recite the Our Father or the Hail Mary). They can be mental, as in *meditatio*, or meditation (as when we talk to God quietly in our minds). They can even be wordless, as in *contemplatio*, or contemplation (as when we rest quietly and wordlessly before the tabernacle). They can also be communal, done together in families, and prayer groups and especially in *liturgia* (as when we gather as God's people to celebrate the sacraments).[1]

These types of prayer—*oratio, meditatio, contemplatio, liturgia*—correspond to the physical, emotional/intellectual, spiritual, and communal dimensions of our human makeup, which are echoed in the Apostle Paul's emphasis on the tripartite anthropology of body, soul, and spirit (see 1 Thessalonians 5:23), as well as the corporate dimension of our being members of Christ's body (see 1 Corinthians 12:12). In a special way, all of these elements come together when we gather for Eucharist. We express ourselves physically to God through vocal prayers, songs, gestures, and engaging the senses with art, music, incense, colorful vestments, and the like. Our minds are nourished through the proclamation of God's word and the homilies we hear that seek to instruct our minds and hearts. Our spirits, moreover, are nourished at the pregnant moments of silence, perhaps after the homily or after Communion, when we rest in God's presence in our midst and in our hearts. And we do this together, as God's people, a community of believers gathered out of love for God and a desire to serve him by living for him.[2]

Since each relationship with God is unique, it follows that each of our prayer lives will also be distinct. The key to prayer is to find an appropriate rhythm that incorporates each of these dimensions in a way that best enables each of us to give glory and honor to God. It is also important for us to ask ourselves which form of prayer we rely on the most and which we overlook and need to develop. As noted earlier, for Irenaeus of Lyons, "The glory of God is man fully alive!"³ We become fully alive when each of these dimensions of our human makeup is given to God in prayer in a way that resonates deeply and in sync with our own unique personalities. Our prayer to God should issue forth from the depths of our beings and embrace every aspect of who we are: the physical, emotional, intellectual, spiritual, and the social. Each of us is like a facet of a diamond that reflects the light of God's glory in a way that no one can replicate. Our prayer polishes God's image in us so it can reflect the light of divine grace in a way that is distinct and unique in the world.

Silence in Prayer

Words make sense to us only against the backdrop of the silence that allows them to be heard, understood, and acted upon. Without spaces of silence between them, words cannot be distinguished from one another and devolve into nothing but gibberish. When teaching his disciples to pray, Jesus himself warned against babbling on as the pagans do (see Matthew 6:7). The words of the Our Father are some of the most beautiful in all of Scripture but they become meaningless if we simply recite them without giving our hearts and minds to them.

Prayer needs silence to help us distinguish our words, clarify our thoughts, and understand our hearts. Prayer, like reading, is not possible without at least some element of silence involved. A good prayer is not unlike reading a good book. When something strikes us while reading, it is sometimes important to put the book down and simply rest in the truth of the insight we have gained. A good book leads the reader into many such moments of silence. In a similar way, words provide the foundations of prayer but silence leads us to its heights and allows us to peer into eternity. God speaks to us in silence. With close friends, there are times when words get in the way and silence alone can communicate what lies deep within our hearts.

Prayer is dialogue with God. Whether words are used or not, at its very heart, prayer is nothing more than simply talking or communing with God. In the spiritual life, reading, talking, and praying were once all intimately connected. In *lectio divina*, for example, the monks of late antiquity searched for the deeper spiritual senses of Scripture by quietly enunciating the sacred words with their mouths as they lifted their minds and hearts to God in prayer. Today, we have lost contact with this form of holy reading. We tend to read for information and rarely, if ever, allow the words of Scripture to penetrate our souls and lift our hearts and minds to God. Augustine once said, "For now treat Scripture like the face of God. Melt in its presence."[4] We need to rediscover how prayer, when viewed as talking to God, reading his word as it is inscribed in our hearts, written in the pages of Scripture, and embodied in the person of Jesus Christ, the Word made flesh, can be viewed as the source of many things: communion with God, with others, with ourselves, and in a special and very particular way, the source of the moral life.

Prayer as the Source of the Moral Life

I now will make some concrete observations about prayer as the source of the moral life. These remarks, while not exhaustive, seek to offer an integrated vision of spirituality and morality, contemplation and action, the good life and the blessed life.

We can begin by looking at Alphonsus de Liguori's teaching on prayer and moral life. In the field of moral theology, the patron saint of confessors and moral theologians is most remembered for the four large tomes of his *Moral Theology*, which underwent numerous editions in his lifetime and treated difficult moral cases by seeking both to respect the law and to preserve freedom under it, and *The Practice of the Love of Jesus Christ*, which concentrates on the fostering of Christian virtues outlined by the Apostle Paul in his great hymn of love (see 1 Corinthians 13:4–13). In the field of spirituality, he is known as "the great doctor of prayer"[5] and is most remembered for his wonderful work *Prayer, the Great Means of Salvation* and his more popular *The Way of Conversing Always and Familiarly With God*.[6] If there is one line in all of his many works that best expresses his view toward the relationship between prayer and the moral life, it would be this, which we noted earlier: "He who prays is certainly saved. He who prays not is certainly damned."[7] While this statement may sound overly harsh, even bordering on crude, it nevertheless makes prayer the key to a person's eternal destiny.

To rephrase it in a way that might be more palatable to our present sensitivities, the statement could read something like this: "If you pray, then you will eventually find your way to God; if you do not pray, then you will spend eternity wandering aimlessly about trying to fill a giant hole in your soul that, in the end, can only be filled by God." If you pray, you will be saved; if you don't pray, you will end up wandering off the road leading to God and be lost.

The road to God is the moral life, the good life, the blessed life. Prayer, in other words, is the great means of salvation. It fosters our relationship with God; it makes us "friends of God"; it empowers us through God's grace to live the fundamental commandment of the moral life given us by Christ himself: the love of God and the love of neighbor (see Mark 12:29–31).

Prayer helps us find our way back to God. The image of the journey is an apt metaphor for understanding both the relationship between the spiritual and moral lives and the role played by prayer in their ongoing relationship. The division between spirituality and morality did not exist in the early centuries of the Church. It has its roots in the nominalist outlook of late medieval scholasticism with its focus on particulars (rather than universals) and its emphasis on law (rather than virtue), and in the rise of the seminary system of early modern Catholicism with its focus on a curriculum of specialized courses (for example, dogma, moral theology, ascetical, and mystical theology), which gradually lost touch with each other and developed into separate disciplines that rarely interacted. It reached its height in the Age of Enlightenment with exaltation of reason over faith and its preference for law and duty over virtue and the gifts of the Spirit. In recent decades it has made its way into Catholic moral theological circles, as evidenced in the controversy between the proponents of autonomous ethics versus faith-based ethics.[8]

The reintegration of the moral life with life in the Spirit represents a retrieval of an earlier outlook that envisioned all of human existence as intimately related to and dependent on one's relationship with God. To return to the image of a journey, there is only one way to God: the person of Jesus Christ, who is "the way, and the truth, and the life" (John 14:6). Those who follow him must go through a process of purgation (which focuses on following the Ten Commandments), illumination (which focuses on the acquisition of virtue), and union (which focuses on life in the Spirit and its manifold gifts). This threefold way is an integrated vision of the journey to God. There are not three ways but one way, and prayer is essential at every step. It is integral to the life of discipleship. In fact, it is prayer that enables us to move forward in our journey. And while *oratio* is often associated with the purgative way, and *meditatio* is often associated with the illuminative way, and while *contemplatio* is often associated with the unitive way, we must remember that, in the end, each of these forms of prayer addresses different aspects of our human makeup and that we are all called to practice them in different levels and intensities as we make our way to God.⁹ We must also remember that our journey to God is not a rigid, linear one, where one stage leads neatly to the next and is then left behind but a spiraling upward movement with numerous moments of purgation, illumination, and union that we encounter in ever-tightening cycles and that eventually merge into one.¹⁰ The ultimate goal of our lives is union with God. Prayer will lead us to that goal, and in doing so, will purge us, heal us, enlighten us, and make us whole.

When speaking about prayer and the moral life, it is important to remember that we live in a fallen world. This fact is something we often overlook or pretend to forget. The story of Adam and Eve's sin in the Book of Genesis depicts in figurative terms the reality of a primal, existential fall from grace at the dawn of human history that has affected us all. We have this deep sense that the world around us, and indeed our own selves, are not what they were originally intended to be. Something has gone awry, and we are responsible for it. We have fallen short of God's dream for us. In his encyclical *Veritatis Splendor*, St. John Paul II says that Adam and Eve's decision to eat from the tree of the knowledge of good and evil represents their attempt to place themselves at the center of the moral universe so that *they*, not God, would determine what was good and what was evil.¹¹ Our primal fall from grace has had serious consequences for us. Our minds have become darkened; our wills weakened; our passions unruly and out of sync.

On the moral level, the fire of conscience that was once ablaze with the light of divine grace dimmed to a mere ember so that it was difficult to read and apply the natural law that God had inscribed in our hearts. The most fundamental level of conscience, what the medievals called the *scintilla rationis* (the "spark of reason" or "synderesis") is all that remains of a once robust, enlightened mind that communed, at one and the same time, with the light of graceful reason.¹² In our present fallen state, we may understand that we must do good and avoid evil, the primary principle of natural law, and perhaps what Aquinas identified as those principles we share in common with all other substances (self-preservation), other animals (reproduction, the education of offspring), and by virtue of our rational natures (life in society; the pursuit of justice and the common good).¹³ We can barely go beyond that, however, before we start bickering over derived principles and their application to specific cases. Some even begin to question the very existence of a natural law itself. William of St. Thierry's description in *The Golden Epistle* (*Epistola aurea*) comes to mind of the three types of men: animal men, who follow their sensual instincts; rational men, who live by the light of reason; and spiritual men, who are guided by the promptings of the Spirit.[14] One of the consequences of humanity's primeval fall from grace was a descent from the spiritual to the rational and into the sensual. Paul's reminder that we are engaged in an ongoing struggle between the "law of the spirit" and the "law of the flesh" is a stark reminder of our need for the redeeming light of God's grace (see Romans 8:1–39).

As the great means of salvation, prayer plays an important role in reviving humanity and bringing it back to a grace-filled existence. We sometimes forget that we cannot pray without help. Authentic prayer requires faith, and faith is a God-given theological virtue. Prayer presupposes faith, and faith presupposes grace. Prayer is salvific, because through it grace enters the core of a person's being and brings its transforming power to bear on us. "Everyone receives sufficient grace to pray," says St. Alphonsus.[15] Every man, woman, and child is given access to this grace. Cooperating with this grace is another matter but the opportunity for prayer is always present. Furthermore, prayer is not a mystery accessible only to a few. As Alphonsus said, "There is nothing easier than prayer. What does it cost us to say, Lord, stand by me! Lord, help me! Give me Thy love! And the like? What can be easier than this?"[16] It is all so easy, and yet we cannot pray without the help of God's grace. It is so easy because God's grace abounds and is overflowing, because with him is plentiful redemption.

More specifically, with respect to the moral life, through the light of faith, prayer places us before God in the Creator/creature relationship. It humbles us and enables us to see that we are not God, and it is not our place to decide what is good and what is evil. Prayer, moreover, enlightens the mind. What Pope Emeritus Benedict says about faith in his encyclical *Deus Caritas Est* also applies to prayer, which presupposes faith:

> Faith by its specific nature is an encounter with the living God—an encounter opening up new horizons extending beyond the sphere of reason. But it is also a purifying force for reason itself. From God's standpoint, faith liberates reason from its blind spots and therefore helps it to be ever more fully itself. Faith enables reason to do its work more effectively and to see its proper object more clearly.[17]

"The light of faith," as Pope Francis reminds us in his encyclical *Lumen*

Fidei, "is capable of illuminating every aspect of human existence." It is born of "an encounter with the living God." It steeps us in God's love and transforms us in such a way that it gives us "new eyes to see" and "a great promise of fulfillment."[18] Through this influence of faith, prayer humbly directed to God lifts us out of the darkness that engulfs our rational powers and rekindles the flame of conscience so that we can see more clearly the law inscribed by God in our hearts and, even more importantly, pursue it with a firm and resolute will. The transforming grace of prayer also engages our affections and tames them, bringing them under the gentle rule of reason's reign. Prayer gives us a deeper appreciation of the common good, for it deepens our communion with God and helps us to find our place in God's family. It engages every dimension of our anthropological makeup—the physical, emotional, intellectual, spiritual, and social—and opens them to the quiet movements of God's transforming grace.

Prayer is not meant to be a heavy burden that weighs a person down with obligations that interfere with the living of one's life. It is an action meant to enrich a person's life by inviting God into one's life journey. Prayer is a mainstay of the Christian disciple, who takes up his cross daily to follow in the footsteps of his master (see Luke 9:23). Paul brings out this refreshing aspect of prayer when his says: "Rejoice always, pray without ceasing, give thanks in all circumstances; for this is the will of God in Christ Jesus for you" (1 Thessalonians 5:16–18). This insight brings to mind Jesus' words to his disciples, "… my yoke is easy, and my burden is light" (Matthew 11:30). For the Christian, prayer is like breathing: It is necessary for life; it must be done at all times and without question. It is also like reading in that it opens up different levels of meaning. In addition to a text's literal meaning, the Church recognizes deeper, spiritual senses that it may embody: the allegorical, which relates the text to Christ and his Church; the tropological (or moral), which connects it with the moral life; and the anagogical, which points out the meaning of the words regarding the last things: death, judgment, heaven, and hell. For example, the word *Jerusalem*, which appears countless times in the Scriptures, can refer to the earthly city Jerusalem (the literal sense), the Church (the allegorical sense), the human soul (tropological/moral), or heaven (anagogical).[19]

The Church still affirms the relevance of this ancient form of scriptural interpretation, which says that God is the primary author of sacred Scripture, and the meaning he wishes to reveal through the text is not confined to the surface meaning of the text but also in more hidden, spiritual meanings which are revealed after the text is thoroughly chewed and digested.[20] In a similar way, the act of prayer has different levels of meaning. In addition to the literal words themselves, each prayer tells us something about the quality of our relationship with Christ and his Church (allegorical), our understanding of the responsibilities of discipleship (moral), and the sense of the importance of our actions regarding our eternal destiny (anagogical). Since prayer involves the whole person, it carries with it many multifaceted meanings. It is not only a spiritual act but also a theological and moral act. As we have seen, the words of Evagrius Ponticus ring true: "If you are a theologian, you truly pray. If you truly pray, you are a theologian."[21]

Conclusion

In prayer, we use both words and silence to engage God in conversation, to talk to him, commune with him, read his mind, probe his thoughts, and ask him for help. And the beautiful thing is that God reciprocates! What we seek from him, he also seeks from us: an indwelling of hearts, an intimate friendship, a sense of resting in and being carried by the love of another. At such times, words give way to silence, and silence melts into communion. Prayer leads to a mutual indwelling of hearts, forges a bond that cannot be broken, and unleashes a power that sanctifies and transforms.

In this chapter, we have laid out the boundaries within which prayer can be understood as the source of the moral life. To be sure, it can be called such only in a derived, secondary sense, since, whether we are talking about either revelation or natural law, the ultimate source of the moral life is Christ himself. As the "great means of salvation," prayer is a source of the moral life, because it contributes in a unique way to helping us deepen our friendship with Christ and conform our lives to his. As God's Son, the Word of God made flesh, Christ reveals to us both what it means to be and how we should act as human beings. Indeed, as the International Theological Commission asserts, "[t]he very person of Christ, *Logos* and Wisdom incarnate,…became the living law, the supreme norm for all Christian ethics."[22] If it does anything, spiritual direction should help us take a hard look at how we pray and encourage us to ask ourselves in our journey through life how God may be calling us to relate to him in an even more personal and intimate manner. In the next chapter, we will take a closer look our spiritual journey and its close connection with the moral life.

Reflection Questions

Of the various forms of prayer, with which do you feel most comfortable?

What role does silence play in these various forms?

Why is prayer considered the great means of salvation?

How is it possible to pray without ceasing?

In what sense is prayer the source of the moral life?

CHAPTER TEN

The Spiritual Journey

The vocation of humanity is to show forth the image of God and to be transformed into the image of the Father's only Son. This vocation takes a personal form since each of us is called to enter into the divine beatitude; it also concerns the human community as a whole.
CATECHISM OF THE CATHOLIC CHURCH, 1877

Spiritual direction seeks to help a person make sense of one's spiritual journey, thereby bringing one closer to God in the process. The hectic pace of daily life often makes it difficult for this to happen. Life's numerous distractions draw our attention to the periphery of things, making it difficult for us to delve beneath appearances to see what is really going on in our lives. As a result, we find it difficult to understand where the Lord may be taking us and what he may be asking of us. In spiritual direction, the director accompanies us on our journey, seeking to help us uncover the narrative of our lives and take ownership of it. For Christians, this personal narrative in intimately bound up with that of Jesus' own life journey. In him, the spiritual life (living in the Spirit) and the moral life (living for the Good) are intimately related.

The Metaphor of Journey

Because it is easily recognizable and has little need for explanation, the metaphor of a journey has often been used as a way of describing the spiritual life. At some point, each of us has left the comforts of home and embarked on a journey, be it a simple day's sojourn or an extended trip. Be they long or short, safe or hazardous, direct or circuitous, all journeys share a number of common traits.

Every journey, for example, contains a beginning, middle, and end. The beginning presupposes a certain amount of planning and preparation to ensure that we have the necessary provisions for what lies ahead. It also requires purpose and a sense of direction to keep us on course and prevent us from getting lost. Every journey, moreover, begins with a single step and consists of a series of such steps that ultimately add up and enable us to reach our desired end. Every journey also involves a certain degree of uncertainty. When we set out into the world, often into unfamiliar surroundings, we may anticipate the obstacles we may encounter along the way but we can never be quite sure about what they will be. Unexpected hurdles may cause us to wander off course and choose a more indirect route to our destination. Such hindrances, whether internal or external, can separate us from our stated purpose and leave us in a state of constant wandering. They may even incite us to abandon the journey altogether and return home empty-handed. Surviving this middle part of our journey requires both a resolute purpose to reach our journey's end and the courage and perseverance to face whatever obstacles we may face and eventually overcome them.

What is more, a journey is not complete unless it reaches its final destination. While we carry this desired end in our minds and hearts all during the journey, it becomes increasingly real to us as we draw closer to it and find it well within our grasp. Every journey we walk begins and ends with a single step. What falls between them depends on a variety of factors and makes up the personal narrative of the journey we have taken.

There are many types of journeys. Some can be routine and mundane, like a trip to the grocery store. Others carry more significance, like a class excursion, a semester abroad, or a honeymoon. Still others have a special spiritual significance, like the *Camino de Santiago* ("The Way of St. James") in Spain, or a pilgrimage to Rome or the Holy Land. Life itself has been likened to a journey. It has a beginning, middle, and end. It involves various levels of preparation, contains many challenges and hardships, and can be broken up into numerous stages (infancy, childhood, adolescence, young adulthood, and so on). The purpose of spiritual direction is to help us uncover the latent spiritual significance of our journey through life by enabling us to interpret our past in the light of our present circumstances and our final destination. In doing so, directors have often resorted to the metaphor of the threefold way.

The Three Ways

The Christian life has often been described as a journey of three spiritual stages: the purgative, illuminative, and unitive.[1] These stages share a number of common traits but also remain very distinct. For centuries, they have been a helpful way in which Christians have marked their progress in the spiritual life. They continue to do so today.

Although Scripture does not specifically refer to these terms, certain passages resonate with these ideas. In the Old Testament, for example, Psalm 34:14 is said to correspond to the purgative emphasis on renunciation ("Depart from evil"), the illuminative focus on the virtuous life ("and do good"), and the unitive stress on communion with God ("seek peace, and pursue it"). In the New Testament, Jesus' call to discipleship in Luke 9:23 has been associated with the purgative focus on self-denial ("If any want to become my followers, let them deny themselves"), the illuminative on good works ("and take up their cross daily"), and the unitive on intimate union with Jesus ("and follow me"). A number of passages from the letters of St. Paul have been interpreted in a similar light: the purgative (see 1 Corinthians 9:26–27); the illuminative (see Philippians 3:13–17; 1 Corinthians 4:16); the unitive (see Galatians 2:20; 2 Corinthians 12:2).

Among the Church fathers, Clement of Alexandria (died around 215) outlines a threefold process for achieving perfect *gnosis*, or understanding, of spiritual truth. At first, one shuns evil through fear and mortification of the passions. Then one practices the virtues out of hope. Finally, one does good simply out of love for God.[2] In a similar vein, John Cassian (died circa 435) speaks of the three degrees of a soul's ascent to God: fear, hope, and love. The first is characteristic of slaves; the second, of mercenaries working for a reward; the third, of children of God.[3] Augustine of Hippo (354-430), in turn, presents this process in terms of incipient love, growing love, full-grown love, and perfect love.[4] The first two stages correspond respectively to the purgative and illuminative ways; the third and fourth, to the unitive.

Among the medieval authors, Bernard of Clairvaux (1090-1153) says that a person loves God first solely on account of the gifts God bestows, then for God's sake and the hope of benefits, and finally out of disinterested love.[5] William of St. Thierry (died 1149) presents the three ways in terms of a progression from the animal to the rational to the spiritual states,[6] while Aelred of Rievaulx (circa 1110-1167) speaks of the carnal kiss, the spiritual kiss, and the intellectual or mystical kiss.[7] Saint Bonaventure (circa 1217-1274) refers explicitly to the purgative, illuminative, and unitive ways,[8] while Thomas Aquinas (1224/25-1274) speaks of beginners who focus on the avoidance of sin, the proficient who exercise the virtues, and the perfect who cling to God and take their delight in him.[9]

Through these and other authors, the purgative, illuminative, and unitive ways made its way into the fabric of the Church's spiritual doctrine. Alphonsus de Liguori was acquainted with these stages from his vast knowledge of the Church tradition, the lives of the saints, and more directly through his close reading of the works of Teresa of Ávila (1515-82) and Francis de Sales (1567-1622).

Although traditionally referred to as the "three ways," these terms actually represent different stages in a single journey. The purgative way is for those who at the outset on their journey must turn away from evil through fasting, prayer, and ascetical practices. The illuminative is for those who have made progress in the spiritual life and have become proficient in the life of virtue. The unitive is for those who have achieved mystical union with God and are closely in touch with the inspirations of the Spirit.

It would be a mistake, however, to think that one stage abruptly ends when another begins or that one is somehow left behind when another arrives. On the contrary, the purgative way is subsumed into the illuminative; the illuminative into the unitive. When seen in this light, determining where a person is in his or her spiritual journey is usually a question of which of these stages is predominant in a person's life as his or her relationship with God deepens.

Those who reach the state of union with God continue to make good use of the various prayer forms and ascetical practices used in the earlier stages. To convey this nuance, the cyclical image of an upward-moving spiral (as opposed to the more linear metaphor of the journey) has been offered as a more accurate way of describing how these various stages or ways relate.[10]

The doctrine of the three ways is a metaphor that can be used by spiritual directors as they help those who come to them to deepen the relationship with God. When coupled with insights from psychology and theology, it can help people arrive at a sense of where they are in their spiritual journey and what concrete steps they need to take. Beyond the ministry of spiritual direction, it can also be used to raise awareness of what goes on when people gather for Eucharist, which has distinct moments of purgation (such as the penitential act), illumination (sharing the word), and union (Communion).

The three-way doctrine is an important component in the ministry of spiritual direction and is often highlighted in courses for adults in Catholic spirituality. It can be used as a helpful metaphor for teaching people to deepen any relationship where there is the potential of intimacy (for example, with God, between husband and wife, between two friends). It is sometimes adapted in RCIA programs to help people understand their role in the Church, especially when they gather for liturgy. It can be applied to almost any ministry that uses the metaphor of the journey to explain how a person begins, progresses, and arrives at a destination.

Interpreting Our Spiritual Journey

No two journeys are alike. Although the distance covered may be similar (perhaps even identical), travelers process their experiences in ways that make their journeys uniquely their own. The same is true for the spiritual journey. While we are all called to share in the intimate life of the divine, the road we travel, while sharing many common characteristics, is uniquely our own. What can we say about the interface of our life journey with the threshold of the sacred?

To begin with, the metaphor of the journey and its corollary of the three ways give us a means of finding both purpose and an awareness of incremental growth in our spiritual experience. They do so by helping us to internalize our outward journey through life and connect it with the internal spiritual journey to holiness. These metaphors lay the groundwork for our deeper incorporation into the mystery of Christ's passion, death, and resurrection. They show us that our outward journey through life is intimately related to our inward, spiritual journey and enable us to find meaning in our suffering. They also assign value to the role of detachment and self-discipline by seeing them not as ends in themselves but as preconditions for receiving deeper insights into our relationship with ourselves, others, and God.

The metaphors of the journey and the three ways also help us to see the roles played by the commandments, the virtues, and the gifts of the Spirit in the spiritual life. The Ten Commandments, typically associated with the purgative way, represent prescriptions from God that he has revealed in the Scriptures and inscribed in our hearts as the natural law. They provide the basic skeletal structure of the moral life and highlight the role of detachment and self-discipline in the initial stages of finding our way to the threshold of the sacred. The three theological virtues (faith, hope, and charity) and the four moral virtues (prudence, justice, fortitude, and temperance) are connected with the illuminative way. They show us that a mature spiritual life internalizes the commandments of God so that the soul can embrace and readily enact them. It does so, because it has acquired over time, either by diligent practice or the assistance of divine grace, the necessary dispositions allowing it to respond spontaneously (as a kind of second nature) to knowing and doing what is good. The gifts of the Spirit flow from the unitive way and enable us to respond to the promptings of the Spirit in our lives. They are supernatural dispositions that build on the commandments, presuppose the life of virtue, and lead us into mystical union with Christ for an intimate life with the triune God.

While the threefold way—that of purgation, illumination, and union—corresponds to the ways of the commandments, the virtues, and the gifts, it is incumbent to say something about how these various paths or stages of the spiritual life interrelate. The variety of opinions on this matter reflects the unique experiences of those involved. Some say they relate to one another in a strictly linear fashion with the purgative being left behind for the illuminative, and the illuminative for the unitive. Others accept this linear format but insist that the earlier stages are not left behind but subsumed into later stages. Still others reject the linear structure altogether and say that the three stages are repeated throughout a person's life in an upward spiraling motion that eventually merges into a single point on the threshold of the sacred.[11]

This variety of interpretations likely reflects the diversity of individual perspectives in coming to grips with their own spiritual experience and should remind us that metaphors are useful only insofar that they accurately reflect personal experience. A fuller understanding of our spiritual experience will come about by juxtaposing these various interpretations upon each other and allowing them to exist in a tension that will preserve a dynamic dimension of the spiritual journey and prevent it from becoming static. Even if, as suggested earlier, the understanding of the threefold way as an upward spiraling motion resonates with the experience of the greatest number of people, the other interpretations can still offer valuable insights into a person's spiritual journey and should be listened to and examined.

We must also be aware of the gap that exists between any teaching about the spiritual life and actual lived reality. Although a teaching such as that of the three ways stems from concerted attempts of saintly men and women to describe their genuine spiritual experiences, we need to recognize that no formulation, however articulate, will ever fully capture the experience itself, let alone replace it. When dealing with metaphors such as those of the spiritual journey and the threefold way, we need to hold them gently, learn what we can from them, and avoid allowing them to shape or dictate our own experience. Such metaphors are not meant to tell us what and how to feel but to assist us in interpreting and making sense out of our own lives. They represent tested truths of those who have gone before us and traveled similar paths. If care is not taken, they can get in the way of a genuine face-to-face confrontation with our own experiences and actually become a hindrance to our own spiritual growth. They should be employed only if they resonate with our own experience and actually help us to make sense out of them.

Finally, when trying to find meaning in our lives, it is important for us to remember that, as powerful as they are, the metaphors of the journey and the threefold way are not the only ways of describing the spiritual life. We should take care not to impose metaphors on others. Instead, we should seek to find a metaphor that speaks to our experience and with which we can easily identify. Other metaphors that have been used to describe the spiritual journey include: spiritual adoption, learned ignorance, spiritual betrothal and marriage, spiritual friendship, the cloud of unknowing, and so on. When trying to describe our spiritual experience, we would do well to focus on those images that arise out of our own experience. While the metaphor of a journey speaks to a wide rage of personal experiences, we may sometimes wish to employ alternative images to serve as an organizing theme for our spiritual narrative.

Conclusion

The metaphors of the journey and the three ways can serve as useful guides to help us interpret our experiences of the sacred. That of the journey resonates with nearly everyone's experience and lends itself very easily to an extension to life in general and the spiritual life in particular. That of the threefold way represents the wisdom of respected spiritual masters who have reflected on their experience and saw that their journey to God included variously related stages of purgation, illumination, and ultimately union.

Helpful as they may be, such metaphors should be seen not as a detailed road map to the sacred but as practical guideposts that can validate our experience and encourage us to carry on. As interpretive markers, they can assist us in making sense of our spiritual lives and in moving us forward in our relationship with God. If care is not taken, however, they can also get in the way of our encounter with the divine and hinder authentic spiritual growth. They can do so by causing us to focus our attention too much on them (and our relationship to them) rather than the personal experiences they are meant to interpret. Each of us has a unique relationship with God that can never be fully replicated. While metaphors such as those of the journey and the threefold way can help us understand that relationship, they can never take the place of our own experience and need not drown out our own voices in articulating it.

In the end, there are many paths to sanctity and many metaphors that can be used to describe the means to attain it. Although they may not be perfect and can even hinder spiritual growth if not used appropriately, the metaphors of the journey and the threefold way are tested, well-tried means of interpreting our encounter with the sacred that can speak to our experience and help us come to an even deeper awareness of God's presence (and, at times, seeming absence) in our lives. The challenge before us is to use them wisely so they channel our experiences in ways that both express and, in the end, validate our deepest desires for union with the divine. Spiritual direction is a place where we can find help to interpret our spiritual experience and discover those metaphors—be it a journey, the threefold way, or otherwise—that best capture its unique features. In the next chapter, we will see that the way of virtue is one such tried-and-true metaphor, one deeply rooted in the Christian tradition.

Reflection Questions

In what sense is the moral and spiritual life a journey?

How is that journey related to the threefold way?

Where does that journey lead?

When does it end?

How can spiritual directors help along the way?

CHAPTER ELEVEN

The Way of Virtue

⇅

The theological virtues are the foundation of Christian moral activity; they animate it and give it its special character. They inform and give life to all the moral virtues. They are infused by God into the souls of the faithful to make them capable of acting as his children and of meriting eternal life. They are the pledge of the presence and action of the Holy Spirit in the faculties of the human being. There are three theological virtues: faith, hope, and charity.

CATECHISM OF THE CATHOLIC CHURCH, 1813

The purpose of spiritual direction is to help us grow in virtue and become ourselves in the faith. It means drawing closer to God and becoming increasingly like him in all things. God's very being reflects the transcendental qualities of the one, the true, the good, and some would even add the beautiful. Since God is good, those who seek to draw closer to him are called to be good. This call to goodness lies at the very heart of the moral life; the spiritual life, in turn, is built upon this foundation. For Catholics, spirituality and morality are thus intimately related. You cannot have one without the other. Separating them does a grave injustice to our very understanding of God and what it means to be a follower of his Son, Jesus Christ.

The Good Life

God wants all of us to be happy. According to Aristotle, happiness (or *eudaimonia*) consists in seeking that beyond which nothing more can be desired.[1] It is the best possible life for a human being. For Thomas Aquinas, such life consists not in seeking wealth, honors, fame, glory, power, some bodily good, pleasure, some good of the soul, or any other created good. It lies only in seeking the *visio Dei*, the vision of God himself.[2] This vision requires both objective and subjective aspects of the good. It involves God's vision of us (the objective) and our vision of God in the beatific vision (the subjective).[3]

The good life, moreover, presupposes some basic things about our human makeup. It assumes the existence of a transcendent being, as well as our capacity to receive it, be filled by it, and rest in it. We are *capax Dei* ("capable of God"), as Aquinas would say;[4] God, in turn, is *capax hominis* ("capable of man"). As we have seen, "God became man so that man might become divine."[5] God made us and became one of us—and we were made for him. By *visio Dei* we mean that God and man are capable of entering into an intimate relationship of love with each other, one that both reflects the very nature of God himself and has a transforming, divinizing effect on human existence.

The Christian narrative is all about the divine initiative to right the wrong of humanity's sinfulness so we might once again share in the intimate life of the Godhead. God entered our world in the mystery of the Incarnation; gave himself to us completely in his public ministry and especially in the mystery of his passion and death; became nourishment for us in the mystery of the Eucharist; and remains a source of hope for us in the mystery of his resurrection and ascension into heaven. If Jesus himself is the Way, as the Gospel of John reminds us (see John 14:6), then the way to happiness lies in following him. The earliest Christians, who were known as followers of the Way (Acts 9:2), glorified God through their imitation of Christ in their life of discipleship. As we have seen, "The glory of God is man fully alive."[6] We become fully alive by sharing in this basic gospel narrative. The good life, the happy life, the virtuous life consists in following Jesus and allowing him to conform our narrative unto his. Like him, we also are called to enter the worlds of others, give ourselves to them completely, become nourishment for them, and be for them a source of hope. As Jesus said, "If any want to become my followers, let them deny themselves and take up their cross and follow me" (Mark 8:34).

To a great extent, our understanding of the good depends on how we view both God and ourselves. As Christians, we believe that we are created in the image and likeness of God, yet also fallen and deeply flawed. Christ came to free us from sin and restore in us the capacity to relate to God and share in his intimate life. He came to redeem every aspect of our flawed human condition: the physical, emotional, intellectual, spiritual, and social. These dimensions of our human makeup are also reflected in our actions. In other words, every human action—that is, every deliberated action of reason and will—contains physical, emotional, intellectual, spiritual, and social elements to it. Our human makeup and the actions flowing from them reveal a circular relationship between being and action. Actions flow from being and, in turn, help shape the soul.

For example, a man buys a gun with the intention of murdering someone and eventually carries out his plan. This heinous crime has tragic consequences both in the external world (the murder of another human being) and in the internal word (the murderer's soul has become disfigured and less what it was created to be). Similarly, a woman knows of a poor single-parent family in her neighborhood and sends the mother a substantial amount of money as an anonymous Christmas gift. This virtuous action has both outward and inward repercussions: the family will enjoy itself during the Christmas holidays; the woman's act of kindness beautifies her soul. The implication is clear. Our actions tell others who we are. They are expressions of being, and they cannot be treated apart from the one performing them. The Catholic tradition describes this intimate relation between being and action through its teaching on the virtues and vices. The Gospel of Matthew puts it this way: "…Every good tree bears good fruit but the bad tree bears bad fruit. A good tree cannot bear bad fruit, nor can a bad tree can bear good fruit" (Matthew 7:17–18). The same is true of the human person.

All human beings are good on the metaphysical level because they have been created in the image and likeness of God. On the ethical level, however, they span the gamut of good and evil on account of their fallen nature and propensity toward sin. The Catholic doctrine of original sin describes the effects of this original fall from grace. Having lost its intimate friendship with God, humanity became vulnerable to diseases of body and soul, and ultimately to death itself. Our human makeup was thrown out of sync: our minds were unruly; our hearts became faint; and our passions revolted against the gentle rule of reason's reign. To act in a virtuous manner is to act in accord with reason and to follow the *via media* or "middle way" between excess and defect.

The vices operate against the virtues by focusing on excesses or defects of this golden mean, thus opening the door to sin and corruption.

Virtues are acquired or infused dispositions of the soul that enable us to do good and avoid evil. They are either acquired through training and practice or infused by the power of divine grace. They cover the three primary dimensions of the human soul: (1) the rational, which contains reason and will (also known as the rational appetite), (2) the irascible, which refers to the soul's hot-tempered or spirited dimension, and (3) the concupiscible, which concerns the soul's pleasure-seeking aspect. After the fall, these powers of the soul became weakened and fell out of touch with each other. The virtues seek to bring them back into sync. They do so by strengthening them, putting them back into harmonious relationship with one another, and enabling them to follow the gentle rule of reason's reign. They operate not only on the natural level but also on the supernatural.

On the natural plain there are four cardinal virtues that can be acquired through diligent training and practice: prudence, justice, fortitude, and temperance. Prudence perfects the practical reason and enables it to find appropriate means to any given end. It helps us to look for the most practical moral ways to achieve one's goals. If a young man wishes to get into a good college, the prudent thing to do would be for him to develop good study skills that will enable him to get good grades.

Justice strengthens the will and enables a person to give others their due. It helps us to judge not by appearances but on the basis of the dignity inherent in all human beings. For example, a woman has found a wallet in the street that contains both a large sum of money and the owner's identity. A just person would return the wallet and its contents to its rightful owner rather than keep it for oneself.

Fortitude controls the irascible (or spirited) appetite and helps us to deal with whatever obstacles may cross our path. It tells us when to retreat from a seemingly insurmountable threat and when to stand firm, resist, and even attack. If someone is bullied at school because of race, a brave person would not join in the bullying but stand up to the bullies and take the targeted person under his or her wing.

Temperance tames the concupiscible appetite and helps us to take all things in moderation. It helps us to curb our appetites and to steer a middle course between defect and excess, between too much of a good thing and too little. If a man knows that he overeats and drinks, he exercises temperance by moderating his intake of food and beverages and starting a daily exercise regimen to enjoy better health.

It is also important to note that the movement of divine grace can penetrate these naturally acquired virtues and transform them into infused virtues focusing entirely on God. In such a scenario, the virtuous person might perform the same actions described above but do them not merely for their natural human ends but for God. The external actions themselves might seem the same but the intention behind them is very different.

Divine grace also endows the soul with the three infused theological virtues: faith, hope, and charity. Faith enlightens our minds, enables us to believe in God, and causes us to accept all that he has revealed. According to Josef Pieper, "To believe always means: to believe someone and to believe something."[7] Christians believe the testimony of the apostles that Jesus Christ rose from the dead.

Hope focuses our wills on the coming of God's kingdom, helps us to trust in Christ's promises, and enables us to rely on the myriad gifts of his Spirit. Pieper reminds us that the hope is the virtue of the *status viatoris*, "to be one on the way."[8] Christians view themselves as pilgrims on an earthly sojourn that will ultimately lead to life after death.

Charity fills our hearts with love for God alone, deepens our desire to be in union with Christ, and enables us to love our neighbors as ourselves. According to Pieper, "all human happiness…is fundamentally *the happiness of love*."[9] Christians find their happiness not in any earthly or human treasure but by participating in the divine life of the God of love. Taken together, these virtues have a transforming, divinizing effect on the soul. They help us to put on the mind of Christ, making us more like him. They enable us to enter in an intimate friendship with God and share in the divine nature. They elevate us and lift us across the threshold of the sacred.

The Divinized Person

To understand how the virtues work in a person's life, it is important to remember that grace builds on nature and ultimately transforms it. Through the movement of divine grace in our lives, the Holy Spirit empowers us to act beyond our natural capacities and participate in the intimate community of love known as the Blessed and Most Holy Trinity. God always meets us where we are and then helps us to take the next step in our journey into the mystery of his love.

When applied to the virtues, it means that the moral life begins with the cultivation of those virtues that we can acquire by our own efforts. These are the cardinal virtues of prudence, justice, fortitude, and temperance, which are also known as the moral virtues since they are largely concerned with human action in the world. These natural virtues come about by education and practice. A young child learns how to ride a bike by riding a tricycle, graduating to a bike with training wheels, and finally to one without training wheels. It requires a good deal of determination and practice. Much the same can be said for the acquired virtues. Prudence enables our practical reason to achieve a good end. Justice strengthens the will to give everyone what is due to them. Fortitude controls the irascible appetite, enabling us to confront obstacles that get in the way of the good by either overcoming them, getting around them, and even retreating from them. Temperance moderates the pleasure-seeking passions of the soul, especially with regard to food, drink, and sex. These naturally acquired virtues perfect nature as much as human effort alone will allow. They enable us to enact the good in an immediate and spontaneous manner, as if doing so were an integral part of us, as if it were second nature to us. The goal is natural happiness, which comes about by submitting all the powers of body and soul to the governance of reason, which does not oppress the soul but liberates it and enables it to enact the good and thereby become its natural best.

In time, the transforming power of grace brings about a radical change in our natural powers and enters our lives with the infusion of the virtues of faith, hope, and charity. According to Aquinas, these virtues are called "theological" because their object is God, because he infuses them in us, and because they are made known to us only through divine revelation.[10] As gifts from God, these virtues place us in relationship to him. Faith enables us to believe in his existence and to trust him with our lives. Hope helps us look forward to the coming of his kingdom with a sense of urgency and expectation. Charity instills in us a desire to love God with all our hearts and makes us want to reach out to others in the way that God reached out to us so that we could once again share in the divine friendship. These virtues are intimately bound up with one another. In the order of development, faith comes first and gives rise to hope, both of which bear fruit in charity. In terms of their dissolution, the loss of charity results in the loss of hope and ultimately in the loss of faith. Of the three virtues, charity is the most perfect, hope comes next, followed by faith.[11]

Through these three theological virtues, divine grace enables us to look upon God as the one thing that matters and to focus everything in our lives on him. It makes us want to not merely conform our lives to the will of God in humble submission but to make our will and God's uniform and truly one. From this transformation of reason and will, the power of divine grace continues to pour itself into the soul by penetrating its spirited and pleasure-seeking passions. It enters the acquired moral virtues and redirects them to a supernatural end, thus infusing them with the power of God's transforming love. These infused cardinal virtues differ from the acquired ones in that they direct our activity not toward our natural end but toward our ultimate end. We can do this only under the influence of divine grace, which empowers us to place God at the center of everything we do.

Based on the insights of Thomas Aquinas, Pieper summarizes the presence and movement of these seven virtues in the life of the believer:

> First: the Christian is one who, in *faith*, becomes aware of the reality of the triune God. Second: the Christian strives, in *hope*, for the total fulfillment of his being in eternal life. Third: the Christian directs himself, in the divine virtue of *love*, to an affirmation of God and neighbor that surpasses the power of any natural love. Fourth: the Christian is *prudent*; namely, he does not allow his view on reality to be controlled by the Yes or No of his will but rather he makes his Yes or No of the will dependent upon the truth of real things. Fifth: the Christian is *just*; that is, he is able to live "with the other" in truth; he sees himself as a member among members of the Church, of the people, and of any community. Sixth: the Christian is *brave*, that is, he is prepared to suffer injury and, if need be, death for the truth and for the realization of justice. Seventh: the Christian is *temperate*; namely, he does not permit his desire to possess and his desire for pleasure to become destructive and inimical to his being.[12]

This succinct description of the moral life of the Christian emphasizes the centrality of the theological and cardinal virtues in our lives and the wide scope of actions they cover. As clear and accurate as it may be, however, it is not quite complete. The transformation of the human person into a divinized organism does not end merely with the presence of the theological virtues and the infused cardinal virtues in our lives. God still has more to do. When these virtues operate in our lives, we are still the primary subjects of the moral action. God's grace works within the boundaries of our natural powers, and we remain the primary subjects of the moral action. At some point, however, the movement of divine grace endows us with gifts that enable us to be sensitive to the promptings of the Holy Spirit, who then takes over and becomes the principal agent in our actions. Remaining completely free, we follow the Spirit's lead in a divine and human dance that transforms us from the inside out to divinize us and make us partakers in the divine goodness. At this point the good and virtuous flow into the blessed life, the mystical life. In the words of St. Paul, "I have been crucified with Christ; and it is no longer I who live but it is Christ who lives in me" (Galatians 2:19–20).

The Practice of the Love of Jesus Christ

When Christ lives in us, the practice of virtue comes easy, because they are fully integrated with one another and focused only on the task of being good and allowing it to flow over into our actions. This close inherence was made visible in the person of Jesus Christ, who embodied in his life the intimate love of the triune God and shared it with all who would listen to him and open their hearts to his words: "Let anyone with ears to hear listen!" (Mark 4:9).

According to Thomas Aquinas, charity is the form of all the other virtues, because it directs the acts of all the other virtues to God as their last end.[13] For this reason, it is considered the "Queen of Virtues," a title that the Apostle Paul would readily have embraced: "And now faith, hope, and love abide, these three; and the greatest of these is love" (1 Corinthians 13:13). Earlier, the apostle points out the main qualities of authentic Christian love:

> Love is patient; love is kind; love is not envious or boastful or arrogant or rude. It does not insist on its own way; it is not irritable or resentful; it does not rejoice in wrongdoing but rejoices in the truth. It bears all things, believes all things, hopes all things, endures all things (1 Corinthians 13:4–7).

One of the most profound treatments of this great hymn of love comes from the pen of Alphonsus de Liguori in his work *The Practice of the Love of Jesus Christ* (1768). This book of spiritual reading represents his mature thought on Christian action in the world and reveals his integrated understanding of the moral and spiritual life. In it, he tells us why we should love Jesus Christ, why he deserves our love, how much confidence we should have in his love, and why we are obliged to love him. He then comments at length on each of the elements of love highlighted by Paul and concludes with a summary of the virtues that must be practiced by those who love Jesus Christ.[14]

One passage in particular brings together the great wisdom of the past on the meaning of love:

> The spiritual masters describe the signs of true love. Love, they say, is *fearful*; it fears displeasing God. It is *generous*, because, trusting in God, it is never dismayed from undertaking even the greatest tasks for his glory. It is *strong*, because it conquers all its evil appetites, even amid the most violent temptations and the darkest desolation. It is *obedient*, because it immediately seeks to carry out God's commands. It is *pure*, because it loves God alone, and only because he deserves to be loved. It is *ardent*, because it would inflame all people and see them consumed with divine love. It is *inebriating*, for it makes the soul live as if it were beside itself, as if it no longer saw or felt or had any senses left for things of this world, and was wholly intent on loving God. It is *unifying*, for it tightly binds together the will of the creature and the will of the Creator. It is *yearning*, for it fills the soul with desire to leave this world, to fly to a perfect union with God in its happy homeland, so as to love him with all its strength.[15]

According to Joseph Oppitz, Alphonsus seems to have extracted the nine qualities of love listed above from meditations on the Canticle of Canticles (Song of Songs), one of his favorite books of the Old Testament. He expands on Alphonsus' presentation and describes these nine qualities of love thus:

1. It is *"filially fearful"* (*amor timorosus*), that is, it is a childlike love, the love of a child who fears to lose the grasp of the hand of the mother and father it loves; a child who wants to bring only joy to

those it loves and is, therefore, fearful lest it bring them disappointment and rejection.
2. It is a *generous love*, and its generosity arouses zeal for deeper expressions of love.
3. It is a *strong love* because it is supported by the passion and cross of Christ. As such, it is sacrificial and long-suffering and persevering in its love despite temptations to the contrary.
4. It is an *obedient love* and this desire to do whatever the Beloved wishes appears in its whole attitude toward authority, in its docility to spiritual guidance, in its seeking for and responding to divine inspiration, and in its unity with the divine will.
5. It is a *pure love*, that is, its motivation is energized by its fixed gaze and focus on its Beloved.
6. It is an *ardent love*, that is, it wants to set the whole world on fire with love and wishes all people to know the Beloved.
7. It is an *inebriating love*, that is, a love which makes one "crazy with love," almost as if one were drunk with joy over the Beloved's presence and his constant gift-giving, that is, his incarnation, passion, the Eucharist, Mary, etc. It is this kind of love which at times leads to the so-called "holy follies" of the great saints, as for example the Redemptorist brother, St. Gerard Majella.
8. It is a *unitive love* which unites the wills of the Beloved and the one loved. Obviously, as in the Canticle, this brings about an intense yearning to be in the presence of the one loved and an intimacy which is verbal in communicating that love and which is truly alive, especially in the Real Presence of holy Communion.
9. It is a *hopeful love* that is always looking forward to a deepening of the love-relationship here, and hereafter in the final, total, unending, and effortless love in heaven.[16]

It would be difficult to find a more sensitive and comprehensive treatment of what it means to love than *The Practice of the Love of Jesus Christ*. Here, Alphonsus teaches us not only what it means to love but also how to turn to God in prayer. He does so by ending each chapter with a section titled, "Prayers of Love and Affection," which encourages us to open our hearts to God so he can dwell within us and empower us to love the way Jesus did. He understands that to practice the love of Jesus Christ, we must open our hearts and ask for God's help. Living in the good, from this perspective, means living in God. The role of spiritual direction is to help us become more aware of our relationship to God and to live more fully in his goodness.

Spiritual Direction: Living in the Good

The purpose of the virtues is to enable us to live in God and thereby live in the good. The purpose of spiritual direction is to unleash the power of the virtues in our lives. The two go hand in hand. Our actions are not isolated events disconnected from each other and from our own internal lives. They flow from our very souls and reflect who we are. Spiritual direction helps us to uncover the continuity (or lack thereof) between our actions and our inner lives. The virtues propel us to do what is good and avoid what is evil. They do so not in mere isolated cases but in a constant and consistent manner that enables us to do good freely and spontaneously. The more virtuous we become, the easier it is for us to do what is good and the more difficult it becomes for us to do evil. Spiritual direction helps us to uncover (and ultimately recount) the narrative by which we define our lives and to walk along the way to true freedom.

The virtues do not limit human freedom but enhance it. They presuppose an understanding of freedom that is not merely the ability to choose between contrary forces ("freedom of indifference") but one that pursues the excellence of living in God and thereby living spontaneously in the good ("freedom for excellence").[17] While the former understanding of freedom requires that our wills are free from any internal or external influences (including virtue), the latter recognizes that a person's soul needs to be shaped by various internal and external forces so that it can achieve its greatest potential. A musician, for example, must undergo rigorous study, training, and practice in order to master a musical instrument and play it well and naturally. In a similar way, we are called to a life of virtue so that we can do good with ease, without even thinking about it. Just as a musician internalizes the rules of music in order to be free to create something of great beauty, so we are called to internalize the moral skill of doing what is good in order to build God's kingdom both within our hearts and within our midst. Spiritual direction helps us become aware of our desire for God, our need for virtue, and our love of the spontaneous excellence of true freedom. In doing so, it encourages us to examine the connection between who we are and what we do.

The virtues remind us that our actions have both internal and external effects. They influence the world around us and help shape our souls and the type of people we become. There is no standing still in the moral life. We are either living in God and pursuing a life of goodness and holiness or retreating from him and living a life based on purely self-centered concerns. Although a gap will always exist (at least in this life) between who we wish to become as moral persons and who we really are, we are all challenged to make efforts to narrow the gap between vision and reality so that it gradually lessens and, under the influence of grace and in God's good time, ultimately disappears. If we are making such efforts, then it is clear that we desire to live the virtuous life and are making headway (however so slight) along the way. If we are not, then the good will become more and more difficult to pursue, and our lives will slowly degenerate into a downward spiral of viciousness. Spiritual direction helps us examine the gap between vision and reality and make concrete decisions about how to narrow it.

To live a life of virtue is to discover our deepest potential and unleash it upon the world to affect change for the better. Virtuous men and women refuse to compromise their values and settle for less. They recognize that the goodness within their hearts must express itself in the goodness inherent in their actions. They seek to pour themselves out in service to others and transform everything they touch. This transformative power can hardly restrain itself from doing good. It changes the lives of others by healing their souls and improving their life circumstances. "The Good," according to Pseudo-Dionysius (circa 500), "is self-diffusive."[18] The truth of this saying is evident in the lives of all who seek to wear the mantle of goodness and truth. Virtuous men and women can befriend others only because God himself has first befriended them. Their love for him propels them to do the same. To live the virtuous life is to live for God and others. It means being so rooted in the good that, in the end, the good is all that matters. To serve the good is to serve God. Living in the service of the good is the world's one and only hope.

Spiritual direction can help us identify those virtues that we have and need to strengthen, as well as those that we lack and need to acquire. It does so by helping us to understand where we stand in relationship to God, neighbor, and ourselves. The Alphonsian approach to direction encourages us to reflect on our lives, to get in touch with our feelings, to surface our needs, and to make practical decisions about the future. When applied to the moral life, it enables us to examine the role the virtues play in our lives, to engage our hearts regarding them, to name those we lack, and to resolve to do something to turn things around and make things better. In doing so, it makes us more aware not only of our various strengths and weaknesses but also of where we are on our journey to God and what practical steps we should take next.

Conclusion

For Christians, the life of virtue is integral to moral life; the moral life, in turn, goes hand in hand with the spiritual life. Separating them does violence to the very notion of life in the Spirit. If spiritual direction seeks to help us become ourselves in the faith, then growth in virtue must be one of its central aims. After all, faith itself is a virtue. To become oneself in the faith presupposes both an understanding of what faith is and how we can deepen it. It also presupposes an awareness of how to grow in faith and how it relates to the other virtues.

The virtues are dispositions of the soul that enable us to pursue good and avoid evil. They strengthen every dimension of the soul—the rational, the volitional, the irascible, and the concupiscible—and empower us to enact the good in a free and spontaneous manner, as if doing so were second nature to it. There are seven major virtues: the cardinal virtues of prudence, justice, fortitude, and temperance; and the theological virtues of faith, hope, and charity. These virtues work together to release us from the bondage of sin and help us to find happiness in doing what is good. They strengthen our weak human nature and, by the grace of God and the power of prayer, make us capable of living the good life, something we could not do when left to our own devices.

Our virtuous actions help to mold the world around us. They also polish our souls and make them reflect God's image more clearly. Virtuous people have beautiful souls: internally, their spirits sing; externally, their actions contribute to making the world a better place, a good place. Spiritual direction assists us in making sense out of our lives by looking at them through the lens of faith. By helping us walk in the way of virtue, it helps us follow the way of goodness that, as outlined in the next chapter, lies at the very heart of the way of the Lord Jesus and the gifts of his life-giving Spirit.

Reflection Questions

What is the good life?
How does the good life make us happy?
What do virtues have to do with the good life?
How do they change us?
How do they make us free?

CHAPTER TWELVE

The Gifts of the Spirit

The moral life of Christians is sustained by the gifts of the Holy Spirit. These are permanent dispositions which make man docile in following the promptings of the Holy Spirit.
CATECHISM OF THE CATHOLIC CHURCH, 1830

Yet another important focus of spiritual direction is life in the Spirit. If becoming ourselves in the faith means living the gospel on a deep level of awareness, then getting in touch with the deep movements of the Spirit in our lives is a basic requirement for all genuine spiritual growth.[1] The gifts of the Holy Spirit (wisdom, understanding, counsel, knowledge, fortitude, piety, and fear) provide us with important help for living the Christian life. Most people, however, know very little about them and are sometimes even hard put to list them in their correct order. Traditional catechetical sources do not help very much. Even the *Catechism of the Catholic Church* does not go much beyond merely telling us what they are and when we receive them.[2] Can nothing more be said? Just what are they? How are they experienced? How are they used? What does life in the Spirit truly mean? Spiritual direction is a perfect place where people can ask such questions and even find relevant answers for their lives.

Intimacy With God

The gifts should be understood primarily in the context of our relationship with God. Each of us is called to a deep intimate friendship with the triune God. Father, Son, and Spirit—the community of love par excellence—has freely chosen to create, redeem, and sanctify us. The Spirit, the personal bond of love existing between the Father and the Son, is the means by which we are able to share in the intimate life of God. The Spirit is not some otherworldly abstraction but a palpable, living reality meant to be experienced in the present life. He is the inherent divine love seeking to commune with the human heart and make his abode there. Each one of us is called to be a temple of the Holy Spirit. The same Spirit, who descended in tongues of fire on the heads of the disciples at the birth of the Church on the first Pentecost, wishes to burn within our hearts and reveal God's love to us in a very personal and intimate way.

As creatures, however, we cannot experience God through our own efforts. To discern his presence in our lives we need to be touched by his healing and elevating grace. We also need to be instructed in the language of silence that will enable us to maintain an ongoing dialogue with the Father, through the Son, in the Spirit. The gifts of the Spirit are those helps given to us by God that allow us to enter more deeply into and to sustain an intense, loving relationship with the very foundation of our existence. Without them, we would be like birds without wings. We would not be able to enter into the fullness of love God has planned for us. Nor would we be able to share that intimacy with others and so expand the circle of God's love in the world we inhabit.

Although spiritual direction does not actually bestow the gifts, it can serve as a valuable instrument to help us understand the role they play in the moral and spiritual life. It can do so by helping us get back in touch with our baptismal calling and use our renewed commitment to give glory and honor to God. In this sense, it can mediate the life of the Spirit for us and help us take full advantage of the gifts God has given us. It can also teach us to listen to the silence, the language of divine love, and serve as an instrument of increasing intimacy with the divine. For this reason, it is a place where we can come to know Jesus personally, live in his Spirit, and learn to live the gospel on a deep level of consciousness.

What Are the Gifts?

The seven gifts of the Holy Spirit are strong dispositions of being and action given to us by God at baptism and strengthened in us at confirmation.[3] The theology of the gifts has its roots in early Christian reflections on Isaiah 11:1–2, a text modern interpreters generally agree is a prophetic description of the qualities of a virtuous king. Traditional scholastic language refers to the gifts as "infused habits," that is to say, God-given ways of thinking and acting that make us sensitive to the promptings of the Spirit in our lives. Contemporary reflection on the gifts draws a distinction between the reception of the gifts and their use. For more than forty years, the charismatic renewal has done much to raise awareness of the presence of the Spirit in the life of the believing community and to encourage the use of the gifts in the daily practice of the spiritual life.[4]

Because they are gifts, none of us can ever have an intrinsic right to them. They are not ours "by nature"—and never will be. This state of affairs sets up an interesting set of possibilities. On the one hand, it means we can lose the gifts if we choose to separate ourselves from the love of God. The power of human choice is such that we can shut ourselves off from God's gratuitous grace and be totally separated from him and the gifts he wishes to bestow. On the other hand, it means that, by cooperating with God's grace in our lives, we can gradually become more familiar with the gifts and thus be more adept at using them for what they are intended. To receive a gift does not necessarily mean it will be put to use. Have you ever received a gift-wrapped present, yet never opened it? Gifts are given to be opened and used. The gifts of the Spirit allow us to participate in the intimate life of the Trinity. They presuppose our cooperation with God's grace in our lives and may thus be thought of as complements to our genuine attempts at living the virtuous life.

Spiritual direction provides us with an excellent opportunity of getting in touch with the movement of the Spirit in our lives. It does so by helping us examine our lives, identify our deepest needs and desires, and listen to what the Lord is saying. The goal of spiritual direction is to help us draw closer to God so we will live the gospel on a deep level of awareness. The closer we come to God, the more we realize that everything is "gift." The seven gifts of the Holy Spirit are prime examples of this basic insight. Usually identified as the intellectual and appetitive gifts, they help us live the Christian moral and spiritual life by enlightening our reason and strengthening our will and emotions.[5]

What follows is a brief description of these gifts and how each of them may be discerned and used in the context of spiritual direction.

Gifts of the Intellect

The gift of wisdom enables us to make correct judgments about divine things. It steeps us in the way of truth and tells us when we are in danger of departing from it. We are able to make these judgments not by way of natural reasoning but because of our close union with God that comes from living a life of Christian love. Our loving union with God gives us knowledge of him that goes beyond the bounds of our normal way of thinking. The love of God has a connatural, cognitive element associated with it. Those who love God with all their heart, mind, and strength are given an intuitive knowledge of God that has important repercussions for how they live and profess their faith. A person may not be well-educated but very wise because of the individual's closeness to God. Holiness brings a person closer to God and thus more knowledgeable about the things of God. In this respect, wisdom complements the virtue of charity and is the highest of the Spirit's gifts. To have it is to enjoy a knowledge of God that arises in the heart and overflows into the rational cavities of the mind.

In spiritual direction, wisdom comes forward whenever directors encourage directees to ponder those they love—God, family, friends—and consider what truths they have learned from them. Considerable time must be spent to allow them to reflect on their lives, letting their true feelings about loved ones to surface. They should be encouraged to look beneath their feelings and identify whatever passing insights and intuitions they associate with the beloved. The emphasis here should be on getting in touch with the way loved ones shape their attitudes and way of being in the world. It should encourage them to explore the inroads love makes into their hidden awareness and unconscious thoughts. Those inroads will ultimately lead to the source of all love and to the things cherished by him.

The gift of understanding is an interior light imparted to us by God that enables us to go beyond the limitations of our natural powers of reason and come to a deep knowledge of the mysteries of the faith. This gift presupposes the ongoing presence of faith in our lives. Without faith there can be no understanding. Without understanding, faith is unable to penetrate the mysteries in which it inspires belief. A child can know the answer to a math problem but not understand how to get to it. Similarly, the gift of understanding helps us delve behind the tenets of our faith and see why they are true and how they interact. Both faith and the gift of understanding presuppose a person's cooperation with God's grace and desire to arrive at a deeper appreciation of the mysteries of the faith. Without the virtue of faith and the gift of understanding we would be left to our own natural powers and would make very little progress in our journey toward God. With them, there is no telling what we may be able to grasp under the gaze of God's illuminating light.

In spiritual direction, understanding is at work whenever we ask directees for a fuller explanation of something that has been shared. As they reflect in silence on what they have said, they try to come to a deeper insight into the meaning of a particular incident in their lives. At times, and seemingly out of nowhere, they are blessed with an insight they have never seen before. "This is new to me," some might say. "I never thought of it that way before." The insight has come not from them but from something beyond them, yet also within them. Through sharing with us, they come to a better understanding of themselves and their relationship with God and others. They feel more at home in the faith and have a much better grasp of the way it fits into their lives and leads them from one moment to the next.

The gift of counsel enables us to examine our options for action and to make prudent decisions under the guidance of the Holy Spirit. It complements the virtue of prudence which, whether acquired or inspired by grace, relies solely on the working of practical reason for its conclusions. The gift of counsel takes the process one step further. A person will often know how a close friend would react in a certain situation. Similarly, our close friendship with God gives us unique access to him when it comes to making practical decisions about how we should conduct our daily affairs. The gift of counsel brings the virtue of prudence to its perfection. While prudence seeks the practical rational means for living a life of virtue, counsel places the conclusions of prudence under the direct scrutiny of the Holy Spirit.

In spiritual direction, counsel is operative whenever we encourage directees to make sound, practical judgments about Christian living. We encourage them to prayerfully reflect on their responsibilities before God and help them to integrate them with the demands of everyday life. We help them to make such decisions out of love for Christ and a desire for true discipleship. Although their resolutions may not make much sense outside the vantage point of faith, they are rife with meaning and deep spiritual insight when considered in light of the Christian vision that sustains and motivates them. True counsel comes from God and is all about living in friendship with Christ. It asks those seeking guidance to look at the repercussions of their faith in God in the warp and woof of daily life.

The gift of knowledge helps us to make proper judgments about the meaning and content of our beliefs. Unlike the gift of wisdom, which enables us to make judgments about the divine content of our faith, knowledge is concerned with what is specifically human or created. Like the gift of understanding, it is generally associated with the virtue of faith. Rather than representing God's aid in helping us to *grasp* the meaning of our faith (as understanding does), it represents the help God gives us through the Holy Spirit to make correct *judgments* about the implications of our faith in daily life. The Spirit blesses us both with a certainty that a particular attitude or action is in accordance with the faith and a sense of freedom that we are giving flesh and bones to what we believe. The gift of knowledge has both speculative and practical dimensions associated with it. Without it, we would have to make such judgments based solely on our powers of rational reflection.

In spiritual direction, knowledge is present whenever we encourage directees to handle worldly things in a Godly way. For example, we might encourage them to bring their problems from home or work to God in prayer and ask him for guidance concerning what to do. In doing so, we help them to live in the world without being of it, and to discern the proper use of material things in the building of the kingdom. We encourage them to look upon creation as something given by God for humanity to care for and nurture. We help them to recognize their responsibilities to use the things of this world in a way that engenders the true values of the kingdom. We help them to navigate life in a way that befits a Christian, one that leads them to embrace the deepest truth about themselves.

Gifts of Will and Affection
The gift of fortitude enables us to pursue any task to its end without fear of loss or failure. It gives us both an assurance that no danger or peril will separate us from the love of God and a confidence of ultimate victory in the face of insurmountable odds. The gift of fortitude perfects the virtue of fortitude by allowing the direct influence of the Spirit to inspire and direct the will of the believer when obstacles arise in the course of life's struggles, especially in the

face of persecution and the danger of death. Since it enables us to face dangers with a courage beyond the limits of human nature, it is something that can be explained only as a grace-filled movement in the soul by the Holy Spirit.

In direction, fortitude shows itself whenever we encourage those seeking guidance to deal with the obstacles preventing them from living authentic Christian lives. We help them overcome difficulties as they never thought possible, and retreat from those they cannot until a better opportunity arises. We help them discipline their will by enabling them to persevere in the faith in the midst of all kinds of temptations, trials, and persecutions. We help them to focus their energies on the most important things and to strive to reach them no matter what, despite difficulties standing in their way.

The gift of piety strengthens our affections and moves us to honor and serve God out of a deep sense of filial devotion. Through this gift, the Spirit helps us to recognize that we are adopted sons and daughters of God and calls us to act accordingly. Piety complements justice (that virtue which seeks to give everyone their due) by seeking to render to God the reverence and respect only he deserves. Our recognition of God enables us to see ourselves for who we truly are. As something that comes to the soul through the movement of the Holy Spirit, this gift awakens in us a sense of the holy that human nature alone cannot easily sustain. It elicits from us a sense of gratitude for everything God has given us. From such thankfulness comes an awareness of the presence of God in the circumstances of daily life and in the lives of the people we serve. The gift of piety enables us to receive the Father's love with open arms and to respond to that love with the gratefulness of admiring children. We can look to St. Thérèse of Lisieux's "little way" of spiritual childhood for an expression of deep reverence for the gift of piety and its impact on the daily life of the believer.[6]

In direction, piety comes forward whenever we help directees deepen their reverence for God and manifest it sincerely and authentically in the concrete circumstances of their lives. We enable them to see that this gift comes not from some identifiable manmade source but from the Spirit, who hungers and thirsts for the justice of God's kingdom. We encourage them to look upon life with a deep sense of gratitude for all God has given them and thus deepen their sense of being gifted by God. The pious view all things in the light of God's providential and benevolent care. They live the devout life not out of a sense of duty or obligation but out of a deep and endearing love for God and creation.

The gift of fear fills us with a deep reverence for God. Through it, we recognize our smallness before our Creator and become afraid we may withdraw ourselves from his love. Fear of the Lord is a healthy element of the spiritual life. Although it does not have as much significance as the other gifts, it protects us against the sin of presumption and constantly reminds us that we can do nothing meritorious apart from God's saving grace. A boy may be afraid of his father either out of the fear of being punished or out of a fear of disappointing him. The gift of fear refers to the latter, which is typically referred to as "filial fear." It comes to us from the Holy Spirit and complements the theological virtue of hope. It perfects hope by reminding us constantly that we can gain salvation only by relying completely on God's love and mercy. In this respect, fear of the Lord and hope in the Lord cling to one another and motivate believers to take advantage of anything that will help them develop and maintain a close relationship with God.

In direction, fear of the Lord is at play whenever we help those seeking guidance see their smallness before God and their insignificance in the vast scheme of things. We help them get in touch with a sense of awe at the beauty and majesty of God, one that deepens their sense of wonder in a loving God who chooses to befriend the likes of them and dwell in their hearts. This deep sense of awe inspires them to do all in their power to avoid offending God. It deepens their hope in God's presence in the world and helps them to see the vestiges of God's glory and majesty in the created world.

These descriptions help us understand the meaning of the gifts of the Spirit and how they operate in our lives. Spiritual direction can bring a deeper level of awareness to the equation by giving us a deeper awareness of the movement of the Spirit in our lives and what it means to respond to its holy promptings.

Led by the Spirit

To be led by the Spirit means that we are committed first to a life of prayer. Prayer is the space in our lives where we turn over to God. We can do this in many ways: through petitions, meditation, the reading of Scripture, contemplation—to name a few. Since we are both individual and social by nature, it follows that our prayer must preserve a delicate balance in our lives between personal devotion and membership to Christ's body, the Church. Spiritual direction helps us examine the way we pray and how we can deepen it. It helps us to look at these various dimensions of our life of prayer, determine what is lacking in it, and how it can be improved. By showing us how to talk with God in a more personal, intimate way, it offers us a possibility of our spirits communing with the Spirit of God. As a result, we are able to share more deeply in the divine life and allow the gifts of the Spirit to manifest themselves in our thoughts, words, and actions.

Prayer is the air we breathe that helps us to live a life in the Spirit. If we are not aware of the Spirit's presence in our lives, it may be because we have not spent enough time seeking the Lord in prayer. Any close relationship needs to be nurtured by time spent in the presence of the other. The same is true of our rapport with God. We nurture our relationship with him when we seek him in prayer with body, mind, and spirit. If we do not pray, we can never be on intimate terms with God. If we do not pray, we will not understand what it means to live a life led by the Spirit. If we do not pray, we may know about the gifts but we will never know what it means to possess them and to use them. Spiritual direction helps us examine our relationship with God and ask challenging questions about the nature of that relationship and the direction it is taking: How do we pray? How do we respond to the promptings of the Spirit in our lives? How do the gifts manifest themselves in our judgments, decisions, and actions? These and other questions arising during the direction process help us to recognize God as our deepest need and to see prayer as the means to fill it.

To draw close to God in prayer means we are responding to the movement of grace in our lives and are open to the promptings of the Spirit. The gifts represent those specific helps God gives us to follow his will more closely in the daily circumstances of our lives. *Wisdom* enables us to make sound judgments about the things of God. *Understanding* helps us to grasp more fully what we believe. *Knowledge* does the same regarding the things of the earth. *Counsel* helps us discern the right course of action. *Fortitude* gives us confidence in the Lord in the midst of adversity. *Piety* fills us with a sense of reverence for God. *Fear of the Lord* gives us a sense of dread at the possibility of offending him. Taken together, the gifts assure the believer of God's concrete presence and action in the face of every possible challenge. They are the winds that blow the sails of our souls and enable us to navigate our way through the difficult waters of life. Without them, none of us would make very much headway in the spiritual life. Spiritual direction teaches us how to sense these winds and put them to good use.

When talking about their presence in the life of believers, it is important to think of the gifts as working in harmony and as having a synergetic effect on us. "The whole is greater than the sum of the parts," we might say. They operate in concert with one another and rarely in isolation. They do not bring notice to themselves or even to the person upon whom they are bestowed. Their purpose is to give glory to God by transforming us ever more closely unto his image and likeness. That is not to say they are always in use. In any given circumstance, the Spirit activates them as the need arises. The direction process helps us to nurture our relationship with God through prayer and to be open to the promptings of the Spirit in our lives. It all comes down to cooperating with God's free offer of grace, of which there is always abundance.

Conclusion

There is much more to the seven gifts of the Spirit than meets the eye. For this very reason, a second pair of eyes, those of a good spiritual director, can help us to appreciate them as vital aids given to us by God for our own spiritual health and the well-being of the entire Christian community. The gifts are more than a list to be memorized, having little relation to daily life. Each of them plays a specific role in our lives and is given to us by God to enable us to be more closely attuned to the movements of the Spirit. The gifts presuppose many things: cooperation with God's grace, living a life of virtue, seeking the Lord through a life of prayer. What they require is eclipsed only by the benefits they reap: "love, joy, peace, patience, kindness, goodness, faithfulness, gentleness, and self-control" (Galatians 5:22–23). The fruits of the Spirit are the results of a life thoroughly opened to the influence of the Spirit.

When these qualities exist in our lives, it is probably because we have been open to the promptings of the Spirit and have made good use of the gifts—perhaps without ever being aware of it. "The wind blows where it chooses" (John 3:8). The Spirit moves in its own way—and in its own time. It does so on the wings of prayer and the gifts it bestows. Spiritual direction is a valuable tool for helping us appreciate the presence of the Spirit in our lives. It inspires us to identify the gifts we have received, ponder them, and use them for the good of others. The next chapter will look at some practical suggestions for how the direction process can move us further along the path of virtuous living and become more sensitive to the Spirit's promptings in our hearts.

Reflection Questions

What are the gifts of the Spirit?
How do the gifts differ from the virtues?
Which gifts are associated with the intellect?
Which gifts are associated with the will and affections?
What does it mean to be led by the Spirit?

CHAPTER THIRTEEN

Attending to the Virtues and Gifts in Spiritual Direction

⇵

The Holy Spirit gives to certain of the faithful the gifts of wisdom, faith and discernment for the sake of this common good which is prayer (spiritual direction). Men and women so endowed are true servants of the living tradition of prayer.

CATECHISM OF THE CATHOLIC CHURCH, 2690

If the virtues and gifts are to provide the content, and spiritual direction the format, for a paradigm shift in the practical orientation of the Church's moral and spiritual teaching, the question arises about how they should relate on the concrete level of implementation. On this score, it is important to remember that form gives shape to matter—not vice versa.[1] The dynamics of the spiritual direction process, in other words, must provide the context, space, and atmosphere for people seeking guidance to speak freely about their needs and desires concerning the virtues and gifts of the Spirit. When seen in this light, the language of the virtues and gifts must not be imposed from without but fostered from within the dynamics of the "holy conversation" that is spiritual direction.

A Guiding Language

In the present context, the process of spiritual direction must be able to animate the language of the virtues and the gifts of the Spirit so that it will come alive for directors and directees. It must, in short, be able to "inhabit" this language and become fluent in it. A close look at the values and goals of each reveals that this can and should be so. Intimacy with God is the ultimate end of spiritual direction, as well as the Church's teaching on the virtues and gifts. That end is sought through self-disclosure and loving attention, the threefold marks of friendship (benevolence, reciprocity, mutual indwelling), and such important relational skills as active listening, personal reflection, giving and receiving counsel, and one's own personal rhythm of prayer. What is more, both have deep roots in sacred Scripture and seek to address the person on every level.

Connecting the virtues and gifts to spiritual direction also offers a practical point of convergence for the ongoing discussion about the relationship between spirituality and morality. Each of these dimensions of Christian life can be examined on different levels (like the experiential, the doctrinal, the analytical)[2] and have been found to interface on a broad range of issues, not the least of which is the preeminence of right relationship for the moral and spiritual life. The anthropological, covenantal, and transformational dimensions of spiritual direction make it particularly receptive to a virtues-and-gifts approach to the moral and spiritual life. The possible benefits to each are encouraging. In the process of spiritual direction, the proponents of the virtues and gifts will find a concrete locus for instilling the Church's teaching concerning the nature of the moral and spiritual life. There people will be given the opportunity not merely to learn about the virtues and gifts but to understand how they work in the warp and woof of their daily lives. Spiritual directors, in turn, will discover that the virtues and gifts provide a framework of substantial content that the process can break open and make available to those serious about growth in the moral and spiritual life. Spiritual direction thus becomes a discipline for growth in the school of virtues and the gifts of the Spirit. The virtues and gifts, in turn, bring into focus an emphasis on leading a person to friendship and intimacy with God.

As it has developed and matured over the years, the process of spiritual direction is especially suited to helping a person grow in the virtues and gifts of the Spirit. The virtues and gifts, in turn, provide a well-established and highly nuanced language with which the director can help directees articulate their spiritual experiences and come to a deeper understanding of their relationships with the divine.

Some Observations
The use of virtues and gifts as the guiding language for spiritual direction invites comments concerning how it should be used and the influence it will have upon those involved in the ministry. The following remarks seek to raise some legitimate concerns that might arise in such an arrangement.

To begin with, directors would be in a better position to help their directees if they had a thorough knowledge of the Christian virtues. An acquaintance with Aquinas' treatment of the general nature of virtue and Alphonsus de Liguori's treatment of love in *The Practice of the Love of Jesus Christ* could provide a general blueprint for the moral and spiritual life and serve as useful touchstones for many aspects of their ministry. This knowledge of the classical representation of the virtues should be complemented by recent attempts to develop an ethics of virtue appropriate for today's world and become an integral part of training programs for spiritual directors. Directors, moreover, need to be sensitive to the influence of the historical and cultural factors involved in any formulation of virtue theory, as well as the relational triangle of God, humanity, and world that forms the backdrop of all mature theological reflection on the moral and spiritual life. Directors should take care not to turn the direction session into a classroom but introduce the language of the virtues and gifts when they think it will help directees have a better grasp of where they are in their spiritual journey and how God may be asking them to grow.[3]

A corollary to the above observation would be the need for directors to have a close familiarity with the corresponding vices associated with each of the Christian virtues. Such knowledge will enable directors to identify disordered patterns of behavior in the directee's life and provide him with a language that will first name the habitual disorder and then point out the direction for gradual, developmental growth. Aquinas' presentation of the vices, when coupled with some of the more recent descriptions of the virtues and the sound insights of the psychological sciences, will help the director to articulate areas in the directee's life requiring further examination. Spiritual direction should be a place where a directee can feel free to bring to the surface those dark, secret areas of life (addictions, recurrent sins, unspoken prejudices) so that they can be named, owned, and appropriately addressed.[4]

A theoretical knowledge of the virtues and vices provides the director with a sense of what the directee should be detached from (il distacco) *and united with* (l'unione). Theoretical knowledge, however, can only go so far. Spiritual direction is both a science and a practical art that needs to be realized creatively in very specific and concrete circumstances. For this reason, directors must pay close attention to how they use their theoretical knowledge in the direction session. Such knowledge is to be used not as an intrusive form of control but as a helpful diagnostic tool and curing salve. Directors' approach to directees should be one of presence, careful listening, and prudent counsel. A thorough knowledge of the virtues puts directors in touch with some of the most valuable treasures of the Christian tradition.

A director should always focus on the directee and look to the virtues as a storehouse from which the director can take out both new and old as the occasion permits. For example, rather than saying, "Well, Aquinas would say that you lack temperance in the way you deal with food and drink and that you are struggling with the vice of gluttony," a better way of addressing an issue would be something like, "From what you have shared, it seems that you sometimes find it difficult to control your appetite for food and drink. Is that correct?" Since one of the goals of the direction process should be to make that tradition come alive in the person receiving direction, special care should be taken to ensure that it is presented in a way that encourages rather than hinders growth in the moral and spiritual life.[5]

It would also be wise at some point in the direction process, preferably at the beginning, for the director to go over some of the classical teaching on virtues with the directee and briefly outline some of the ways the director will be employing them. This sharing of knowledge emphasizes the mutuality of the direction process and avoids making the directee overly dependent on the director's knowledge of the material. At some point, the director may even wish to suggest some spiritual reading that will cover these general principles in a straightforward and easily digestible manner. Directors would do well to keep an eye out for popular presentations of the virtues that would be useful to their directees in their moral and spiritual lives. In addition to spiritual reading, directors should be open to questions on the virtues in general or any one of the virtues or vices in particular. The goal would be to have the language of the virtue and gifts become a shared possession, one that both the director and directee can turn to for guidance when trying to make sense of the directee's spiritual journey.[6]

All during this time, it is essential for the director to foster an honest, trusting, and open relationship with the directee. Only then will the directee feel free enough to share with the director the most intimate details of his or her moral and spiritual experience. The story of one's ongoing faith experience is the meeting place for the virtues, the gifts, and the spiritual direction process. Once it is shared, director and directee can engage in serious theological reflection and begin to ask questions about its meaning for the moral and spiritual life of the directee. If it is not shared in an honest and open manner, then both can become engaged in a mutual form of self-deception. The directee will assume a persona that does not correspond to his or her true experience but that is acceptable to the director. The director, in turn, will be responding to a mask and may not have the sensitivity or wherewithal to ask the directee to remove it. Spiritual direction should be a place where an atmosphere of confidentiality and trust enables directees to reveal their true self to the director and, ultimately, to God.[7]

The convergence of the virtues and the direction process in the directees' personal narrative of their experience of the divine should also resonate with the biblical narrative. Directors should look for possible parallels with the Scriptures and suggest them to directees at appropriate times. The Exodus story; Jesus' parables; and the narrative of his passion, death, resurrection, and ascension are just some of the Bible stories where possible parallels may exist. Directors should also encourage directees to read the Scriptures meditatively (as in *lectio divina*) and to listen actively for passages that resemble their experiences. Knowledge of the various spiritual senses of Scripture (allegorical, moral, and anagogical) will help directees delve below the literal meaning of the text and find adequate points of reference for growth in their moral and spiritual lives. Reading the Scriptures in this way can give directees a greater appreciation of the direction process and convey a deeper awareness of how God is working in their lives.[8]

One of the main purposes of the direction process is to help directees come to a deeper understanding of the various ways in which God has gifted them. Giftedness has many dimensions, ranging from the Holy Spirit itself—often referred to and named Gift—to universal gifts given to all humanity (such as creation and life) to more particular gifts given to believers (such as the infused virtues and the gifts of the Spirit), to special gifts given to individuals (such as personal talents, including public speaking, writing, listening, building, gardening, cooking). The director's goal should be to raise directees' awareness of the various ways in which they have been gifted by God, to deepen their gratitude for those gifts, and to deepen their resolve to use those gifts for the service of others. We are sometimes more conscious of our weaknesses than of our various gifts and talents. Directors should encourage those who come to them to humbly recognize the truth about themselves by naming and taking ownership of the gifts and talents with which they have been blessed.[9]

One special gift that God gives to everyone is the grace to pray. A person's prayer life should be not a mere otherworldly pursuit but deeply rooted in the spiritual and moral issues of the day. Aquinas makes a powerful point when he places his treatment of prayer within his treatise on justice. Prayer, in his mind, is an interior act of the virtue of religion, an allied virtue of justice, and it's an important way in which we give God his due. Directors need to be knowledgeable in the ways of prayer (*oratio, meditatio, contemplation, liturgia*) so they will be able to help their directees respond to the issues facing them in moral and spiritual life. This means helping directees discern the correct paths of action in the circumstances facing them. It also means encouraging them to strike a proper balance and rhythm in their daily routine so every anthropological dimension of their lives will be oriented to God: the physical, emotional, intellectual, spiritual, and social. Prayer is to the moral and spiritual life what breathing is to life itself. The Apostle Paul tells us to "pray without ceasing" (1 Thessalonians 5:17). Spiritual direction should be a place where directees can examine how they pray and look for ways of making it a more integral part of their daily lives.[10]

As the direction process unfolds, the language of the virtues should eventually help directees name areas that are preventing them from growing in intimate friendship with God. In responding to these areas, the director should encourage directees to confront those areas of darkness in their lives by giving them to God in prayer and by developing realistic and practical means for dealing with them. This twofold movement of prayer and practical resolution gives concrete expression to the theological notion of cooperation with God's grace. It also reveals another way in which the spiritual and moral dimensions of Christian existence converge in the spiritual direction process. Prayer is a practical way of responding to the concrete problems of the moral and spiritual life. It helps us to recognize limitations, accept them for what they are, and humbly turn to God for help. Practical resolutions, in turn, reveal the shape and content of our spirituality in the circumstances of daily life. It encourages us to take concrete steps to turn our lives around and deal with the problems facing us in constructive ways.[11]

As the direction process unfolds, the classical language of the virtues should also help the directee to name those areas that are helping him to grow in friendship with God. In responding to these areas, the director should encourage the directee to celebrate his relationship with the divine by resolving never to take it for granted. Growth in intimacy with God should gradually become the center of the directee's conscious awareness and ultimately permeate everything he does. Through prayer, the directee should be encouraged to place his relationship with God in God's hands. The directee should also be encouraged to find concrete ways in which that friendship can be deepened. For example, try to spend some time alone with God, attend a prayer meeting, pray a daily rosary, or start a regimen of spiritual reading. Finally, the directee should be encouraged to explore the ways in which one's relationship with God affects one's relationship with others—and vice versa. For example, try to be a little kinder to those you find especially difficult to deal with, try to see the face of God in the strangers you meet. Pray for them.[12]

These observations in no way exhaust the various ways in which the virtues can benefit the process of spiritual direction and serve as a practical and concrete locus for integrating the spiritual and moral dimensions of life. They seek only to demonstrate what use the virtues might have for the direction process and to show how that process can provide an experiential context for coming to a deeper understanding of the moral and spiritual. While they can be added to (or adjusted), they represent an initial attempt at demonstrating what a decidedly concrete and practical turn might look like for recent theoretical discussions on the relationship between spirituality and morality.

Conclusion

There are many models of spiritual direction, and this text in no way replaces a balanced variety of approaches with a monolithic system that would rob the ministry of one of its greatest riches. But an unwarranted proliferation of models might also produce the contrary effect of disorienting directors about the purpose, scope, and method of their ministry.

The use of the virtues and gifts in the process of direction is meant to provide a solid basis for growth in the moral and spiritual life, one that directors can refer to with confidence and without hesitation. It is also meant to be flexible enough to allow us to adapt its insights to our own special preferences regarding the approach and implementation of our ministry. As such, the union of the virtues and spiritual direction can serve as a valuable touchstone that directors and directees alike can use as a source of wisdom, creative insight, and continuity with the Catholic moral and spiritual traditions.

There are, of course, many questions still to be asked and many difficulties that will be encountered in the initial stages of implementation. Those interested in uniting the virtues and gifts with the process of spiritual direction can receive solace from the knowledge that the attempt is not without precedent in Church history.[13] They may also be encouraged by the reception their attempt will be received with by those demonstrating a renewed interest in the virtues and the classics of Christian spirituality.

Certainly not all directors will accept this effort to unite the virtues and gifts with the process of spiritual direction. But doing so hopes to provide a concrete, practical space where questions concerning the moral and spiritual spheres of a person's life can be explored, integrated, and even celebrated. It also hopes to offer spiritual directors an opportunity to share mutual areas of concern and competence in the hope of discovering common ground for future collaboration on the nature and scope of the moral and spiritual life. As will be revealed in part four, spiritual direction may even provide an opportunity for opening dialogues with people of other faiths.

Reflection Questions

Why are the virtues and gifts important for the moral life?

What do they tell us about ourselves?

How do they help us grow in our relationship with God?

Why should spiritual directors be familiar with the virtues?

In what way do the virtues provide a bridge between spirituality and morality?

PART FOUR

Dialoguing With Other Traditions

Part four examines how the Alphonsian model of direction in its concern for integrating spirituality and morality can help people from other religious, philosophical, and ethical traditions. It offers a very broad description of spirituality (chapter fourteen), presents natural law and interspirituality as two possible ways of employing the model (chapter fifteen), asserts that this approach to direction can help people understand and embrace their own traditions on deeper levels (chapter sixteen), provides a suggested template for how to use the model in such situations (chapter seventeen), and offers practical suggestions on how to bridge the gap between the ideals presented by such traditions and the circumstances of everyday life (chapter eighteen). It asserts that the model can be adapted to help people from other traditions to become themselves in their faith and, in doing so, prepare them for honest dialogue with those of differing views and vantage points.

CHAPTER FOURTEEN

An Open View of Spirituality

I learned both what is secret and what is manifest, for wisdom, the fashioner of all things, taught me. There is in her a spirit that is intelligent, holy, unique, manifold, subtle, mobile, clear, unpolluted, distinct, invulnerable, loving the good, keen, irresistible, beneficent, humane, steadfast, sure, free from anxiety, all-powerful, overseeing all, and penetrating through all spirits that are intelligent, pure, and altogether subtle.
WISDOM OF SOLOMON 7:21–23

One way in which this Alphonsian approach to spiritual direction can reach out to members of other religious, philosophical, and ethical traditions is to use it in conjunction with a very broad understanding of spirituality. Although the model itself arose within the purview of Roman Catholicism, it can be adapted by other Christian and non-Christian traditions to much benefit by incorporating a wider understanding of spirituality into the direction process.

Toward Defining Spirituality
Of the many attempts to define spirituality, probably the broadest and most universal comes from the hand of Walter H. Principe, who calls it "…the way in

which a person understands and lives within his or her historical context that aspect of his or her religion, philosophy or ethic that is viewed as the loftiest, the noblest, the most calculated to lead to the fullness of the ideal or perfection being sought."[1] The strength of this definition is its all-embracive character. The only element lacking in it is its failure to emphasize the social or communal aspect of our human makeup in the concept. If the words "or group" were added at appropriate places, it would become much more serviceable to the needs of the direction model outlined in this book. In other words, no single religious, philosophical, or ethical tradition can claim the term *spirituality* exclusively for itself.

According to this adapted definition, every person (or group) has a spirituality, although each may have varying levels of awareness of just what that is. The direction process developed in this book can help people come to a deeper understanding of their spirituality and help them live it out in a more focused and conscientious manner. Taking a closer look at the various elements of this definition will shed light on how other religious, philosophical, or ethical traditions might use the Alphonsian model.

Spirituality is the way in which a person (or group) understands and lives. It therefore embraces the whole of life and involves not merely ideas but also putting them into action. It pertains not only to a person's (or group's) understanding of life and its meaning but also to how that particular understanding manifests itself in daily life.

Within his or her (or their) historical context. Spirituality is impacted by the circumstances in which the people find themselves. High ideals must be lived out in everyday life. Although a gap often exists between the spiritual vision in question and the way it is lived, a key component of any spirituality concerns whether the people involved are working to narrow it.

That aspect of his or her (or group's) religion, philosophy, or ethic. Spirituality embraces religion and any vision dealing with matters of ultimate concern. One's ultimate concern has a direct impact on one's spirituality. People's belief systems supply the underlying foundation upon which they build their spiritualities. What is of ultimate concern to people (power, possessions, pleasure, love, happiness) represents their fundamental, life-defining option, their "god," if you will.

That is viewed as the loftiest, the noblest, the most calculated. Spirituality deals with the way people live out what matters most to them. As one author says, it "is about what we do with the fire inside of us, about how we channel our eros."[2] It is about what we are passionate about and about how we strive to make our dreams a reality.

To lead to the fullness of the ideal or perfection being sought. One element common to all spiritualities is that they put forth some kind of a vision to be embraced and actively pursued. People want to make what matters to them most a reality. Whatever that vision may be, they actively pursue it, because they believe achieving it will fulfill them and make them happy.

Levels of Spirituality

In addition to this concrete and very flexible definition of spirituality, Principe also speaks about three different (albeit related) levels of spirituality: the experiential, the doctrinal, and the analytical.

The experiential level, according to Principe, "is the *real* or *existential* level."[3] It pertains to the lived reality of those seeking to conform their lives to a particular vision. It recognizes the disparity that often occurs between a particular ideal and the way it is embodied by its adherents in different historical periods and even in various cultures and geographical areas. Every spirituality has this vital, lived component, and there is always a gap between the vision itself and its lived manifestation. The goal at this level is always to recognize the distance between the two and to try to minimize it as much as possible. A vibrant spirituality would be one that undergoes intense self-examination regarding the relationship between its vision and lived reality and then implements concrete structures and practices that narrow the distance between them. A feeble (possibly dying) spirituality is one that neglects to do so and allows the distance between vision and reality to steadily increase. When applied to spiritual direction, this first level of spirituality would be concerned with the actual experiences of those receiving and giving spiritual direction: struggles with faith, experiences of abandonment, difficulties at prayer, and tensions in friendships, for example. It would also be interested in the extent to which those experiences are taken into account by the particular model of direction employed and the efforts made to ensure they are addressed.

The second level of spirituality, the doctrinal, pertains to *"the formulation of a teaching about the lived reality."*[4] Such teaching arises as a result of extended reflection on the experience of those who have embraced a particular spiritual tradition. It seeks to concretize that experience through structures and practices capable of communicating that experience from one generation to the next. Religious, philosophical, and ethical traditions are handed down through time as a result of such teachings. The Gospels, for example, are the teachings of Christ reflected upon and written down by his closest followers in the early generations of Christianity. Similarly, *The Rule of Benedict* is a moderate monastic teaching that sought to temper the rigors of early monastic asceticism and emphasize the cenobitic or communal aspect of this particular call. In like manner, the *Catechism of the Catholic Church* is an attempt to bring together in one place the various doctrines (teachings) of the Church so that members of the faithful could have easier access to them. Every spiritual family seeks to set down either in writing or in oral tradition the teachings it holds most dear. These doctrines are not imposed from without but shared from within. They spring from lived, existential experience and seek to give cohesion and continuity to that lived reality. In the context of spiritual direction, there are a variety of models arising from many schools of spirituality. Although the one being shared here has arisen within the Alphonsian tradition of the Redemptorist order in the Catholic Church, it is flexible enough so that its basic insights can be used by other Christian and non-Christian traditions.

The third level of spirituality, the analytical, concerns "the *study* by scholars of the first and especially the second levels of spirituality."[5] Critical analysis should accompany all human endeavors and is especially important for spirituality. With it, scholars are able to gauge developments in a particular tradition and make helpful observations that can serve to move that tradition forward. Without it, a tradition runs the risk of losing its bearings and perhaps even its self-identity. The academic study of spirituality is "a field-encompassing" endeavor, because it embraces a number of disciplines (such as theology, religious studies, philosophy, sociology, anthropology).[6] While there is always a risk that such study can become removed from a tradition's lived reality and teaching, the advantages of such study far outweigh the disadvantages. Scholars must take care to offer unbiased, critical analysis of the spiritual tradition they are studying. Through carefully controlled comparative analysis, they also can offer valuable interreligious insights that can foster dialogue and mutual understanding. Such analysis can take place through any number of means: lectures, workshops, courses, articles, books, monographs, video recordings, and the like. The goal is to apply critical thinking to the first two levels of spirituality in order to ameliorate the tradition to which they belong.

When applied to spiritual direction, this level assures serious analysis and critical reflection upon the particular model of direction employed and the experience of those giving and receiving direction under this model. Such study will uncover ways in which the model can be improved, point to the common ground it shares with other models, and offer sound counsel for how the model can be appropriated by other religious, philosophical, and ethical traditions.

Each level of spirituality should not be considered in isolation from the others but viewed as intimately related to them. Each has the potential of enriching the others and, in doing so, further one's own self-understanding. A person's lived experience of a particular spiritual tradition can deepen as a result of reading a critical scholarly study of that tradition. Scholars, in turn, can benefit greatly in their analysis by stepping into the traditions they are studying and seeking to experience them from the inside out rather than from a perspective of academic distance. A circular relationship exists among these various levels. Experience informs teaching and, together, both assist in critical analysis. Scholarly study, in turn, sheds light on the internal workings of a tradition's teaching and leads to more appropriate ways of passing it into the realm of real, existential, lived experience.

The present study takes this interplay among the three levels very seriously, especially with regard to adapting its use in flexible ways to other traditions. The aim of this model of direction is to facilitate ways in which people can become themselves in their faith and, in doing so, come to a deeper awareness of their role in the world. The model seeks to address the lived experience of those seeking guidance and welcomes whatever critical reflections scholars can offer to sharpen and refine the process. Assessment plays an important role in the process of spiritual direction and is addressed, on the one hand, by focused supervision that ensures both confidentiality and accountability on the part of the director and, on the other hand, by careful scientific analysis of both the implementation and experience of the process of skilled theologians.

Some Observations

This definition of spirituality and its three related levels has great importance for spiritual direction and the moral life. The following observations will focus on the relevance they have for adapting the Alphonsian model of direction to other religious, philosophical, and ethical traditions.

To begin with, the intention is not to impose a specific definition of spiri-

tuality on any tradition but to use one broad enough in its focus so that it can address the concerns of any tradition, regardless of its assumptions and spiritual underpinnings. Other understandings of the spiritual life are welcome and may complement the approach adopted here. The attempt is merely to find a fundamental point of departure to apply to the Alphonsian model developed in this book to as wide a number of traditions as possible. This broad definition of spirituality enables directors to sift through any spiritual tradition and separate those elements genuinely useful to all traditions from those more specific to itself.

In the light of this definition, directors should encourage the directee to get in touch with her deepest values and then identify the specific dispositions that would enable her to enact them in daily life. This grouping of values represents the vision of who the directee wishes to become. Many of these values may flow from a particular religion or spiritual tradition. Others may be more personal or rooted in a specific cultural-social milieu. The aim of direction would be to help directees identify the ideals that underlie their vision of reality.

Once the directee has identified and named these deepest values, the director should then encourage him to reflect on how they manifest themselves in his daily life. Much of this part of the process involves active listening and allowing the directee to put together and share the narrative of his life. In reflecting back this narrative, the director should encourage the directee to look at those aspects of it where the vision is clearly manifest and those where it is not. The director should likewise help the directee to uncover those areas in life where there is a gap between the values espoused and the lived experience.

Once directees recognize the manifestations and gaps in the realization of their vision of daily life, directors should encourage then to look at their positive and negative feelings about them. This moment in the process is important for moving the directee from the level of mind to that of heart. Intimacy with the divine, with others, and with oneself involves a dual involvement of self-disclosure and loving attention.[7] Directees can take true ownership of their vision only by delving into this affective area and making an inventory of the vast range of feelings arising from this journey of self-understanding.

Such sharing should give directees a deeper awareness of their spiritual needs. At this point directors should encourage directees to name them, regardless of how large or small they may seem. Identifying them and expressing them first to oneself and then to the directors will pave the way for helping them to eventually express these needs to God. If the directees' traditions do not allow for belief in a personal God, then they should be encouraged simply to rest with these needs in silence and be open to a deepening self-awareness and self-understanding. Since it may take a while for directees to identify their deepest needs, the director must be encouraging and patient.

Helping people identify their values, feelings, and needs ultimately leads to the question: "What is the next step?" The direction process now seeks to move from the level of mind to the level of heart and finally to the level of action. At this point, directors should encourage directees to identify those small steps that they can take to narrow whatever gaps might exist between the vision they espouse and their lived experience. Growth in the spiritual life comes about by meeting people where they are and then encouraging them to take the next step toward achieving the desired end. The resolutions formed at this stage of the direction process should be small, measurable, and within the directees' grasp. Directors should elicit such resolutions from directees and should serve as a sounding board for a realistic evaluation of the probability of their being actually implemented.

From beginning to end, both the director and the directee should converse with one another in an atmosphere of revered silence. The direction session should begin and end with moments of silence. Throughout their conversation, moreover, they should be conscious of the silence between the words, phrases, and sentences they share. Authentic spiritual insight into one's life arises in the midst of such silence. By befriending silence and embracing it as an important element in the process of direction, the director and the directee will come to appreciate the role it plays in their relationship and in their own individual spiritual growth.

Throughout the direction process, the director should keep clear the distinction between the first and second levels of spirituality. The model being employed represents the second level of teaching and is meant to serve the directee's level one experience of lived, existential reality. The director must take care not to look upon the model as an end in itself by trying to fit the directee's experience into a preexisting mold. Since a spiritual direction relationship normally lasts for an extended time, it does not matter if every step does not take place during a specific session. Over time, each of these areas—the reflective, affective, needful, and active—will take place in time. It is important for the director and directee to be patient with the process and not allow it to become a false priority.

Since the three levels of spirituality are interrelated, the director should encourage the directee to learn as much as possible about the particular religion, philosophy, or ethic he espouses. This learning process can take place through spiritual reading and participation in related seminars and workshops. The director, moreover, should make an effort to explain the basics of the direction process to the directee and receive adequate supervision to ensure that he remains faithful to the directee, to the process of direction, and to his own lived experience. If the director does not come from the same spiritual tradition of the directee, appropriate efforts should also be made to familiarize himself as much as possible with it. Doing so, will allow for more quality sharing during the direction session and open up avenues for further discussion and self-reflection.

Finally, both the director and directee should be aware that no definition of spirituality and no exposition of its various levels will ever be exhaustive. For this reason, they should familiarize themselves with other approaches to the field and be reconciled to the fact that the tools they are utilizing are feeble instruments that need to be continually evaluated and refined. The purpose behind using this particular definition of spirituality along with its associate levels lies in its universal applicability and its power to keep the levels of experience, teaching, and analysis logically distinct yet relevantly connected. This understanding of spirituality is broad enough to allow virtually anyone to enter into the process of self-understanding that underlies and supports the model of direction under consideration.

Conclusion

This chapter adapts a broad understanding of spirituality to a particular model of spiritual direction to make it relevant for adherents of other religious, philosophical, and ethical traditions. It thus seeks to give that model as wide an application as possible. Such an understanding should help the director to adapt the Alphonsian approach developed in this book in a way that meets the directee's specific concerns.

These concerns normally span a wide gamut of values, dispositions, character traits, and actions. The model of direction presented here seeks to help directees identify as far as possible those dispositional powers of mind and heart that best lead to the embodiment of the vision or ideal being pursued in the concrete circumstances of their daily lives. In doing so, it opens a window to the ways in which it can speak to those belonging to other religious, philosophical, and ethical traditions.

A broad, universal understanding of the nature of spirituality should enable directors to enter into dialogue with a much wider audience. The common element in this adaptation is the shared humanity of those involved in the direction process. The next chapter will examine the various dimensions of this common *humanum* and offer another way in which this particular approach to direction can be adapted to other religious, philosophical, and ethical traditions.

Reflection Questions

What are the strengths of having a broad definition of spirituality?

Are there any weaknesses?

How can such an understanding of spirituality be put to use in the direction process?

How do the three levels of spirituality interrelate?

How do they interact in the direction process?

CHAPTER FIFTEEN

Natural Law and Interspirituality

↕

In diverse cultures, people have progressively elaborated and developed traditions of wisdom in which they express and transmit their vision of the world as well as their thoughtful perception of the place that man holds in society and the cosmos. Before all conceptual theorizing, these wisdom traditions, which are often of a religious nature, convey an experience that identifies what favors and what hinders the full blossoming of personal life and the smooth running of social life. They constitute a type of "cultural capital" available in the search for a common wisdom necessary for responding to contemporary ethical challenges.
INTERNATIONAL THEOLOGICAL COMMISSION,
IN SEARCH OF A UNIVERSAL ETHIC, 12

In addition to employing a broad, all-embracing understanding of spirituality, other ways in which this particular approach to spiritual direction can reach out to other religious, philosophical, and ethical traditions would be to focus on natural law (and the common humanity shared by all), and interspirituality (an approach that concentrates on the common elements of spiritual experience in those traditions).

I. Natural Law

By identifying those elements that all people share, efforts can be made to identify those goods that promote human life in general so that it can grow and prosper wherever it appears. These key anthropological factors should be both directly observable in all human cultures and rooted in common sense. The moral life flows from the common identity shared by all human beings and forms the basis of the natural law.

It would likely be impossible to assert that everyone would agree on what the commonly shared human characteristics might be, or even whether a common understanding of the makeup of human nature can be universally accepted. Unanimity rarely occurs in a world of such widely diverse cultures, philosophies, and religious outlooks. Differences in opinion, however, should not inhibit sincere attempts to arrive at such a common understanding as a point of departure and as a way of inviting others to engage in constructive dialogue.

The Catholic Church has reflected a great deal on the nature of the human person and its moral ramifications. It has a rigorous natural law theory dating before St. Thomas Aquinas. Its most recent expression is an International Theological Commission's 2009 document *In Search of a Universal Ethic: A New Look at the Natural Law*.[1] The point of this document is that the world needs to resolve the mounting ethical dilemmas it faces. The framers of the document recognize the plurality of religious and philosophical traditions at work in today's world and call upon each tradition to examine its own approach in finding this common ethical language. They take another look at the Church's venerable tradition of natural law in the hope of helping to clarify the Catholic position and possibly even helping other traditions do the same for their own.

The document claims to have "…no other aim than helping to reflect on this source of personal and collective morality."[2] It proposes "a rationally justifiable foundation" for a universal ethic, and invites experts and spokespersons of the great religious, wisdom, and philosophical traditions of humanity "to proceed to an analogous labor beginning from their sources, to reach a common recognition of the universal moral norms based on a rational approach to reality."[3] It also affirms the United Nations' *Universal Declaration of Human Rights*[4] as "one of the most beautiful successes of modern history" and sees it as an important step in rooting natural law theory in human rights and the dignity of every person.[5]

The following is an attempt to correlate the basic inclinations of Aquinas' natural theory, as adapted by the authors of *In Search of a Universal Ethic*, with the thirty articles of the *Universal Declaration*, followed by some observations on how these human inclinations and rights can be introduced into the process of spiritual direction. Although there have been several attempts to expound a theory of natural law from a variety of philosophical perspectives,[6] Aquinas' natural law theory is being used here because of its time-honored place in the Catholic tradition, and because it is the one employed by the framers of *In Search of a Universal Ethic*. It bears noting, moreover, that Alphonsus de Liguori was heavily influenced by the thoughts of Aquinas and leans heavily on him in his dogmatic works and in his *Moral Theology*.[7]

Primary Precepts of the Natural Law

Aquinas develops the primary precepts in the *Summa Theologiae*, I-II, q. 94, a.2. They may be paraphrased as follows:

1. An inclination to do and pursue good and avoid evil
2. An inclination toward self-preservation (shared with all substances)
3. An inclination toward procreation and the education of offspring (shared with all animals)
4. An inclination toward knowing the truth about God and toward living in society (shared with all rational creatures).

The first human inclination is also known as the first principle of practical reasoning and flows from the notion that all things seek what is good. The next three inclinations flow from what human beings share in common with all other substances (to desire to simply exist), with the animal world (the desire to have and to rear offspring), and with all rational creatures (the desire for truth and life in society). According to Aquinas, human beings are naturally inclined to act according to reason and thus according to virtue. For this reason, all acts of virtue, when considered as virtuous (that is, specifically under the aspect of virtue), belong to the natural law.[8]

The authors of *In Search of a Universal Ethic* find the presentation of the natural law in Thomas Aquinas' *Summa Theologiae* extremely useful for its purposes, since it emphasizes the dignity of the human person and its power of discernment. They develop these basic inclinations in a more personal and existential manner and note that "[s]uch precepts remain very general but ... form the first substratum that is at the foundation of all further reflections on the good to be practiced and on the evil to be avoided."[9] They also make an interesting observation regarding the relationship between natural *law* and natural *justice*. While the former focuses on human inclinations (an anthropological category), the latter on human rights (a legal category).[10] They also point to the UN's *Universal Declaration of Human Rights* as "...one of the highest expressions of the human conscience in our time, and it offers a solid basis for promoting a more just world."[11]

What follows is a brief presentation of these basic human inclinations identified by Aquinas in his natural law theory, a correlation of these inclinations with the thirty articles of the *Universal Declaration of Human Rights*, and relevant observations regarding how this correlation can be used in the ministry of spiritual direction.

From Natural Law to Natural Right

A correlation of the thirty articles of the UN *Declaration* with the primary precepts of the natural law would have great value in the attempt to adapt the model of direction developed in this book to other religious, philosophical, and ethical traditions. For the sake of simplicity, an abbreviated version[12] of these rights is being used and the breakdown would look something like this:

1. An inclination to do and pursue good and avoid evil
    - All articles apply (nos. 1-30)
2. An inclination toward self-preservation
   (shared with all substances)
    - Right to life, liberty, personal security (a. 1)
    - Freedom from slavery (a. 4)
    - Freedom from torture and degrading treatment (a. 5)
    - Freedom from arbitrary arrest and exile (a. 9)
    - Right to adequate living standard (a. 25)
3. An inclination toward procreation and the education of offspring
   (shared with all animals)
    - Right to marriage and family (a. 16)
    - Right to rest and leisure (a. 24)

- Right to education (a. 26)
4. An inclination toward knowing the truth about God and toward living in society (shared with all rational creatures)
   - Right to equality (a. 1)
   - Freedom from discrimination (a. 2)
   - Right to recognition as a person before the law (a. 6)
   - Right to equality before the law (a. 7)
   - Right to remedy by competent tribunal (a. 8)
   - Right to fair pubic hearing (a. 10)
   - Right to be considered innocent until proven guilty (a. 11)
   - Right to free movement in and out of the country (a. 13)
   - Right to asylum in other countries from persecution (a. 14)
   - Right to a nationality and the freedom to change it (a. 15)
   - Right to own property (a. 17)
   - Freedom of belief and religion (a. 18)
   - Freedom of opinion and information (a. 19)
   - Right of peaceful assembly and association (a. 20)
   - Right to participate in government and in free elections (a. 21)
   - Right to social security (a. 22)
   - Right to desirable work and to join trade unions (a. 23)
   - Right to participate in the cultural life of community (a. 27)
   - Right to a social order that articulates this document (a. 28)
   - Community duties essential to free and full development (a. 29)
   - Freedom from state or personal interference in the above rights (a. 30)

Although some of the rights may be applicable to more than one category, the above correlation shows that the *Universal Declaration* adequately addresses each of these primary inclinations of human nature. The correlation indicates that the *Universal Declaration* focuses on areas pertaining to knowing the truth about God and life in society but does not neglect the other inclinations. All of the articles in the *Universal Declaration* pertain to the primary principle of doing and pursuing good and avoiding evil. The question now arises: How can this correlation be applied to spiritual direction?

When Applied to Spiritual Direction

This movement from natural law (*lex naturalis*) to natural right (*ius naturale*) can be useful in attempts to adapt the spiritual direction approach in this book to other religious, philosophical, and ethical traditions. This direction process seeks to help the directee to deepen her understanding of the moral and spiritual life by identifying those attitudes and dispositions necessary for a prosperous life. When employing the above correlation of natural inclinations and natural rights, the process would look like this:

1. The director welcomes the directee and, after some initial small talk, invites the directee to enter with a minute or two of silence. This atmosphere of silence is meant to permeate the entire conversation. If the directee believes in God, silent prayer would be appropriate during this time.
2. At the close of this period of silence, the director invites the directee to reflect on what's been happening in the directee's life in relation to the person's needs or inclinations. The UN declaration may be made available in either its extended or abbreviated versions.
3. As the directee unfolds the narrative of her life, the director should employ active listening and reflect back those areas where these inclinations (and the rights flowing from them) have been met or frustrated.
4. In the course of the conversation, the directee should focus on one or more of the areas that have been uncovered. At that point, the director should invite the directee to share feelings about these issues. The director should also invite the directee to identify those attitudes and dispositions that will bring these inclinations along.
5. Once the directee has shared feelings about what has been shared, the director should invite the person to identify what needs have arisen during the course of the conversation that will help the person. The director should encourage the directee to list all needs, large and small, and eventually help the person focus on the deepest needs of the moment.
6. Once the needs have been identified, the director should encourage the directee to focus on what needs to be done to move forward. What concrete steps need to be taken? How should the steps be

accomplished? In what order? The director should encourage the directee to be as practical and concrete as possible.
7. Once the directee has made some practical resolutions, the director can invite the directee to conclude the session with another minute or two of silence. Again, if the directee believes in God, silent prayer would be appropriate during this time.

The process outlined above should emphasize mutual respect for those involved in the direction process and a reverence for silence and active listening. The director should seek not to impose from without but only suggest and elicit responses from the directee. The focus during this type of direction session should be on the common experience of their shared humanity by means of a reflection on the basic inclinations of human existence and the rights flowing from them.

II. Interspirituality

Yet another useful tool in adapting the model of direction proposed in this book would be to concentrate on *The Snowmass Guidelines for Interreligious Understanding* as set forth by Thomas Keating in the context of Wayne Teasdale's notion of interspirituality. These authors focus on the elements common to the spiritual experiences of all religious traditions as a means to mutual understanding and human solidarity.

Guidelines for Interreligious Understanding

These guidelines are designed to encourage dialogue among the various religions by focusing on the common spiritual experiences they share. They are listed as follows:

1. The world religions bear witness to the experience of the Ultimate Reality to which they give various names: Brahman, the Absolute, God, Allah, (the) Great Spirit, the Transcendent.
2. The Ultimate Reality surpasses any name or concept that can be given to It.
3. The Ultimate Reality is the source (ground of being) of all existence.

4. Faith is opening, surrendering, and responding to the Ultimate Reality. This relationship precedes every belief system.
5. The potential for human wholeness—or in other frames of reference, liberation, self-transcendence, enlightenment, salvation, transforming union, moksha, nirvana, fana—is present in every human person.
6. The Ultimate Reality may be experienced not only through religious practices but also through nature, art, human relationships, and service to others.
7. The differences among belief systems should be presented as facts that distinguish them, not as points of superiority. In the light of the globalization of life and culture now in process, the personal and social ethical principles proposed by the world religions in the past need to be rethought and reexpressed.[13]

While these basic guidelines were originally simply listed without commentary, Keating later refined and actively promoted them as a means toward authentic interreligious sharing. They, in turn, were adapted by Wayne Teasdale in his book *The Mystic Heart: Discovering a Universal Spirituality in the World's Religions*.[14]

Interspirituality Defined

Using Keating's guidelines as a spiritual backdrop, Teasdale goes on to offer the basic features of a universal communal spirituality. "Interspirituality," the term he uses to describe this emerging phenomenon is "[t]he common heritage of humankind's spiritual wisdom; the sharing of mystical resources across traditions."[15] This spirituality, he claims, will share the following characteristics:

1. It will be contemplative.
2. It will be interspiritual and intermystical.
3. It will be socially engaged.
4. It will be environmentally responsible.
5. It will engage other media.
6. It will be cosmically open.
7. It will aim for integration.[16]

Teasdale further develops Keating's guidelines and explains why the above characteristics tap into the spiritual experience of the world's great religions. He gives an extensive explanation of each and shows how they relate to one another in a cohesive and integral way. When taken together, both the guidelines and characteristics of this emerging universal communal spirituality can be a useful tool in adapting the model of spiritual direction presented in this book to other traditions.

When Applied to Spiritual Direction

The process of spiritual direction proposed in this book can be easily adapted to follow the seven guidelines for religious understanding and the main features of interspirituality. The focus when conducting such a session would be to concentrate on those elements of the directee's spiritual experience that have relevance across the traditions. The process of such a session would look something like this:

1. The director greets the directee and they spend a few minutes in silence in order to recognize the presence of the Ultimate Reality in their midst. During this time they should seek to put aside their thoughts, quiet their hearts, and rest in the stillness.
2. After some time, the director invites the directee to share those moments since their past meeting where that Ultimate Reality has made its presence (or absence) felt in a poignant way. The point is to allow the directee to identify those moments in his life where the veil between the Ultimate and Present Realities has become very thin or the gap between them very great.
3. Once these experiences have been shared, the director should encourage the directee to speak about the relevance of that experience for his life. The director should encourage the directee to examine his feelings about what happened, and to look for underlying patterns that fit into the overall narrative of his life.
4. Both the director and directee should try to be aware of the pregnant silences that come and go during their conversation, since those moments can be times when the Ultimate Reality is trying to break through and touch the silence that is between them and within their hearts.

5. In the course of the conversation, the director should ask the directee if he has become aware of any needs as a result of the experience that has been shared. Attention should be given not only to personal needs but also those of social, environmental, and cosmic significance. As these needs are shared, the director should help the directee to identify those that are most pressing and in need of personal attention.
6. Once some specific needs have been identified and prioritized, the director should encourage the directee to focus on what practical goals to take in order to meet them. The director should invite the directee to be as concrete as possible. It is usually better to focus on one rather than several needs. It is also normally better to concentrate on small, achievable steps that serve a larger end.
7. Finally the session ends by returning to the silence that has permeated the entire conversation and reverence it by resting in it. This silence has been the backdrop against which the session has taken place and must now be brought to the fore. Doing so reminds both the director and directee that what was shared serves a greater purpose and has significance beyond the session.

The basic features of our direction model hold up well when it is adapted to the various guidelines of interreligious understanding and the characteristics of interspirituality. It can serve as a point of departure for reflecting on one's spiritual experience and, as a result, help a person to come to a deeper self-awareness and self-understanding. The flexibility of the model allows its use in a wide variety of spiritual contexts and enables it to be adapted by traditions other than the one from which it arose.

Conclusion
This chapter has looked at ways in which the Alphonsian model of spiritual direction can be adapted to meet the needs of other religious, philosophical, and ethical traditions. It has examined two very different approaches to the moral and spiritual life—natural law and interspirituality—and shown how they can be of help in this process of adaptation.

Rather than going into an in-depth study of these approaches, the aim here was simply to list their main characteristics and show how they could be absorbed in the Alphonsian model of direction and used to great benefit. Natural law can be used to help the director and directee focus on the elements of their common humanity. Interspirituality, in turn, concentrates on the common elements of spiritual experience existing across religious traditions. These approaches highlight what people of different backgrounds share in common and should enable directors to adapt the Alphonsian model of direction to meet the needs of others, regardless of their assumptions about the meaning of life and purpose of human action.

When coupled with the broad understanding of spirituality developed in the previous chapter, these approaches offer directors valuable tools for meeting people where they are, helping them look at their experiences, encouraging them to come to grips with their feelings, and opening up for them a better understanding of themselves and the world in which they live. If nothing else, they should help both director and directee have a deeper appreciation of the common ground upon which they stand and from which they engage the world. In the next chapter, we will explore how the Alphonsian model of direction can help people come to a better understanding of their own religious, philosophical, or ethical traditions.

Reflection Questions

How can natural law be used to adapt the Alphonsian model of direction to people from other religious, philosophical, and ethical traditions?

How can natural rights be used to do so?

In what ways can interspirituality be helpful?

How do these approaches make the Alphonsian model more flexible?

Are there any dangers in adapting the model in these ways?

CHAPTER SIXTEEN

Embracing One's Tradition

⇅

By including the dead in the circle of discourse, we enrich the quality of the conversation. Of course we do not listen only to the dead, nor are we a tape recording of the tradition. That really would be the dead faith of the living, not the living faith of the dead.
JAROSLAV PELIKAN, *THE VINDICATION OF TRADITION*[1]

In the previous chapter, natural law and interspirituality were identified as two possible ways in which our approach to spiritual direction could be adapted to other religious, philosophical, and ethical traditions. This chapter emphasizes how the model can help people come to a deeper awareness of and take ownership of their own traditions. The goal will be to offer a way for people to engage the sacred texts of their traditions and make them their own.

Naming One's Tradition
Paul Tillich, one of the great Protestant theologians of the last century, once wrote that faith pertains to matters of ultimate concern.[2] N. Max Wildiers, in turn, has said that all mature theological reflection involves the reflective interplay of three concepts: God, the human person, and the world.[3] What is more, Geoffrey Wainwright, basing himself on the typology of H. Richard Niebuhr's

Christ and Culture, identifies five types of Christian spirituality: (1) Christ against Culture, (2) Christ of Culture, (3) Christ above Culture, (4) Christ and Culture in Paradox, and (5) Christ, the Transformer of Culture.[4] Jaroslav Pelikan calls tradition "the living voices of the dead," and not "the dead voices of the living."[5] These insights from noted theologians have particular relevance for adapting our model of spiritual direction for other religious, philosophical, and ethical traditions. The word tradition comes from the Latin *trado, tradere*, which means "to give up, hand over, deliver, transmit, surrender, consign."[6] In this context, the word concerns wisdom that is passed on, handed over, and surrendered from one generation to the next. Each generation is a vital link in the handing on of this living wisdom.

In light of the above, our approach to spiritual direction does not wish to impose any single religious tradition on anyone but simply help others to identify those matters of ultimate concern in their lives. It also wishes to enable them to come to a deeper encounter with their understandings of God, the human person, and the world in which they live. These understandings should lead them to take a particular stance toward the culture in which they live. In other words, their matters of ultimate concern should place them *against* the world, *of* it (that is, immersed in it), *above* it, *in paradox* (or tension) with it, or as a *transforming* leaven for it. It should also enable them to take ownership of their traditions, identify strengths and weaknesses in them, and find practical applications for their daily life. The goal is to enable people to encounter the living voices of their traditions, make them relevant for their present circumstances, and give them the strength to move forward in life with more confidence in their own self-understanding.

The process of naming one's tradition is no easy task. It involves listening to the living voices of the past and probing them to discover their subtle nuances and interpretations. It means sifting through them, being able to discern their various strengths and weaknesses, and looking at the values they seek to inculcate in their followers. Most of all, it means taking ownership of them and making them one's own in a way that fosters one's human identity so that one can move forward in life and actually become one of those living voices for future generations. Listening to these voices enables people to develop in continuity with them as they seek to interpret it in a way that has practical relevance for their lives.

Preparing for Direction

Our model of spiritual direction seeks to help others to interpret their tradition so that they can name it, take ownership of it, and live it out in the warp and woof of daily life. It encourages those belonging to other religious, philosophical, and ethical backgrounds to engage their traditions in constructive, practical ways. Doing so requires preparation before entering into a direction session. Such preparation should involve engaging one's sacred texts in a contemplative, reflective manner that leads to resolute action.

One way of achieving this goal would be to employ the four Rs of *Read, Reflect, Rest,* and *Resolve.* This fourfold process of reading differs somewhat from classical monastic *lectio divina* ("holy reading"), which focuses more on the interior life through reading, meditation, prayer, and contemplation. The four Rs approach, by way of contrast, seeks to move the reader toward practical and resolute action and, in doing so, prepares people for the direction session with a greater sense of where they stand in relationship to their particular tradition and what it requires from them morally. While there is considerable overlap in the two approaches, the one employed here seems better suited to helping people face the challenges of the turbulent waters of the moral and spiritual life. Let us take a deeper look at this fourfold movement.

1. Read. Every tradition usually has a canon of sacred texts. For example, Jews have the Hebrew Scriptures; Christians, the Old and New Testaments; Muslims, the Koran; Hindus, the Upanishads; Buddhists, the Tripitaka and the Sutras. Even strictly philosophical and ethical traditions have key texts to which they turn for guidance. When preparing for a direction session, people should look at a text from their tradition and engage it reflectively. The text itself should not be very long and should be read slowly several times over. The purpose here is not to focus merely on what the texts says but on what its significance is for the individual. The reading should be done in silence and in a quiet place. A process of active listening should be employed so that the reader seeks to receive from the text the wisdom it seeks to impart for her. In a culture that has become overwhelmed by information, people need to learn how to sit with a text in a contemplative manner. They need to chew the words and digest them to release their deeper senses. The search for wisdom is a never-ending process, one that requires discipline, determination, and endurance. People must be patient with the text. They must learn to stay with it, even wrestle with it, until it reveals to the reader a relevant meaning.

2. Reflect. The next step in the process of preparation would be for people to reflect on the significance of the reading for their lives. One way of going about this would be to seek connections between the book being read and the book of one's life. No one can discover these connections but the individual, and care must be taken to do so in a manner that reflects both the integrity of the sacred text and the dignity of the person. The point here is that the sacred text must have some relevance for the concrete circumstances of one's daily life. Otherwise it becomes a dead voice from the past with little practical significance. During this process of reflection people should look for patterns and similarities between the wisdom revealed in the text and the narrative of their lives. They should seek to identify areas in their lives that correspond to the wisdom of the sacred text and places where it falls short. There will usually be a gap between the ideal presented in the sacred text and the way it is embodied in real life. The size of this gap should be noted and an effort should be made to identify practical steps for reducing it.

3. Rest. Once people have reflected on the text, its connection to their lives, and the gap between the ideal the text presents and how it is embodied in their lives, it is time to put the text down and simply rest in the wisdom garnered from the text and the light that it has shed on them. Doing so allows them to get in touch with a deeper, spiritual level of their human makeup. This movement from mental reflection to restful silence allows them to absorb the text in ways that go beyond words and concepts. It allows one to get in touch with one's feelings toward both the gap in one's life and what needs to be done to narrow it. During this time, the text's meaning gently takes root in a person's soul and inspires it to strive for the fullness of the ideal being sought. This movement from words to wordless silence gives depth to the person's apprehension of the text and enables her to respond to it freely and openly. It gives people time to embrace the soul of the text and take it to heart. This quiet resting with the sacred text allows for a deeper reading, one that goes beneath the words to the silent spaces between them that make the various words and sentences possible. Such resting will eventually lead to even deeper insights that directees can take hold of and apply. It enables the reader to make the text her own and interpret it in a way that leads to genuine human fulfillment.

4. Resolve. "What is this text asking of me?" The purpose of engaging the sacred text in this way is to gently move people to action. To do so, they must move out of the period of silent rest, ask themselves this very simple question, and try to identify concrete steps that will enable them to give the text life in the concrete circumstances of daily life. This last stage of the preparation process is critical, for it asks people to look at the possible ways in which they can narrow the gap between vision and reality, between the ideal and the real, between the persons they wish to become and the persons they actually are. The goal of this stage in the process is to be as concrete and practical as possible. Rather than coming up with big, grandiose schemes for growing in the life of virtue, people would benefit much more by focusing on small, gradual steps that could be easily implemented. Over time, one small step will follow another and people will eventually draw nearer to their desired goals. At this stage of the process, people should try to identify as many small, practical steps as possible. During the direction session itself, the director will help them discern which of these to take on and follow. Above all, the resolutions should be action-oriented, practical in scope, and relatively easy to implement.

This fourfold process of preparation that involves reading the sacred text, reflecting upon it, resting in it, and resolving to act from it should prepare directees for the direction process in a way that should enable them to talk openly and freely about the specific areas of growth in need of attention. Since the efficacy of this process will depend on the values conveyed by the texts themselves, efforts must be made to ensure that those selected reflect the best of the tradition in question and can be interpreted in a way that enables people to connect them with their life narratives.

Five Non-Christian Religious Traditions

Now that we have seen a particular way of approaching a sacred text—one that shares much in common with the approach of *lectio divina* or "holy reading," but with more of an emphasis on resolute action—we now can underscore the values embodied in some of the major world religions besides Christianity: Judaism, Islam, Taoism, Hinduism, and Buddhism. At the very outset, it is important to mention that none of these traditions speak with a single voice. As with Christianity itself, each contains a multiplicity of voices that give different emphases and nuances to each tradition.

This is not the place to outline the variances in the various subgroups within the world's five major non-Christian religions. Our sole purpose is simply to highlight in very broad strokes the chief moral values that each major religious tradition seeks to inculcate in the minds and hearts of their followers.

To do so, I will simply list the major commonly accepted moral values of each tradition, point out where relevant texts in each tradition can be accessed, and briefly comment on how they can interface with the four Rs approach and be brought to a direction session.

Judaism

The moral values of Judaism are primarily found in the Torah, especially in the Decalogue or the "Ten Words." They involve words or commands with respect to God and neighbor. The following values offer an insight into the scope and depth of this tradition.

1. Love God.
2. Honor God.
3. Worship God.
4. Love your neighbor.
5. Do not hate.
6. Do not speak falsely of another.
7. Do not take revenge or bear a grudge.
8. Do not use hurtful words.
9. Judge fairly.
10. Distance yourself from falsehood.
11. Honor your parents.
12. Honor others.
13. Visit the sick.
14. Invite and be hospitable to guests.
15. Give joy to the bride and groom.
16. Console those who mourn.
17. Do not stand over your brother's blood.
18. Return lost objects.
19. Do not steal.
20. Do not covet and do not desire.
21. Pay on time.
22. Do not deceive.
23. Go beyond the letter of the Law.
24. Walk in God's ways.
25. Bury the dead.

The Chosen People were called to respond to God's choice by the holiness of their lives: "Speak to all the congregation of the people of Israel and say to them: You shall be holy, for I the Lord your God am holy" (Leviticus 19:2). These moral values of the Jewish tradition point out the way to holiness of life and are delineated in the law and the prophets. There, the history of salvation of God's people is presented in a variety of ways and using a number of diverse literary genres to accentuate such themes as election, promise, law, and covenant. These values are also found in the Jewish wisdom literature with its focus on the contemplation of the nature of things in the created order.[7] For more on these topics and other relevant texts, see Torah.org.[8]

Islam

Muslim ethics can generally be summarized as a "morality of obedience." To do good means to obey God's commandments; to do evil is to disobey them. Within Islam, there were some (the *mou'tazilita*) who maintained that human reason could recognize good from evil; others (the *ach'ariti*) came to a completely opposite conclusion, saying that good and evil are known only through God's revelation.[9] Another factor to consider is what Howard Kainz calls "the two religions of Islam:" one has its origins in Mohammed's early days in Medina, is devoid of anti-Semitism, and calls for peaceful conversion; the other, stemming from the prophet's later days in Mecca, calls for violent jihad in order to conquer the world for Islam. Despite such fundamental differences in outlook, a number of common ethical norms appear across Islam, although they would be applied differently, depending on one's interpretation and the degree of one's adherence to the religion of Islam.[10] They can be delineated as follows:

1. Charity
2. Contentment
3. Courtesy
4. Courage
5. Dignity
6. Discipline
7. Firmness
8. Frankness
9. Forgiveness
10. Frugality

11. Generosity
12. Good Speech
13. Gratitude
14. Honesty/Fair-Dealing
15. Hope
16. Humility
17. Justice
18. Kindness
19. Loyalty
20. Mercy
21. Moderation/Balance
22. Patience
23. Perseverance
24. Prudence
25. Purity
26. Repentance
27. Respect
28. Responsibility
29. Righteousness
30. Self-Restraint
31. Sincerity
32. Spirituality
33. Tolerance
34. Trustworthiness
35. Unity
36. Wisdom

Islam considers itself as a return to the original natural religion of humanity. Depending on the particular tradition to which one belongs, however, these moral values come either through a reasoned reflection on the consistency of nature or by the divine positive revelation of God.[11] In many ways, the tensions within Islam today reflect these different interpretative approaches to morality and the nature of God's revelation to man. For more on these topics and other relevant texts, see the Internet site, *Islamic Information Portal*.[12]

Taoism

Taoism puts forth Ten Precepts by which individuals are to conduct their lives. Many of these appear in other religious traditions and give credence to the possibility of humanity possessing a shared moral patrimony. These precepts have both personal and communal implications, and may be listed as follows:

1. Do not kill but always be mindful of the host of living beings.
2. Do not be lascivious or think depraved thoughts.
3. Do not steal or receive unrighteous wealth.
4. Do not cheat or misrepresent good and evil.
5. Do not get intoxicated but always think of pure conduct.
6. I will maintain harmony with my ancestors and family and never disregard my kin.
7. When I see someone do a good deed, I will support him with joy and delight.
8. When I see someone unfortunate, I will support him with dignity to recover good fortune.
9. When someone comes to do me harm, I will not harbor thoughts of revenge.
10. As long as all beings have not attained the Tao, I will not expect to do so myself.[13]

According to Taoism, the primordial principal immanent in the entire universe consists in a dynamic of permanent change reflected in two contrary poles, the yïn and the yang; people are called to take this natural process of transformation to heart by letting themselves go and adopting an attitude of nonaction.[14] For more on these topics and other relevant texts, see the Internet site, *Taoist Ethics*.[15]

Hinduism

In the various Hindu traditions both the universe and human society are controlled by a fundamental order known as *dharma*. The *Upanishads*, the sacred texts of Hinduism, highlight the following key virtues:

1. Ahimsa (nonviolence)
2. Mind and sense control
3. Tolerance
4. Hospitality
5. Compassion
6. Protection
7. Respect
8. Wisdom
9. Austerity
10. Celibacy
11. Honesty
12. Cleanliness

Hinduism's moral teaching is intimately tied up with the belief "in an infinite cycle of transmigrations (*samsāra*), with the idea that good and bad actions committed during the present life (*karman*) have an influence on successive births."[16] A person's behavior, in other words, has concrete consequences for the afterlife. For more on these topics and other relevant texts, see the Internet site, *The Heart of Hinduism*.[17]

Buddhism

The moral teaching of Buddhism is based on the four noble truths taught by Buddha after his experience of illumination, the noble eightfold path, and the five precepts flowing from it.

The Four Noble Truths
1. Reality is suffering and dissatisfaction.
2. The origin of suffering is desire.
3. The cessation of suffering is possible (with the extinction of desire).
4. There is one way that leads to the cessation of suffering: the noble eightfold path.

The Noble Eightfold Path
1. Right view
2. Right aspiration
3. Right speech
4. Right action
5. Right livelihood
6. Right effort
7. Right mindfulness
8. Right concentration

The Five Precepts
1. Not to harm any living being and not to take life.
2. Not to take that which is not given.
3. Not to practice sexual misconduct.
4. Not to speak false words or lie.
5. Not to drink intoxicating products that diminish self-control.

Six Key Virtues
1. Charity
2. Uprightness
3. Forbearance
4. Dispassion
5. Dauntlessness
6. Contemplation

Marked by a profound altruism "expressed in a resolute attitude of nonviolence, amicable benevolence and compassion," Buddhist ethics shares much in common with the golden rule.[18] For more on these topics and other relevant texts, see the Internet site, *The Buddhist Society*.[19] See also, *Buddhist Ethics*.[20]

From this brief, admittedly condensed and schematic presentation of the key moral values of the five major non-Christian religions, it should be clear that, despite differences in doctrinal beliefs, these traditions share a great deal of moral wisdom in common. The authors of *In Search of a Universal Ethic* go so far as to speak of a common moral patrimony shared by many of these traditions:

The form and extent of these traditions can vary considerably. Nevertheless, they testify to the existence of a patrimony of moral values common to all human beings, no matter how these values are justified within a particular worldview. For example, the "golden rule" ("And what you hate, do not do to anyone" [Tobit 4:15]) is found in one form or another in the majority of wisdom traditions. Furthermore, these traditions generally agree in recognizing that the great ethical rules not only impose themselves on a specific human group but also hold true for each individual and for all peoples. In fact, several traditions recognize that these universal moral behaviors are demanded by the very nature of man: they express the manner by which he is to enter, in a creative and harmonious way, into a cosmic or metaphysical order that transcends him and gives meaning to his life. This order is, in fact, filled with an immanent wisdom. It carries a moral message that human beings are capable of discerning.[21]

By identifying where and how those values common to all the great traditions appear in one's own sacred texts, and by meditating on them through a process of *Read, Reflect, Rest,* and *Resolve,* these important moral values can be appropriated on a deeper level of awareness and embodied in one's life in practical ways that enable one to be faithful to one's own tradition while respectful of the expression of those same values in other traditions.

Although time and space do not allow an exploration of how this same dynamic might apply to adherents of other philosophical and ethical traditions, it appears likely that there will be a similar overlap on the level of moral content. A good treatment of these moral convergences appears in chapter one of *In Search of a Universal Ethic.*[22] C. S. Lewis provides a similar offering in "Illustrations of the Tao," an appendix to his book on moral theory, *The Abolition of Man.*[23] Richard T. Kinnier, Jerry L. Kernes, and Therese M. Dautheribes do much the same in their essay "A Short List of Universal Moral Values."[24] Sir John Templeton's *Discovering the Laws of Life, Worldwide Laws of Life, Agape Love,* and *Wisdom from World Religions* highlight much of this common moral patrimony.[25] Those interested in accessing readings from a variety of religious, philosophical, and ethical traditions can also go to the *Internet Sacred Text Archive.* This site claims to be "the largest freely available archive of online books about religion, mythology, folklore, and the esoteric on the Internet.

The site is dedicated to religious tolerance and scholarship, and has the largest readership of any similar site on the Web."[26]

Conclusion

In this chapter, we have examined how, by embracing their own traditions and probing their sacred texts, members of other religious, philosophical, and ethical traditions can benefit from an adaptation of the Alphonsian model of direction. Our purpose is not to impose one tradition upon another but simply to help people come into deeper contact with their own traditions by entering into dialogue with it and discovering its relevance for their daily lives.

People make such contact by engaging texts that embody the esteemed moral values of their own traditions. The fourfold approach of *Read*, *Reflect*, *Rest*, and *Resolve* seeks to help people reflect on the sacred text in a way that enables them to draw connections between the text and the narrative of their own lives. By reading the text, reflecting on it, resting in it, and then making practical resolutions about their lives, they will be prepared for and ready to make the most of the direction session.

The goal throughout this process is to help people get in touch with the living voices of their traditions and make them their own. Only by taking ownership of these traditions and cultivating the best they have to offer will people be able to embrace them as a guiding light for their lives. Only then will they be able to engage in traditions other than their own in authentic dialogue. We have seen that, despite deep doctrinal differences, many of the world's major religious traditions share a common moral patrimony that unites them in a dogged pursuit of virtuous action. By focusing on this common heritage, members of different religious, philosophical, and ethical traditions can grow in mutual respect and understanding. Doing so is one of the most pressing needs and great challenges that humanity faces in years ahead. In the next chapter, we will look at the dynamics involved when employing this model of direction to other traditions.

Reflection Questions

What does it mean to engage one's tradition?

Why is it important to name and embrace one's tradition in the direction process?

Why is it important to engage the sacred texts of one's tradition?

How does the fourfold process of read, reflect, rest, resolve help us engage these texts?

How can such texts and the values they represent be used to help a person become himself or herself in their faith?

CHAPTER SEVENTEEN

A Suggested Template

The whole point of seeing through something is to see something through it. It is good that the window should be transparent, because the street or the garden beyond it is opaque. How if you saw through the garden too?
It is no use trying to 'see through' first principles. If you see through everything, then everything is transparent. But a wholly transparent world is an invisible world. To "see through" all things is the same as not to see.
C. S. LEWIS, *THE ABOLITION OF MAN*[1]

The previous three chapters have shown how a broad understanding of spirituality (chapter fourteen) can be combined with theories of natural law and interspirituality (chapter fifteen), along with using one's own tradition as a point of departure (chapter sixteen) to show how our model of spiritual direction can be adapted to those of other religious, philosophical, and ethical traditions. In this chapter, we wish to establish a template for how such a direction session might proceed. This template would eliminate any specific reference to Christianity and focus instead on the model's underlying dynamics of listening and dialogue. Those involved in the session might employ one or more of the tools cited in chapters fifteen and sixteen. The goal of the session would be to help directees become themselves within their specific belief system.

The Model's Underlying Dynamic

As seen in earlier chapters, our model represents an adaptation of the Alphonsian approach to mental prayer to the direction process. Since the model was developed with the Catholic tradition, it presupposes such basic doctrines such the faith in God, the Trinity, the Incarnation, redemption in Christ, and life in the Spirit. As fundamental as these beliefs are to Catholics, they can be separated from the underlying dynamics of the model itself. In doing so, the model can be adapted to members of other traditions without posing the threat of proselytism. The goal is not to impose or indoctrinate but simply to help directees come to grips with their own traditions and reach an assessment of its immediate and practical implications for their lives. What is more, only by owning one's tradition can a person enter into constructive dialogue with those from other traditions. The model's underlying dynamics can be summarized as: (1) Immersing Oneself in Silence, (2) Reflecting on One's Life, (3) Getting in Touch with One's Feelings, (4) Naming One's Needs, (5) Identifying the Next Step, and (6) Ending in Silence. Taken together, these steps form a basic template that can be used in constructive ways to help directees of other traditions.

1. *Immersing Oneself in Silence.* Silence is an essential characteristic of the direction process. Every session should begin and end in silence. Resting in silence and continuing to dialogue against a backdrop of silence will help directors and directees alike to listen both to the movements of their hearts and to each other. Authentic dialogue requires silence. Words make sense, only against the backdrop of the silence that allows them to be heard, understood, and ultimately acted upon. Without spaces of silence between them, words cannot be distinguished from one another and devolve into nothing but gibberish. For this reason, an atmosphere of silence should permeate the entire session. This backdrop of silence helps to foster a contemplative attitude toward life and allows the direction session to stand out from the other activities of the day. When beginning a session, directors should invite directees to spend some time in quiet getting in touch with themselves and their area of ultimate concern. A period from one to three minutes should be sufficient. When directors feel that enough time has passed, they can end this period of silence by simply saying, "Let's begin."

2. *Reflecting on One's Life.* At this stage of the process, the silence becomes the backdrop for a conversation that follows. The main topic of this conversation should be the life of the directees and their engagement with the sacred

text they have reflected on prior to the session. During this time, directors listen actively to what their directees are saying and help them get in touch with the significance of the text they have reflected on. The goal is to help directees find parallels between the sacred narrative and the narrative of their own lives. They are to help them discover patterns and connections between the two so that the text becomes alive for them. "The living voices of the dead," we might say, are meant to speak to the directees and help them make sense of their lives.[2] Directors should not impose any particular interpretation on their directees but seek only to elicit possible parallels between the two narratives. In the end, only the directees can determine if a particular interpretation has relevance for them and requires their response. Directors should seek to help their directees unpack the text and find its significance for their lives. When such meaning comes forth, it will be time to move the process into an examination of one's feelings and affections.

3. *Getting in Touch with One's Feelings*. Once directees have had the opportunity to examine a sacred text and find its relevance for their lives, directors should gradually and gently encourage them to move from mind to heart. They should encourage their directees to delve into their feelings and emotions about the particular text they have reflected upon. This is a critical stage in the process. Directors should be sensitive, yet probing. They should engage very carefully in active listening and seek to elicit from their directees their authentic feelings regarding the discussion that has just taken place. The goal in all of this is to enable directees to look not only at their thoughts but also at their feelings about the narrative under discussion. Directors should anticipate a wide rage of responses regarding their directees' engagement with the narrative of their lives and the text that confronts them. They should seek to help their directees embrace both narratives—that of the selected sacred text and that of their lives—and seek to uncover the hidden meaning that it holds for them. Directors should encourage their directees to share freely and openly what they are actually feeling about the insights gained from their reflections.

4. *Naming One's Needs*. After the period of reflection and the subsequent deepening that takes place by getting in touch with and expressing one's feelings, the process moves on to identifying ones needs. This stage of the process represents a further deepening of the process of reflection, since it entails looking at the vision or ideal presented by one's tradition in the area of moral concern and taking a hard look at one's present reality. One's needs can be

thought of as the distance between the ideal presented by one's tradition and the reality of where one stands in relation to it. These needs can pertain to any one of a number of key anthropological factors: the physical, emotional, intellectual, spiritual, and social. At this stage of the direction process, directees should be encouraged to name their needs that fall anywhere along this anthropological spectrum and then ask themselves if the gap they have identified between vision and reality is increasing or decreasing. Before moving to the next stage of the process, they should ask themselves if they are willing to commit themselves to narrowing that gap by taking small practical steps that will produce effective change.

5. *Identifying the Next Step.* Once directees have committed themselves to doing what they can to narrow the gap between the ideal presented to them by their tradition and the reality of their present lives, it remains for them to identify practical steps for doing so. At this point directors should encourage their directees to focus not on abstract, grandiose, (and largely impractical) schemes but to find small, concrete ways of moving closer toward their desired goal. The gap between vision and reality will not disappear overnight but only through a consistent program of practice involving easily realizable steps that will gradually move them closer to their intended end. Once these steps are identified, directors should help their directees to prioritize them and put together a prudent and practical plan of implementation. This plan should be elicited from the directees, not imposed, and consist of small things they believe they can implement in a steady, consistent way. The goal for directors should be to meet their directees where they are and accompany them as they identify ways of narrowing the gap between their vision of the moral life and their real life situations. They should be encouraged to be practical and realistic, and admonished not to bite off more than they can chew.

6. *Ending in Silence.* As stated earlier, the direction session should begin and end in silence. Silence should also be the backdrop against which the conversation takes place. The purpose of having silence at the close of the session is to give directees a chance to gather together what was said and begin to integrate it into their lives. This is the time for them to gather their thoughts and feelings about what was shared. It should also be a time for them to hold their needs before their eyes and commit themselves to do what they said they would do to better their situation. Silence speaks. It has a way of validating the session. When directors and their directees close by resting in the silence

that surrounds them, they gather all that has been said in a pensive, reflective manner. If the conversation was sincere, the silence they share will bring them a sense of peace. If not, it will challenge them to be more open with each other the next time. Silence marks off the direction session from the rest of life and reminds directors and directees alike that their sharing has enabled them to delve beneath the appearances of things and focus on things that really matter. By ending in this way, it allows directors and directees to go back into life with a greater awareness of their need to listen both to what is going on around them and also within them.

Taken together, the above steps comprise a basic template for spiritual direction that can be used to adapt our model to those from other religious, philosophical, and ethical traditions. This template should be thought of as a helpful guide rather than a method to be implemented at all times at any cost. It may very well be that some of the steps may not be covered in a single one-hour session. The goal is that over the course of time (and through several sessions) directors and directees will be able to establish a rhythm in their conversations that will enable to deal with each of these elements.

Observations

Having established a base with which our model of direction could be adapted to those from other traditions, we are now in a position to make some remarks regarding some of the underlying assumptions involved with using such a model.

To begin with, it is important that at the very first session directors and directees talk about their expectations regarding spiritual direction. During this opening session, issues such as frequency of the sessions, payment (if there is any), and levels of confidentiality should be addressed. At this time, it is also appropriate for directors to explain the model of direction being used and give their directees some information and reading material regarding it. In addition to being a time for directors and directees to get acquainted with each other, the first session should also be used as a time to explain the model and answer any questions regarding it. It is very important that the model be explained and to emphasize that the template being used has been specifically tailored to reach out to those coming from other traditions.

In the early sessions of the spiritual direction relationship, some time should be spent helping directees talk about their understanding (or lack thereof) of

God, the world, and the human person. Even if they do not come to the surface in a particular session, these three concepts generally form a backdrop against which the conversation takes place. Helping directees come to a deeper awareness of their stance toward these key ideas will enable them to better understand their own tradition and where they fit in it. Directors should be careful not to impose their own ideas but to elicit from their directees their genuine belief regarding these fundamental ideas.

Another topic that should be addressed early on in the sessions is the directees' understanding of prayer. The word *prayer* can mean different things to different people, even those coming from the same tradition. Directors should allow their directees to speak openly and honestly about what prayer means to them (if anything at all), how they do it, why they do it, how often they do it, and why they do it. The notion of prayer will obviously involve their understanding of God, or lack thereof. Prayer can be dialogical, a means for calming oneself, a way of relieving stress, a method of raising consciousness—or a combination of two or more of these. By talking about prayer with their directors, directees will have an opportunity to examine a fundamental concept of the spiritual life and see where it fits into their lives.

During these sessions, directees are typically encouraged to speak about their lives in the context of the teachings presented to them by their particular religious, philosophical, or ethical tradition. In doing so, they eventually construct a larger "life narrative" with various plot turns and dramatic climaxes. This narrative will change as it is told and retold. Directors should encourage their directees to continually shape and reshape their narrative by incorporating past memories into it, along with new events, and their outlook for the future. By being given the opportunity to tell and retell the stories of their lives, directees will gradually be able to take ownership of their lives and interpret it in a manner that will enable them to engage the world in better, more constructive ways.

The purpose of spiritual direction is to help people become themselves in their faith. Regardless of their tradition, directees need to be encouraged to examine just what it is they believe. What is of ultimate concern to them? How do they deal with it? How does this concern affect the way they live their lives? By looking at these questions of ultimate concern and assessing the level of their commitment to them, they will be able to take an honest look at their ethical standards and overall approach to the moral life. Faith pertains not merely to content (what I believe) but also to personal trust (whom I believe). When in direction, directees should be encouraged to explore the various tenets of their belief system and, more importantly, look at the people who seek to embody them.

During these sessions, directees should also be encouraged to look at just what is meant by the moral life. Are their ethical standards rooted in eternal principles? Do they flow from human nature? Are they settled by mere convention? Do they change? If so, how? What does their tradition say about the origins of good and evil, right and wrong? How do they relate to one another? How does one react to evil when confronted with it? How does one deal with the evil one discovers within oneself? These and similar questions should be elicited from directees. The focus, however, should not be on abstractions but on the concrete manifestations of these questions in their lives.

Finally, in the direction session, directees should be encouraged to engage the sacred texts of their particular tradition and do so in a way that they can find meaning in them that is relevant for their lives in practical ways. Directors should help their directees engage these texts and interpret them in a way that makes them living voices that speak to them in the concrete circumstances of their daily lives. A living tradition is one that resonates in the lives of those who stand in it and seek to follow it. Directees must take hold of the texts in question and make them their own. They must look to these texts for guidance and seek out the counsel of those who have steeped themselves in their wisdom.

Conclusion

This chapter shows that our model of spiritual direction, although rooted in the Catholic spiritual tradition of Alphonsus de Liguori, can be adapted to other religious, philosophical, and ethical traditions by following a simple six-step template that extracts the underlying dynamics of the direction process from its overt doctrinal claims. Doing so allows directors to use the model with members of other traditions without having to worry about the danger of imposing one particular set of teachings over another. It also affords directees the opportunity to explore their tradition in a manner that accentuates the personal relevance of that tradition for the concrete circumstances of their lives.

Although firmly rooted in the Catholic tradition, our model is flexible enough to assist members of other traditions in their attempt to become themselves in their faith. The template is not a distillation or reduction of the model to its bare minimum but a practical adaptation that encourages active listening and open dialogue with directees coming from other traditions. Such exploration is essential for ecumenical and interreligious dialogue, for it helps people to probe their own traditions and take ownership of them. Doing so is a necessary prerequisite for any and all attempts at mutual understanding and respect across the traditions.

When used in conjunction with a broad definition of spirituality, the theories of natural law and interspirituality, as well as an encounter with the sacred texts of one's own tradition, this template can go a long way in helping those from other traditions to probe their beliefs of ultimate concern and connect them in practical ways to their everyday lives. The goal is not to impose a particular view of morality from without but to help people to foster an understanding of and respect for their respective traditions that will resonate in their lives and bear fruit in ways that uphold humanity's common moral patrimony. Our final chapter will look at the challenge of living in the gap between the ideals presented by any particular tradition and its embodiment in the concrete circumstances of daily life.

Reflection Questions

How can spiritual direction based on the underlying dynamics of the Alphonsian model help those from other traditions?

Do these dynamics lose anything when removed from their Catholic (and specifically Alphonsian) framework?

Do they gain anything?

What are the strengths of this approach to spiritual direction?

Are there any weaknesses?

CHAPTER EIGHTEEN

Living in the Gap

⇵

When Jew and Christian, Hindu and Buddhist, Muslim and agnostic come together for prayer, the world will listen. And God will listen, too.
WILLIAM JOHNSTON, *BEING IN LOVE*[1]

Whether our model is used within the Catholic tradition or outside of it, one of its key features must be to help directees live in the gap between vision and reality and to help them find concrete ways of narrowing the distance between the two. To achieve this aim, directors need to be sensitive to the different attitudes their directees might have about the ideal they are striving to realize in their lives, help them to identify the gap, name it, take ownership of it, and accompany them in a search for practical ways of living in the gap and narrowing it.[2]

Attitudes Toward the Vision

A look at Christianity's vision of the ideal life may prove helpful for our present concerns. Jesus' Sermon on the Mount (Matthew 5—7) represents the heart of the Christian ideal and has been interpreted in various ways. In his book *The Sources of Christian Ethics*, Servais Pinckaers identifies five contrasting views. One interpretation views the sermon as a series of counsels rather than commands and hence does not apply to everyone. Another sees it as an impossible ideal that is designed to inspire us and goad us on to achieve as much of it as we can. Yet another claims that it represents an interim morality to be lived during what the early Christians thought was to be the short interval of time between Christ's first and Second Comings. A fourth interpretation considers it as means of social transformation to be carried out literally through peaceful, nonviolent means. Still another says that its primary function is to make us aware of our sinfulness and thus lead us to renewed faith and repentance.[3] Even from this brief summary, it should be clear that, in addition to the Christian ideal itself, one's *attitude toward it* will say a lot about the degree to which it will be implemented.

A similar set of attitudinal postures can be attributed to those belonging to other religious, philosophical, and ethical traditions. Some may think that the vision or ideal in question is only universally applicable for a select few. Others may see it as an unreachable goal designed only to inspire. Still others may view it as something that could be practiced but only for a short while. Still others may take it literally and consider it universally applicable. Others may look at what the ideal tells them about themselves and how much they fall short of making the ideal a reality in their lives. It is also quite possible for a person to have a number of different (perhaps even conflicting) attitudes toward the vision or ideal in question.

One of the ways in which directors can serve directees would be to help them identify the various aspects of the ideal they espouse and examine their underlying attitudes toward them. In doing so, their directees would be in a better position to look at how they can take better ownership of their ideal and allow it to shape their lives in both implicit and explicit ways. People's understanding of the moral life is shaped, at least in part, by the ideals they embrace as matters of ultimate concern and how they view the moral demands stemming from them. Even though the official teachings of a particular tradition may be clearly delineated, people often assimilate them in different ways.

For this reason, a gap will often exist between the official teaching of a particular tradition and how people have embraced it and made it their own. This distance can be large, small, or somewhere in between. People can have varying degrees of awareness of it, or none at all. The goal should be to help directees identify their matters of ultimate concern and how they manifest them in their daily lives. Doing so requires the courage to take a hard look at oneself, the critical posture to examine areas where one has fallen short of the ideal, and the patience to implement practical steps to move one closer to the ideal in question.

Identifying the Gap

In order to name and take ownership of the gap that exists between the vision and reality, directees need to make realistic assessments of their present situations. Doing so requires honesty with oneself, a desire to look beneath appearances, and a commitment to strip off any false masks they may be hiding behind. Only then can an adequate assessment of the distance between the ideal and the real come about. Since people can be very skilled in the art of self-deception, they often need help in arriving at such valued judgments. Spiritual directors can be just the ones to help them view themselves as they really are.

For the process to continue, taking a clear-eyed look at one's vision or ideal of ultimate concern is not enough. The next step requires directees to make an accurate assessment of their lives. This involves looking at their values, practices, and styles of living. People who espouse a particular religious, philosophical, or ethical tradition need to have a solid understanding of the moral and spiritual values it proposes. They also need to find out if they have watered down those values in any way, and if they actually hold any others explicitly contrary to their ideals. Much of spiritual direction involves helping directees uncover whatever hidden values they hold that may actually go against their deepest-held values and beliefs.

People express their values in life through concrete practices. If they believe in God, they tend to pray and attend church. If they believe that certain meditation practices lead to a higher form of consciousness, they incorporate such practices into their daily or weekly routines. If they believe the material world is an integral aspect of the human makeup, they will seek to take care of their physical well-being by exercising, eating well, and getting regular checkups. They will also seek to care for the environment and make a special effort not to misuse its resources. The self-understanding of directees involves the interplay between their understanding of God (or lack thereof), the human person, and the world. The interplay of these various concepts combine to form a person's spirituality, which manifests itself in life through concrete practices. At this stage of the process, directors should encourage their directees to look at how their ideas of God, themselves, and the world shape the way they live. What are the various manifestations of these concepts in their daily lives? Do these practices coincide with or depart from the ideals they consciously espouse? Which practices do they need to continue? Which do they need to drop? What new practices do they need to incorporate in their lifestyle and way of life?

Once directees have made an honest assessment of their lives, they are in a position to confront the distance between their ideal vision of the moral life and their concrete circumstances. At this point, directors should encourage their directees to understand that, at least in this present life, there will always be a discrepancy between vision and reality in their lives. Nevertheless, the gap can be diminished by means of small, incremental practices that foster different ways of thinking and acting. The goal is always to meet people where they are and help them to see what possible steps could be taken that will narrow the gap and move them closer toward their ideal. Directors can also help their directees by helping them to discover useful strategies for living in the gap between the ideal toward which they are striving and the incomplete realization of it in their daily lives. Such strategies should involve concrete practices capable of producing positive habitual and dispositional change in their day-to-day lives.

Practical Resolutions

After one's focus of ultimate concern has been duly contemplated, a thorough assessment of one's current situation made, and the distance between the ideal and the real in one's life calculated, directees can look at what concrete, practical steps that can be taken to narrow the gap between the ideal and the real in their lives. Directors can help them in a number of ways.

Probably the most important thing they can do is to meet those coming to them where they are. Directors need to rid themselves of any false ideas they may have about where their directees should be in their journey along the moral and spiritual life. They must listen attentively to their directees and help them get in touch with the various needs that have arisen during their assessment of the gap between vision and reality. They can meet them where they are by offering them a safe, nonthreatening place to share what is actually on their minds. Intimacy, we are told, comes from self-disclosure and loving attention. The relationship of spiritual direction should be based on a level of intimate trust that allows both of these aspects to surface. Only from this basic relationship of trust can directees share their authentic concerns with their directors and look for the next practical steps they need to take.

Flowing from this trusting relationship comes the work of prudent reflection on what can be done and implemented to narrow the gap between vision and reality in their lives. Our model of spiritual direction is eminently practical. It encourages directees to take control of their lives by identifying practical steps to help them deal with their concerns and troubles. It makes little or no sense to go through all the trouble of identifying ones needs, and then entertain nothing but abstract ideas for dealing with them. Our model encourages a spirituality of practice. Regardless of the religious, philosophical, or ethical tradition to which they belong, directees should be encouraged to live in the gap they have identified in constructive, practical ways. This means trying to name useful and realistic means that will bring them closer to their desired end. Directors should remind their directees that real, permanent change usually comes not overnight but only through a series of small, gradual steps taken over a long time that eventually bring about a change in lifestyle and moral outlook. At this stage of the process, directors should help their directees identify as many such steps as possible, prioritize them, and bring them together in a plan of action that they can embrace and begin to implement.

Directors should then advise their directees to integrate their prioritized list of concrete steps into their daily lives by means of a specific rule of life. This plan should list the concrete steps they plan to take on a daily basis that would contribute to narrowing the gap between vision and reality, between the ideals they espouse regarding the moral and spiritual life and their actual living out of that ideal. In formulating this plan, directees should be encouraged to start out slowly by adding only one or two practical steps into their daily routine. Only after these small steps have been successfully integrated into their lives should they consider adding further in their program. The goal is to gradually add a series of small steps that will narrow the distance between vision and reality and make their ideal more visible in their lives. Like any journey, one reaches a desired destination by keeping the goal in mind and by heading toward it steadily one step at a time. Living in the gap largely means setting out on a journey and being determined to finish it. It presupposes moving toward one's destination by means of a steady application of small, clearly identifiable practices that always meet people where they are, and then encourages them to move closer toward their goal by taking the next small, incremental step.

Observations

Helping directees from other religious, philosophical, and ethical traditions to live in the gap between their ideal of the moral life and the way they actually live it requires a thorough understanding of the ideal in question, an honest look at their current lifestyle, an assessment of the distance between the ideal and the real, and a decision to take prudent and practical steps to help narrow the gap. This process of living the gap also raises a number of concerns.

To begin with, we should state up front that those who hold a completely subjective and relativistic worldview will benefit little from our model of direction. The danger of what some call "emotivism" or what others call the "dictatorship of relativism" shifts the focus from the external objective good to the internal subjective self.[4] While our model could conceivably be used to help such people, its primary focus is on those whose tradition taps into the common patrimony of moral teaching that has been delineated over the centuries by the world's great wisdom traditions. This common patrimony represents a kind of natural revelation in the moral order, has been collected in a number of places, and should be used in conjunction with the sacred texts of one's own religious, philosophical, or ethical tradition.[5]

Along the way, directors should help their directees assess the progress they are making to live in the gap between vision and reality and gradually narrow it. As part of this assessment, they should help them identify any red flags that might represent an actual widening of the gap rather than a narrowing of it. They should also help them to recognize that growth in the moral life is not always steady and continuous but sometimes reaches certain plateaus that do not display clear signs of improvement. Such moments offer opportunities for directees to prove their mettle by demonstrating their actual level of commitment to the process of moral growth.

If directors are going to be of help to their directees, it is important that they seek to live in and narrow the gap between vision and reality in their own lives by participating in the direction process themselves, receiving ongoing formation in spiritual direction, and by seeking out ongoing supervision. Failure to do so runs the risk of projecting some of their own difficulties and concerns onto those who have come to them for help. In such cases, directors can have a detrimental effect on their directees. Rather than becoming themselves in their faith, they can easily develop a relationship of dependence on their directors and avoid facing their deepest issues in their lives.

When helping their directees to seek adequate means to live in the gap and to narrow the distance between vision and reality, directors should encourage them to look at how they compare themselves with others. Each person is on a unique journey and needs to take into account their unique personalities and current limitations. While the accomplishments of others often inspire directees to growth, if care is not taken they can also spawn attitudes of envy and jealousy that can get in the way of authentic moral and spiritual development. Directors should encourage in their directees a healthy awareness of such dangers and help them to identify moments in their lives when such dangers present themselves.

Living in the gap between vision and reality requires accurate assessments of the directees' moral ideals attitudes toward it, their commitment to it, their failure to embody it in daily life, their commitment to narrowing it, and the practical means they have found for doing so. These accurate assessments, in turn, require brutal honesty on the part of directees with both themselves and others. Directors should seek to lead their directees into honest reflection on the difficulties they face in living out their moral ideals in their daily lives. They should seek to create a trusting, nonthreatening atmosphere where their directees will feel free to divulge their authentic feelings about their current situations.

In addition to being realistic and practical, directors should encourage their directees to be hopeful. Doing so means helping them to keep their eye on their goal, while at the same time encouraging them to take practical steps to get there. The opposite of hope is despair. All too often people give up on the moral life, because they feel that the obligations it imposes are too burdensome and ultimately out of reach. As a result, they let go of their ideal and adopt various rationalizations and means of subtle self-deception to convince themselves that the goal they once sought was nothing but an elusive pipe dream with little or no sound foundation in reality. At such times, directors should help their directees to vent their frustrations, while also encouraging them to seek appropriate means to keeping the vision alive in their hearts and minds.

Finally, in addition to being realistic and hopeful, directors should encourage their directees to befriend their imperfections with the view of one day outgrowing them. Living in the gap means having patience with oneself in life's journey. It means being able to cope with one's inability to live up to one's highest ideals, while at the same time striving to change in such a way so that those ideas may become more visible in the way one treats oneself and others. Matters of ultimate concern are not always in the forefront of our awareness. Directors should help their directees develop practical ways of bringing these matters more to the fore.

Conclusion

Although our model of spiritual direction developed out of the Catholic tradition and, more particularly, from within the moral and spiritual vision of St. Alphonsus de Liguori, it can be adapted to those coming from other religious, philosophical, and ethical traditions. This adaptation is not a "watering down" of the model but an accommodation to the sensitivities of others so that they may benefit from the underlying dynamics of the process. One important feature of this process is the importance of helping directees to "live in the gap" between vision and reality, between their ideal of the moral life, and the way in which they manifest it in their daily lives.

Doing so does not mean becoming disillusioned with one's ideal and simply settling for a lesser, perhaps more attainable, embodiment of it but being at one and the same time focused on the vision as the goal of one's life's journey and taking practical steps toward achieving that end. Such an approach involves a subtle mixture of idealism, realism, and resolute planning. It means being able to focus on matters of ultimate concern, while recognizing one's limitations in achieving those concerns, and committing oneself to incremental steps that will gradually narrow the gap and make it disappear.

Regardless of the tradition they espouse, our model encourages directees not to ignore their shortcomings and imperfections but to befriend or make peace with them in order to look beyond them and hopefully one day overcome them. The goal is to make the traditions they espouse come alive in their minds and hearts, so that the common moral patrimony shared across so many of the great religious, philosophical, and ethical traditions might move to the forefront of their lives and inspire them to embrace the moral vision they espouse with fervor and so work for the wellbeing and benefit of the societies in which they live. Spiritual direction should help people "live in the gap" between vision and reality, between the ideal presented by their tradition and its actual, living embodiment in the here and now.

Reflection Questions

Why is it important to be aware of our attitude toward the ideal life?

How does this attitude affect what we think, say, and do?

Why do people give up on their ideals?

How can spiritual direction help us identify the gap between vision and reality in our lives?

How can it help us live in the gap?

Conclusion

A close bond exists in the Catholic tradition between spiritual direction and the moral life. This relationship is a subtheme in the much wider discussion regarding the interaction of spirituality and morality in general. How these fields interrelate has been the subject of much discussion. At various times in the Church's history, Christian spirituality and Christian ethics have been thought to relate in a variety of ways, anywhere from close identity, to strained interaction, to complete separation. This book has presupposed a distinction between the two, while at the same time maintaining their close integration. For Catholics, the good life leads to happiness. The way of the Lord Jesus is intimately connected to embracing God, the source of all goodness, with one's whole heart, mind, soul, and strength.

Leading the good life, the moral life, however, does not mean that our lives will be free of suffering. Jesus himself said, "If any want to become my followers, let them deny themselves and take up their cross daily and follow me" (Luke 9:23). The moral life is part and parcel of the life of discipleship. It represents the cross that each of us is called to take up with renewed vigor. In *Veritatis Splendor*, his encyclical on the moral life, St. John Paul II sees Christian martyrdom as both a witness to the "inviolability of the moral order" and "an outstanding sign of the holiness of the Church."[1] By refusing to compromise one's beliefs and being willing to give up one's life for what is true and good, the Christian martyr highlights what it means to be truly human.[2] Much the same can be for us. Although few of us may ever be called to martyrdom in the literal sense, we become so in a secondary sense by dying to self and embracing the challenges of living moral lives in a world whose moral sense has been compromised. The word *martyr* comes from the Greek word for "witness." In a very real way, to live the moral life gives witness to the source of all goodness and holiness. To live the moral life is to give witness to God, the source of all goodness, and to take up the cross of discipleship along the way to the good life, the blessed life.

The focus of this book has been to examine the link between spiritual direction and the moral life. In four parts we have sought to trace the general contours of the ministry of spiritual direction (Part One), develop a model of direction based on St. Alphonsus de Liguori's approach to mental prayer (Part Two), examine the virtues and gifts of the Spirit as they relate to the direction process (Part Three), and look to how this model might be of help to members of other religious, philosophical, and ethical traditions (Part Four). Within its chapters, we have examined a wide range of topics pertaining to spiritual direction in general, the Alphonsian model in particular, the relevance of the moral life for the direction process, and the model's usefulness for other traditions. If, in one respect, we have covered a great deal of material, in another, what we have accomplished dwindles in size compared to all that remains to be done.

This book ends with a challenge. The attempt to integrate spirituality and morality in the process of spiritual direction will produce little, if any, fruit if it remains simply at the level of theory or if, even its practical insights, are not implemented by spiritual directors themselves. Theory needs to be learned, internalized, and practiced. Skills must be acquired, honed, and reflected upon. Training workshops need to be organized; retreats held. Outreach to other religious, philosophical, and ethical traditions must be attempted and seriously evaluated. The ministry of spiritual direction has much to learn from an open dialogue with the life of virtue and the gifts of the Spirit. In the end, people's lives are at stake. Either they will grow in their love of the good life, or gradually make compromises and wander away from it. Spiritual direction can do much in assisting people to live in the gap between who they are and who they are called to become. This book has sought to make a modest (yet significant) contribution in helping spiritual directors assist those who come to them bridge the distance between vision and reality in their lives and, in doing so, become more themselves in the living out of their faith.

Appendices and Resources

APPENDIX A

Excerpts from the Writings of St. Alphonsus de Liguori

Note: The following excerpts from the writings of St. Alphonsus provide a general overview of the saint's moral and spiritual vision and may be used for study, personal meditation, or spiritual direction. They come from: Eugene Grimm, ed. *The Complete Works of Alphonsus de Liguori*, 22 vols. (New York: Redemptorist Fathers, 1886-94; reprint ed. 1926-27) [Hereafter referred to as "Grimm."]. The sole exceptions are those excerpts concerning: (1) "The Four Duties of the Confessor," the translations of which come from, R. Schiblin, gen. ed., *Guide for Confessors: From the* Praxis Confessarii of St. Alphonsus Liguori (Esopus, NY: Matthew. St. Alphonsus, 1978) [Hereafter referred to "Schiblin"] and (2) "Conscience," the translations of which come from St. Alphonsus Liguori, *Theologia Moralis*, Vol. I, Books I-III, trans. Ryan Grant (Post Falls, ID: Mediatrix Press, 2017) [Hereafter referred to as "Grant."]. Slight adaptations have been made to the grammar and syntax of the Grimm translations to make them more compatible with present-day usage. The chapter and verse references to Scripture are those of the Latin Vulgate.

The Four Marks of Alphonsian Spirituality

1. Crib. "I bring you good tidings of great joy" (Luke 2:10). Thus said the angel to the shepherds, and thus do I say to you, O devout souls! On this night, I bring you tidings of great joy. And what tidings could be greater to a nation of poor exiles, condemned to death, than for them to be told that their Savior had come, not only to deliver them from death but also to obtain for them permission to return to their country? And this is what I announce to you this night: "A savior is born to you" (Luke 2:11). Jesus Christ is born; and he is born for you, to deliver you from everlasting death, and to open heaven to you, which is our country, from which we had been banished in punishment for our sins.

Discourse for Christmas Night (Grimm, 4:140)

2. Cross. It is a pleasing thing to see a person beloved by some great man and more so if the latter has the power of raising him to some great fortune; but how much more sweet and pleasing must it be to us to see ourselves beloved by God, who can raise us up to an eternity of happiness? Under the old law some might have doubted whether God loved them with a tender love; but after having seen him, shed his blood on an infamous gibbet, and die for us, how can we doubt his loving us with infinite tenderness and affection? O my soul, behold now your Jesus, hanging from the cross all covered with wounds! Behold how, by these wounds, he proves to you the love of his enamored heart: "The secrets of his heart are revealed through the wounds of his body," says St. Bernard.

Reflections and Affections on the Passion of Jesus Christ, 2.7 (Grimm, 5:37-38)

3. Sacrament. They feel great tenderness and devotion who go to Jerusalem and visit the cave where the Incarnate Word was born, the hall where he was scourged, the hill of Calvary on which he died, and the sepulcher where he was buried; but how much greater ought our tenderness be when we visit an altar on which Jesus remains in the Most Holy Sacrament! The Venerable John of Ávila used to say, that of all the sanctuaries there is not one to be found more excellent and devout than a church where Jesus is sacramentally present.

Meditations for the Octave of Corpus Christi 1 (Grimm, 6:214)

4. Mary. God, having determined to manifest to the world his immense goodness, by humbling himself so far as to become man, to redeem lost man, and having to choose a Virgin Mother, sought among virgins the one who was the most humble. He found that the Blessed Virgin Mary surpassed all others in sanctity, as greatly as she surpassed them in humility, and therefore chose her for his Mother.

Sermon for the Feast of the Annunciation 1 (Grimm, 7-8:445)

Solitude of Heart

Let us understand what is meant by solitude of heart. It consists in expelling from the soul every affection that is not for God, by seeking nothing in all our actions but to please his divine eyes. It consists in saying with David: "What have I in heaven? And besides you, what do I desire on earth?...You are the God of my heart, and the God that is my portion forever" (Psalm 72:25). O my God, except for you, what is there on earth or in heaven that can make me happy? You alone are the Lord of my heart, and you shall always be my only treasure. In the end, solitude of heart implies that you can say with sincerity, my God, I desire you alone, and nothing else.

The True Spouse of Jesus Christ, chapter 16, section 2 (Grimm 10-11:488)

God can neither be sought nor found if he is not first known; but how can a soul attached to creatures comprehend God and his divine beauty? The light of the sun cannot enter a crystal vessel filled with earth; in a heart occupied with attachments to pleasures, wealth, and honors, the divine light cannot shine. Hence the Lord says, "Be still and know that I am God" (Psalm 45:11). The soul that wishes to see God must remove the world from her heart, and keep it shut against all earthly affections. This is precisely what Jesus Christ led us to understand when he said: "But when you shall pray, enter into your room, and having shut the door, pray to your Father in secret" (Matthew 6:6).

The True Spouse of Jesus Christ, chapter 16, section 2 (Grimm 10-11:489)

The solitary soul, that is, the soul that is free from all attachments, and in which earthly affections are silent, will unite itself with God in mental prayer by holy desires, self-offerings, and acts of love. It will then find itself raised above all created objects, so that it will smile at the person who sets so high a value on the goods of this earth and submits to so many toils in order to secure their enjoyment, while it regards them as trifles, and utterly unworthy of the love of a heart created to love God, who is infinite good.

The True Spouse of Jesus Christ, chapter 16, section 2 (Grimm 10-11:489-90)

The Presence of God

The spiritual masters call the practice of the presence of God the foundation of a spiritual life. This foundation consists in three things: the avoidance of sin, the practice of virtue, and union with God. The presence of God preserves the soul from sin, leads it to the practice of virtue, and moves it to unite itself with God by means of holy love.

Let us now come to practice of this excellent exercise of the divine presence. This exercise consists partly in the operation of the understanding, and partly in the operation of the will: of understanding, in beholding God present; of the will, in uniting the soul to God, by acts of humiliation, of adoration, of love, and the like.

With regard to the intellect, the presence of God may be practiced in four ways:

1. By imagining that our Redeemer, Jesus Christ, is present, that he is in our company, and that he sees us in whatsoever place we may be.
2. The second method, which is more secure and more excellent, is founded on the truth of faith, and consists in beholding with eyes of faith God present with us in every place, in considering that he encompasses us, that he sees and observes whatever we do.
3. The third means of preserving the remembrance of the presence of God is to recognize him in his creatures, which have from him their being, and their power of serving us.
4. The fourth and most perfect means of remembering the divine presence is to consider God within us. We need not ascend to heaven to find our God; let us be recollected within ourselves, and in ourselves we shall find him.

Allow me to speak of the application of the will to the holy exercise of the divine presence. And it is necessary, first, to know that to remain always before God, with the mind always fixed on him, is the happy lot of the saints; but in the present state it is morally impossible to keep up the presence of God without interruption. Hence we should endeavor to practice it to the best of our ability, not with a solicitous inquietude and indiscreet effort of the mind but with sweetness and tranquility.

There are three means of facilitating the application of the will to this exercise:

1. The first method consists in frequently raising the heart to God, by short but fervent ejaculations, or loving affections towards God, present with us.
2. The second method of preserving the presence of God by the acts of the will is to renew always in distracting employments the intention of performing them all with the intention of pleasing God.
3. The third method is, when you find yourself very much distracted during the day, and the mind oppressed with business,…to retire, at least for a little, to chapel or to your room, in order to recollect yourself with God.

The True Spouse of Jesus Christ, chapter 16, section 3 (Grimm 10-11:495-512)

Conformity to the Will of God

Our whole perfection consists in loving God, who is in himself most lovely: "Charity is the bond of perfection" (Colossians 3:14). But, then, all perfection in the love of God consists in the union of our own will with his most holy will. This, indeed, is the principal effect of love; as St. Dionysius the Areopagite observes, "such a union of will of those who love as makes it to become one and the same will." The more united a person is with the divine will, so much greater will be his love.

Conformity to the Will of God, 1 (Grimm, 2:353)

If then, we would give a full satisfaction to the heart of God, we must bring our own will in everything into conformity with his; and not only into conformity but into uniformity too, as regards all that God ordains. Conformity signifies the conjoining of our own will to the will of God; but uniformity signifies, further, our making of the divine will and our own will one will only, so that we desire nothing but what God desires, and his sole will becomes ours. This is the sum and substance of that perfection to which we ought to be ever aspiring; this is what must be the aim of all our works, and of all our desires, meditations, and prayers. For this we must invoke the assistance of all our patron saints and of our guardian angels, and, above all, of our divine Mother Mary, who was the most perfect of all the saints, for the reason that she ever embraced most perfectly the divine will.

Conformity to the Will of God, 1 (Grimm, 2:357-58)

And, above all, let us dedicate ourselves to serve God in the way in which he wants us to serve him. I say this, that we may shun the deception practiced upon himself by one who loses his time, amusing himself by saying, "If I were in a desert, if I were to enter into a monastery, if I were to go somewhere, so as not to remain in this house, to a distance from these relatives or these companions of mine—I would sanctify myself; I would do such and such penance; I would say such and such prayers." He says, "I would do, I would do"; but in the meantime, through bearing the cross which God sends him with a bad will ...he not only does not sanctify himself but goes on from bad to worse.

Conformity to the Will of God, 6 (Grimm, 2:387)

The Four Last Things

1. Death. We must die. Sooner or later we must die. In every age, houses and cities are filed with new inhabitants, and their predecessors consigned to the grave. We are born but to die. However long our life may be, a day, an hour, will come which will be our last, and the hour is already determined.... In a few years, neither I who write, nor you who read, will be living on this earth. As we have heard the bell toll for others, so will others one day hear it toll for us. As we now read the names of others inscribed in the lists of the dead, so will others read ours.

Meditations for an Eight Days' Retreat, 5.1 (Grimm, 3:331)

2. Judgment. Place yourself, in imagination, in the same situation in which you will be when dying and in your agony, when not more than an hour or less will remain for you. Imagine that in a very short time you will come to your Judge, Jesus Christ, to render an account of your life. Nothing will then so alarm you as remorse of conscience. Put, therefore, your accounts in order, before the arrival of the great accounting day.

Meditations for an Eight Days' Retreat, 6.1 (Grimm, 3:340)

3. Heaven. At present it is impossible for us to comprehend the happiness of heaven, because we understand only earthly enjoyments. Were a horse capable of reasoning, he would, if he expected a rich feast from his master, imagine it to consist in excellent hay and oats; for these are the only species of food of which it has any idea. This is how we form our notions of happiness in heaven. It is beautiful in the summer to behold at night the starry heaven; it is delightful in the spring to stand on the shore when the sea is unruffled, and to see in its bosom the rocks covered with seaweed, and the fishes gliding through the waters; it is also delightful to be in a garden full of fruits and flowers, ornamented with flowing fountains, and enlivened by the flutter and singing of birds; in such a scene one is tempted to exclaim: Oh! What a paradise! What a paradise! But far different are the delights of heaven. To form some imperfect idea of them, let us reflect that in heaven is an all-powerful God, who has pledged himself to make the soul that loves him happy. "Do you wish," says St. Bernard, "to know what is in heaven?" "There is nothing there that gives displeasure; there is everything that delights."

Preparation for Death, 19.1 (Grimm, 1:291)

4. Hell. Think of the horror of a soul on its first entrance into hell. "Am I then," it will say, "really damned? Or am I mistaken?" It will think whether there can be any remedy; but will find that there can be none for all eternity. Millions of ages will pass away, as many as there are drops of water in the sea, or grains of sand on earth, or leaves upon the trees; and hell will still be hell, eternity will still be to come.

Meditations for an Eight Days' Retreat, 7.3 (Grimm, 3:348)

The Way to Converse with God

The paradise of God, so to speak, is the heart of man. Does God love you? Love him. His delights are to be with you; let yours be to be with him, to pass all your lifetime with him, in the delight of those whose company you hope to spend a blissful eternity. Accustom yourself to speak with him alone, familiarly, with confidence and love, as to the dearest friend you have, and who loves you best.

The Way to Converse Always and Familiarly with God, 1 (Grimm, 2:395)

Your God is ever near you, no, within you: "In Him we live, and move, and be" (Acts 17:28). There is no barrier at the door against any who desire to speak with him; no, God delights that you should treat him confidently. Treat with him of your business, your plans, your griefs, your fears—of all that concerns you. Above all, do so (as I have said) with confidence, with open heart. For God does not speak to the soul that does not speak to him. If it were not used to conversing with him, it would little understand his voice when he spoke to it.... God will have himself esteemed the Lord of surpassing power and terribleness, when we despise his grace; but, on the contrary, he will show himself to be a most affectionate friend when we love him; and to this end he would like us to speak often with him familiarly and without restraint.

The Way to Converse Always and Familiarly with God, 2 (Grimm, 2:395-96)

Never, then, forget his sweet presence, as do the greater part of men. Speak to him as often as you can; for he does not grow weary of this nor disdain it, as do the lords of the earth. If you love him, you will not be at a loss what to say to him. Tell him all that occurs to you about yourself and your affairs, as you would tell it to a dear friend. Look not upon him as a haughty sovereign, who will only converse with the great, and on great matters. He, our God, delights to abase himself to converse with us, loves to have us communicate to him our smallest, our most daily concerns. He loves you as much, and has as much care for you, as if he had none others to think of but yourself.

The Way to Converse Always and Familiarly with God, 3 (Grimm, 2:398)

Mental Prayer Is Morally Necessary for Salvation

1. It Enlightens the Mind. Without mental prayer the soul is without light. Saint Augustine says that those who keep their eyes shut cannot see the way to their country. The eternal truths are all spiritual things that are seen, not with the eyes of the body but with the eyes of the mind; that is by reflection and consideration. Those who do not make mental prayer do not see these truths. Neither do they see the importance of eternal salvation and the means they must adopt to obtain salvation.

Mental Prayer and the Exercises of a Retreat 1.1 (Grimm, 3:252)

2. It Disposes the Heart to the Practice of Virtues. Meditation is like fire with regard to iron, which, when cold, is hard, and can be shaped only with difficulty. But placed in the fire it becomes soft, and the workman gives it any form he wishes.... To observe the divine precepts and counsels, it is necessary to have a tender heart, that is, a heart docile and prepared to receive the impressions of celestial inspirations, and ready to obey them. It was this that Solomon asked of God: "Give therefore, to thy servant an understanding heart." Sin has made our heart hard and indocile; for, being altogether inclined to sensual pleasures, it resists, as the Apostle complained, the "laws of the spirit." "But I see another law in my members, fighting against the law of my mind" (Romans 7:23). But a person becomes docile and tender to the influence of grace given it in mental prayer.

Mental Prayer and the Exercises of a Retreat 1.2 (Grimm, 3:254-55)

3. It Helps Us to Pray as We Should. Without petitions on our part, God does not grant divine assistance; and without aid from God, we cannot observe the commandments. From the absolute necessity of the prayer of petition arises the moral necessity of mental prayer; for he who neglects meditation and is distracted with worldly affairs will not know his spiritual wants, the dangers to which his salvation is exposed, the means which he must adopt in order to conquer temptations, or even the necessity of the prayer of petition for all men. As a result, he will give up the practice of prayer and, neglecting to ask God's graces, will certainly be lost.

Mental Prayer and the Exercises of a Retreat 1.3 (Grimm, 3:256-57)

Mental Prayer Is Indispensable in Order to Attain Perfection

All saints have become saints by mental prayer. Mental prayer is the blessed furnace in which souls are inflamed with divine love. "In my meditation," says David, "a fire shall flame out" (Psalm 38:4). Saint Vincent de Paul used to say that it would be a miracle if a sinner who attends the sermons in the mission or the spiritual exercises, were not converted. Now he who preaches, and speaks in the exercises, is only a man but it is God himself that speaks to the soul in meditation. "I will head her into the wilderness; and I will speak to her heart" (Hosea 2:14).

Mental Prayer and the Exercises of a Retreat 2 (Grimm, 3:258)

Saint John Chrysostom compared mental prayer to a fountain in the middle of a garden. Oh! What an abundance of flowers and verdant plants do we see in the garden, which is always refreshed with water from the fountain. Such is the soul that practices mental prayer. It always advances in good desires and always brings forth more abundant fruits of virtue. From where does the soul receive so many blessings? It receives them from meditation, which continually irrigates it.

Mental Prayer and the Exercises of a Retreat 2 (Grimm, 3:259-60)

Saint Ignatius of Loyola used to say that mental prayer is the short way to perfection. In a word, he who advances most in meditation makes the greatest progress in perfection. In mental prayer the soul is filled with holy thoughts, with holy affections, desires, and holy resolutions, and with love for God. There, one sacrifices one's passions, appetites, earthly attachments, and all the interests of self-love.

Mental Prayer and the Exercises of a Retreat 2 (Grimm, 3:261-62)

The Ends of Mental Prayer

1. To Unite Ourselves to God. We must meditate in order to unite ourselves more completely to God. It is not so much good thoughts in the intellect as good acts of the will, or holy desires, that unite us to God; and such are the acts which we perform in meditation—acts of humility, confidence, self-sacrifice, resignation, and especially of love and of repentance for our sins.

Mental Prayer and the Exercises of a Retreat 3 (Grimm, 3:263)

2. To Obtain Grace From God. We must meditate in order to obtain from God the graces that are necessary to advance in the way of salvation, and especially to avoid sin, and to use the means which will lead us to perfection....Above all, in meditation we should ask God for perseverance and his holy love. Final perseverance is not a single grace but a chain of graces, to which must correspond the chain of our prayers. If we cease to pray, God will cease to give us his help, and we shall perish. He who does not practice meditation will find the greatest difficulty in persevering in grace till death.

Mental Prayer and the Exercises of a Retreat 3 (Grimm, 3:264-65)

3. We Ought Not to Seek Spiritual Consolations in Mental Prayer. We must apply ourselves to meditation, not for the sake of spiritual consolations but in order to learn what is God's will concerning us. "Speak, Lord," said Samuel to God, "for your servant is listening" (1 Samuel 3:9). Lord, make me to know your will, that I may do it. Some people continue meditation as long as consolations continue; but when these cease, they leave off meditation. It is true that God is accustomed to comfort his beloved souls at the time of meditation and give them some foretaste of the delights he has prepared for them in heaven. The lovers of the world do not comprehend these things; those who have no taste except for earthly delights despise those that are celestial. Oh, if they were wise, how surely would they leave their pleasures and shut themselves in their rooms to speak alone with God! Meditation is nothing more than a converse between the soul and God. The soul pours forth to him its affections, its desires, its fears, its requests, and God speaks to the heart, causing it to know his goodness, and the love which he bears it, and what it must do to please him. But these delights are not constant, and, for the most part, holy souls experience much dryness of spirit in meditation.

Mental Prayer and the Exercises of a Retreat 3 (Grimm, 3:266)

Principal Subjects of Meditation

The Holy Spirit says, "In all your works remember your last end, and you will never sin" (Sirach 7:40). He who often meditates on the four last things—namely death, judgment, and the eternity of hell and paradise will not fall into sin. But these truths are not seen with the eye of the body; the soul alone perceives them. If they are not meditated on, they vanish from the mind; and then the pleasures of the senses present themselves, and those who do not keep before the eternal truths before their eyes are easily taken up by them; and this is the reason why so many abandon themselves to vice, and are damned. All Christians know and believe that they must die, and that we shall all be judged; but because they do not think about it, they live far away from God.

Mental Prayer and the Exercises of a Retreat 4 (Grimm, 3:267)

After all, the good rule is that we preferably meditate on the truths and mysteries that touch us more and procure for our soul the most abundant nourishment. Yet the subject most suitable for a person that aspires to perfection ought to be the Passion of our Lord.

Mental Prayer and the Exercises of a Retreat 4 (Grimm, 3:268)

Oh, what an excellent book is the Passion of Jesus! There we understand, better than in any other book, the malice of sin, and also the mercy and love of God for us. To me it appears that Jesus Christ has suffered so many different pains—the scourging, the crowning with thorns, the crucifixion, etc.—that, having before our eyes so many painful mysteries, we might have a variety of different subjects for meditating on his Passion, by which we might excite sentiments of gratitude and love.

Mental Prayer and the Exercises of a Retreat 4 (Grimm, 3:268)

The Place and Time Suitable for Meditation

We can meditate in every place, at home or elsewhere, even in walking, in working. How many are there who, not being able to do otherwise, raise their hearts to God and apply their minds to mental prayer without leaving for this purpose their occupations, their work, or even meditate while traveling. He who seeks God will find him everywhere at all times.

Mental Prayer and the Exercises of a Retreat 5 (Grimm, 3:268-69)

The essential condition to converse with God is the solitude of the heart, without which prayer would be worthless, and, as St. Gregory says, it would profit us little or nothing to be with the body in a solitary place, while the heart is full of worldly thoughts and affections. But to enjoy the solitude of the heart, which consists in being disengaged from worldly thoughts and affections, deserts and caves are not absolutely necessary. Those who from necessity are obliged to converse with the world, whenever their hearts are free from worldly attachments, even in the public streets, in places of resort, and public assemblies, can possess a solitude of heart and continue united with God. All those occupations that we undertake in order to fulfill the divine will have no power to prevent the solitude of the heart.

Mental Prayer and the Exercises of a Retreat 5 (Grimm, 3:269)

According to St. Bonaventure, the morning and evening are the two parts of the day which, ordinarily speaking, are the fittest for meditation. But, according to St. Gregory of Nyssa, the morning is the most seasonable time for prayer, because, says the saint, when prayer precedes business, sin will not find entrance into the soul....Prayer, as St. Jerome has written, is also necessary in the evening. Let not the body go to rest before the soul is refreshed by mental prayer, the food of the soul. We can pray at all times and in all places; it is enough for us to raise the mind to God and to make good acts, for in this consists mental prayer.

Mental Prayer and the Exercises of a Retreat 5 (Grimm, 3:270-71)

The Manner of Making Mental Prayer

I. The Preparation: Begin by disposing your mind and body to enter into pious recollection

    A. Act of Faith: "Lord, I believe in your presence here."

    B. Act of Humility and Contrition: "Lord, have mercy on me."

    C. Act of Petition for Light: "Lord, give me light."

II. The Corpus:

    A. The Meditation: May be done in private or in common. When in private, you may use some book, at least at the commencement, and stop when you find yourself most touched. When in common, one reads the subject for the rest and divides it into two parts. The first is read at the beginning, after the preparatory acts; the second, toward the middle of the half hour. One should read in a loud tone of voice, so as to be well understood....It should be remembered that the advantage of mental prayer consists not so much in meditating as in making affections, petitions, and resolutions, the three principal fruits of meditation.

    B. The Affections: When you have reflected on the points of the meditation, and feel any devout sentiment, raise your heart to God and offer him acts of humility, of confidence, or of thanksgiving; but above all acts of contrition and love.

    C. Petitions: Moreover, in mental prayer it is very profitable, and perhaps more useful than any other act, to raise our petitions to God, asking with humility and confidence for his graces: light, resignation, perseverance, and the like; but, above all, the gift of his holy love.

    D. Resolutions: When ending the meditation it is necessary to make a particular resolution, such as, to avoid some particular defect into which you have frequently fallen, or to practice some virtue, such as to suffer the annoyance which you receive from another person....We must repeat the same resolution several times, until we find that we have got rid of the defect or acquired the virtue.

III. The Conclusion: The conclusion of the meditation consists of three acts.
  A. In thanking God for the lights received.
  B. In making a purpose to fulfill the resolutions made.
  C. In asking of the Eternal Father, for the sake of Jesus and Mary, grace to be faithful to them.
Mental Prayer and the Exercises of a Retreat 6 (Grimm, 3:273-81)

Distractions and Aridities

If, after having prepared ourselves well for mental prayer, ...a distracting thought should enter, we must not be disturbed, nor seek to banish it with a violent effort; but let us remove it calmly and return to God.

Let us remember that the devil labors hard to disturb us in time of meditation, in order to abandon it. Let him, then, who omits mental prayer on account of distractions, be persuaded that he gives delight to the devil. It is impossible, says Cassian, that our minds should be free of all distractions during prayer.

Let us, then, never give up meditation, however great our distractions may be. Saint Francis de Sales says that if, in mental prayer, we should do nothing else than continually banish distractions and temptations, the meditation would be made well. Before him St. Thomas taught that involuntary distractions do not take away the fruit of mental prayer.

Finally, when we perceive that we are deliberately distracted, let us desist from the voluntary defect and banish the distraction but let us be careful not to discontinue our meditation.
Mental Prayer and the Exercises of a Retreat 7 (Grimm, 3:281-82)

When a soul gives itself up to the spiritual life, the Lord is accustomed to heap consolations upon it, in order to wean it from the pleasures of the world but afterwards, when he sees it more settled in spiritual ways he draws back his hand, in order to make proof of its love, and to see whether it serves and loves God unrecompensed, while in this world, with spiritual joys. Some foolish persons, seeing themselves in a state of aridity, think that God may have abandoned them; or, again, that the spiritual life was not made for them; and so they leave off prayer, and lose all that they have gained.
Mental Prayer and the Exercises of a Retreat 7 (Grimm, 3:282-83)

In going to meditation, never propose to yourself your own pleasure and satisfaction but only to please God, and to learn what he wishes you to do. And, for this purpose, pray always that God may make known to you his will, and that he may give you strength to fulfill it. All that we ought to seek in mental prayer is the light to know and the strength to accomplish the will of God in our regard.

Mental Prayer and the Exercises of a Retreat 7 (Grimm, 3:284)

The Four Duties of a Confessor

1. Father. In order to be a father to his penitent, the confessor must have charity. He must show his love first of all by receiving everyone who comes to him for confession with kindness—whether they be poor or uncultured or even sinners. Some priests will hear only devout souls; others hear only the wealthy because they do not have the nerve enough to turn these away. But if some poor sinner comes to confession, he will hear him begrudgingly and then curtly send him away. And so it happens, that troubled souls, who often have to force themselves to come to confession, become embittered when they see how rudely they are received. They imagine that there is no one who will help and absolve them, and then they slip back into their habits of sin, in despair of their salvation.

Praxis confessarii, chapter 1 (Schiblin, 7)

2. Doctor. To be able to prescribe the right remedy to his penitent's spiritual sickness, the confessor must know its origin and cause. Some confessors ask for nothing more than the number and the species of the sins. As soon as they are convinced that the penitent is disposed, they send him away almost without a word.

A good confessor acts very differently. First he investigates to find out how the sickness started and how grave it has become. He asks if there is a habit of sin, if there are occasions some time or place or persons or circumstances that provoke him to sin. In this way, he can do a better job of correcting the penitent, of disposing him for absolution, and of giving him profitable remedies for correcting his sins.

Next he makes the pertinent observations. Even though he should treat his penitents as a loving father, still as a doctor he is bound, when it is necessary, to warn and to correct them. This is especially necessary in the case of the very sinful who seldom come to confession. He should warn and correct them. He should warn and correct everyone who needs it, without respect of persons.

Praxis confessarii, chapter 1 (Schiblin, 9-10)

3. Teacher. "For the lips of the priest are to keep knowledge, and instruction is to be sought from his mouth" (Malachi 2:7). It is the confessor's duty to know the law well, in order that he may exercise the office of teacher, for if he is ignorant of it, naturally he cannot teach it to others. Note that St. Gregory calls the task of directing souls through life to eternal salvation the art of arts. "Guidance of souls is the greatest of arts." St. Francis de Sales said that the office of hearing confessions is the most difficult of all, because the confessor's knowledge is for nothing else than eternal salvation; it is the most difficult of all, because it demands a knowledge of all sciences, professions and arts, because moral theology itself embraces so many facets of life, and because it consists in so many positive laws, and sacred canons which he must be able to interpret properly.

Praxis confessarii, chapter 1 (Schiblin, 18)

4. Judge. The last role of a confessor—that of judge—is very important. Judges are obliged to learn the facts, to examine the proofs, and then to pass sentence. The confessor must learn the state of the patient's conscience, then find out his dispositions, and finally impart or deny absolution.

Praxis confessarii, chapter 1 (Schiblin, 22)

Conscience

There is a twofold rule of human acts, one is called remote and the second, proximate. *The remote* or material is the divine law, while the *proximate*, or formal, is conscience. Although conscience ought to conform to the divine law in all things, nevertheless, the goodness or malice of human actions are known to us, inasmuch as it is apprehended by the conscience itself, as St. Thomas teaches: "human reason is the rule of human will which measures is goodness. (1.2.q. 19, art. 4). And more clearly in another place: "A human act is judged virtuous or vicious according to the good perception, in which the will is imposed, and not according to the material object of the act" (Quodlib. 3. art 27).

Theologia Moralis 1.1.1 (Grant, 1:24–25)

Conscience is so defined: "It is a judgment, or practical command or reason, in which we judge something must be done here and now as a good, or something must be avoided as an evil." Moreover, conscience is called a *practical command*, in distinction from *synderesis*, which is the speculative knowledge of universal principles to live well, certainly: "That God must be worshiped, you do not do to another what you would not wish for yourself, etc.," as St. Thomas holds, p. 1, qu. 79, art. 12.

Theologia Moralis 1.1.2 (Grant, 1:25)

…an *invincible* conscience is such that cannot be morally conquered, since no thought or doubt comes into the mind of the one who acts, nor even confusion while he acts, or when he considers the cause of the action.

Theologia Moralis 1.1.3 (Grant, 1:26)

Someone that has an invincibly erroneous conscience, not only does not sin by acting according to it but even that he is held to follow it at any time. The reasoning of each is that he does not sin, because although the action may not be right in itself, nevertheless, it is right according to the conscience of the one who does the act; at anytime one is held to act according to it, if his conscience, which is the proximate rule, so suggests it must be done.

Theologia Moralis 1.1.5 (Grant, 1:26)

The Daughters of Charity

1. Charity Is Patient. The earth is the place for meriting, and therefore it is a place of suffering. Our true country, where God has prepared for us repose in everlasting joy, is paradise. We have but a short time to stay in the world; but in this short time we have many labors to undergo: "Man born of a woman, living for a short time, is filled with many miseries" (Job 14:1). We must suffer, and all must suffer; be they just, or be they sinners, each one must carry his cross. He that carries it with patience is saved; he that carries it with impatience is lost.

The Practice of the Love of Jesus Christ 1 (Grimm, 6:305)

2. Charity Is Kind. The spirit of meekness is peculiar to God: "My spirit is sweet above honey" (Sirach 24:27). Hence it is that a soul that loves God loves also all those whom God loves, namely, her neighbors; so that she eagerly seeks every occasion of helping all, of consoling all, and of making all happy as far as she can.

This meekness should be particularly observed toward the poor, who, by reason of their poverty, are often harshly treated by others. It should likewise be especially practiced toward the sick who are suffering under infirmities, and for the most part meet with small help from others. Meekness is more especially to be observed in our behavior towards enemies: "Overcome evil with good" (Romans 12:21). Hatred must be overcome with love, and persecution by meekness; thus the saints acted, and so they conciliated the affections of their most exasperated enemies.

The Practice of the Love of Jesus Christ 2 (Grimm, 6:316–17)

3. Charity Envies Not. Saint Gregory explains this next characteristic of charity in saying, that as charity despises all earthly greatness, it cannot possibly provoke her envy. "She envies not, because, as she desires nothing in this world, she cannot envy earthly prosperity."

Hence we must distinguish two kinds of envy, one evil and the other holy. The evil kind is that which envies and repines at the worldly goods possessed by others on this earth. But holy envy, so far as from wishing to be like, instead has compassion for the great ones of the world, who live in the midst of honors and earthly pleasures. She seeks and desires God alone, and thus has no other aim besides that of loving him as much as she can; and therefore she has a pious envy of those who love him more than she does, for she would, if possible, surpass the very seraphim in loving him.

The Practice of the Love of Jesus Christ 3 (Grimm, 6:323)

4. Charity Does Not Deal Perversely. Saint Gregory, in his explanation of these words, "deals not perversely," says that charity, giving herself up more and more to the love of God, ignores whatever is not right and holy. The Apostle had already written the same when calling charity a bond that unites the most perfect virtues together in the soul: "Have charity, which is the bond of perfection" (Colossians 3:14). And whereas charity delights in perfection, she consequently abhors that lukewarmness with which some persons serve God, to the great risk of losing charity, divine grace, their very soul, and their all.

The Practice of the Love of Jesus Christ 4 (Grimm, 6:330)

5. Charity Is Not Puffed Up. A proud person is like a balloon filled with air, which seems, indeed, great; but whose greatness, in reality, is nothing more than a little air; which, as soon as the balloon is opened, is quickly dispersed. He who loves God is humble, and is not elated at seeing any worth in himself; because he knows that whatever he possesses is the gift of God, and that of his own he has only nothingness and sin; so that this knowledge of the divine favors bestowed on him humbles him the more; while he is conscious of being so unworthy, and yet so favored by God.

The Practice of the Love of Jesus Christ 5 (Grimm, 6:358)

6. Charity Is Not Ambitious. He that loves God does not desire to be esteemed and, loved by his fellow men: the single desire of his heart is to enjoy the favor of Almighty God, who alone forms the object of his love. Saint Hilary writes, that all honor paid by the world is the business of the devil. The enemy traffics in hell when he infects the soul with the desire for esteem. By thus laying aside humility, the soul runs great risks of plunging into every vice. Saint James writes, that as God confers his graces with open hands upon the humble, so does he close them against the proud, whom he resists: "God resists the proud, and gives His grace to the humble" (James 4:6). He says he "resists" the proud, signifying that he does not even listen to their prayers. And certainly, we know that the desire to be honored by others and self-exaltation at receiving honors from them falls among the acts of pride.

The Practice of the Love of Jesus Christ 6 (Grimm, 6:366)

7. Charity Seeks Not Her Own. Whoever desires to love Jesus Christ with his whole heart must banish from his heart all that is not God but is merely self-love. This is the meaning of those words, "Seeks not her own," not to seek ourselves but only what pleases God. And this is what God requires of us all, when he says: "You shall love the Lord your God with your whole heart" (Matthew 22:37). Two things are needful to love God with our whole heart: (1) To clear it of earth. (2) To fill it with holy love. It follows, that a heart in which any earthly affections linger can never belong wholly to God.

The Practice of the Love of Jesus Christ 7 (Grimm, 6:371)

8. Charity Is Not Provoked to Anger. In order to remain constantly united with Jesus Christ, we must do all with tranquility, and not be troubled at any contradiction that we may encounter. "The Lord is not in the earthquake" (1 Kings 19:11). The Lord does not abide in troubled hearts. Let us listen to the beautiful lessons given on this subject by that master of meekness St. Francis de Sales: "Never put yourself in a passion, nor open the door to anger on any pretext whatever; because, when once it has gained an entrance, it is no longer in our power to banish it, or moderate it, when we wish to do so. The remedies against it are: (1) To check it immediately, by diverting the mind to some other object, and not to speak a word. (2) To imitate the Apostles when they beheld the tempest at sea, and to have recourse to God, to whom it belongs to restore peace to the soul. (3) If you feel that, owing to your weakness, anger has already got footing in your breast, in that case do yourself violence to regain your composure, and then try to make acts of humility and sweetness towards the person against whom you are irritated; but all this must be done with sweetness and without violence, for it is of the utmost importance not to irritate the wounds."

The Practice of the Love of Jesus Christ 8 (Grimm, 6:395)

9. Charity Thinks No Evil, Rejoices not in Iniquity, But Rejoices with the Truth. Charity and truth always go together; so that charity, conscious that God is the only and the true good, detests iniquity, which is directly opposed to the divine will, and takes no satisfaction but in what pleases Almighty God. Hence the soul that loves God is heedless of what people say of it, and only aims at pleasing God. The Blessed Henry Suso said: "That man stands well with God who strives to conform himself to the truth, and for the rest is utterly indifferent to the opinion of mankind."

The Practice of the Love of Jesus Christ 9 (Grimm, 6:400)

10. Charity Suffers All Things. So that we may be able to practice charity in all our tribulations, we must be fully persuaded that every trial comes from the hands of God, either directly, or indirectly through men. We must therefore render God thanks whenever we are beset with sorrows, and accept with gladness of heart every event, prosperous or adverse, that proceeds from him, knowing that all that happens by his disposition for our welfare: "To them that love God all things work together for good" (Romans 8:28). In addition, it is well in our tribulations to glance a moment at that hell which we have formerly deserved: for assuredly all the pains of this life are incomparably smaller than the awful pains of hell. But above all, prayer, by which we gain the divine assistance, is the great means to suffer patiently all affliction, scorn, and contradictions; and is that which will furnish us with the strength which we have not ourselves. The saints were persuaded of this; they recommended themselves to God, and so overcame every kind of torments and persecutions.

The Practice of the Love of Jesus Christ 10 (Grimm, 6:428–29)

11. Charity Believes All Things. Faith is the foundation of charity; but faith afterwards receives its perfection from charity. His faith is most perfect whose love of God is most perfect. Charity produces in us not merely the faith of understanding but the faith of the will also. Those who believe only with the understanding but not with the will, as in the case of sinners who are perfectly convinced of the truths of the faith but do not choose to live according to the divine commandments—such as these have a very weak faith; for had they a more lively belief that the grace of God is a priceless treasure, and that sin, because it robs us of his grace, is the worst of evils, they would assuredly change their lives. If, then, they prefer the miserable creatures of this earth to God, it is because they either do not believe, or because their faith is very weak. On the contrary, he who believes not only with the understanding but also with the will, so that he not only believes but has the will to believe in God, the revealer of truth, from the love he has for him, and rejoices in so believing—such a one has a perfect faith, and consequently seeks to make his life conformable to the truths that he believes.

The Practice of the Love of Jesus Christ 11 (Grimm, 6:430–31)

12. Charity Hopes All Things. The primary object of Christian hope is God, whom the soul enjoys in the kingdom of heaven. But we must not suppose that the hope of enjoying God in paradise is any obstacle to charity; since the hope of paradise is inseparably connected with charity, which there receives its full and complete perfection. Charity is that infinite treasure, spoken by the Wise Man, which makes us the friends of God: "An infinite treasure to men, which they that use become the friends of God" (Wisdom 7:14). The Angelic Doctor, St. Thomas, says that friendship is founded on the mutual communication of goods; for as friendship is nothing more than a mutual love between friends, it follows that there must be a reciprocal interchange of the good which each possesses. Hence the saint says, "If there is no communication, there is no friendship." On this account Jesus Christ says to his disciples, "I have called you friends, because all things whatsoever I have heard of my Father I have made known to you" (John 15:15). Since he had made them his friends, he had communicated all his secrets to them.

The Practice of the Love of Jesus Christ 12 (Grimm, 6:436–37)

13. Charity Bears All Things. It is not the pains of poverty, of sickness, of dishonor and persecution, which in this life most afflict the souls that love God but temptations and desolations of spirit. While a soul is in the enjoyment of the loving presence of God, she is so far from grieving at all the afflictions and ignominies and outrages of men, that she is rather comforted by them, as they afford her an opportunity of showing God a token of her love; they serve, in short, as fuel to enkindle her love more and more. But to find herself solicited by temptations to forfeit the divine grace, or in the hour of desolation to apprehend having already lost it, oh, these are torments too cruel to bear for one who loves Jesus Christ with all her heart! However, the same love supplies her with strength to endure all patiently, and to pursue the way of perfection, on which she has entered. And, oh, what progress do those souls make by means of these trials, which God is pleased to send them in order to prove their love!

The Practice of the Love of Jesus Christ 13 (Grimm, 6:446-47)

The Virtues of Mary

1. The Humility of Mary. "Humility," says St. Bernard, "is the foundation and guardian of virtues"; and with reason, for without it no other virtue can exist in a soul. Should she possess all virtues, all will depart when humility is gone. But, on the other hand, as St. Francis de Sales wrote to St. Jane Frances de Chantal, "God so loves humility, that whenever he sees it, he is immediately drawn to it." This beautiful and so necessary virtue was unknown in the world; but the Son of God himself came on earth to teach it by his own example, and willed that in that virtue in particular we should endeavor to imitate him: "Learn of me, because I am meek and humble of heart" (Matthew 11:29). Mary, being the first and most perfect disciple of Jesus Christ in the practice of all virtues, was the first also in that of humility and merited being exalted above all creatures.

The Glories of Mary, Part 4 (Grimm, 7-8:547)

2. Mary's Charity toward God. Saint Anselm says that "wherever there is the greatest purity, there is also the greatest charity." The more a heart is pure, and empty of itself, the greater is the fullness of its love towards God. The most holy Mary, because she was all humility, and had nothing of self in her, was filled with divine love, so that "her love towards God surpassed that of all men and angels," as Saint Bernardine writes. Therefore St. Frances de Sales, with reason, called her "the Queen of love."

The Glories of Mary, Part 4 (Grimm, 7-8:554)

3. Mary's Charity toward Her Neighbor. Love toward God and love toward our neighbor are commanded by the same precept: "And this commandment we have from God, that he who loves God love also his brother" (1 John 4:21). Saint Thomas says that the reason for this is, that he who loves God loves all that God loves. Saint Catherine of Genoa one day said, "Lord, you will that I should love my neighbor, and I can love none but you." God answered her in these words: "All who love me love what I love." But there never was, and never will be, any one who loved God as much as Mary loved him, so there never was, and never will be, any one who loved her neighbor as much as she did.

The Glories of Mary, Part 4 (Grimm, 7–8:561)

4. Mary's Faith. As the Blessed Virgin is the mother of holy love and hope, so also she is the mother of faith: "I am the mother of faith, love, and of fear, and of knowledge, and of holy hope" (Sirach 24:24). And with reason is she so, says St. Irenaeus; for "the evil done by Eve's incredulity was remedied by Mary's faith." This is confirmed by Tertullian, who says that because Eve, contrary to the assurance she had received from God, believed the serpent, she brought death into the world; but our Queen, because she believed the angel when he said that she, remaining a virgin, would become the mother of God, brought salvation into the world. For St. Augustine says, that "when Mary consented to the Incarnation of the Eternal Word, she opened heaven to us by means of her faith." Richard of St. Victor, on the words of St. Paul, "for the unbelieving husband is sanctified by the believing wife" (1 Corinthians 7:14), also says, that "Mary is the believing woman by whose faith the unbelieving Adam and all his posterity are saved. Hence, on account of her faith, Elizabeth called the holy Virgin blessed: "Blessed are you that you have believed, because those things shall be accomplished in you that were spoken by the Lord" (Luke 1:45). And St. Augustine adds, that Mary was rather blessed by receiving the faith of Christ than by receiving the flesh of Christ.

The Glories of Mary, Part 4 (Grimm, 7–8:564-65)

5. Mary's Hope. Hope takes its rise in faith; for God enlightens us by faith to know his goodness and the promises he has made, that by his knowledge we may rise by hope to the desire of possessing him. Mary then, having had the virtue of faith in its highest degree, had also hope in the same degree of excellence; and this made her say with David, "But it is good for me to adhere to my God, to put my hope in the Lord God" (Psalm 72:28).

The Glories of Mary, Part 4 (Grimm, 7-8:568)

6. Mary's Chastity. Since the fall of Adam, the senses being rebellious to reason, chastity is of all the virtues the one that is the most difficult to practice. Saint Augustine says: "Of all the combats in which we are engaged, the most severe are those of chastity; its battles are of daily occurrence but victory is rare." May God be ever praised, however, who in Mary has given us a great example of this virtue.

The Glories of Mary, Part 4 (Grimm, 7-8:571)

7. Mary's Poverty. Our most loving Redeemer, that we might learn from him to despise the things of this world, was pleased to be poor on earth: "Being rich," says St. Paul, "he became poor for your sake, that through his poverty you might be rich" (2 Corinthians 8:9). Therefore Jesus Christ exhorts each one who desires to be his disciple, "If you will be perfect, go sell what you have, and give to the poor…and come, follow me" (Matthew 19:21). Behold Mary, is the most perfect disciple, who indeed imitated his example.

The Glories of Mary, Part 4 (Grimm, 7-8:575-76)

8. Mary's Obedience. When the angel Gabriel announced to Mary God's great designs upon her, she, through love for obedience, would only call herself a handmaid: "Behold the handmaid of the Lord" (Luke 1:38). "Yes," says St. Thomas of Villanova, "for this faithful handmaid never, in either thought or word or deed, contradicted the Most High; but, entirely emptied of her own will, she lived always and in all things obedient to that of God. She herself declared that God was pleased with her obedience, when she said, "He has regarded the humility of his handmaid" (Luke 1:48), for the humility of a servant properly consists in prompt obedience.

The Glories of Mary, Part 4 (Grimm, 7-8:578-79)

9. Mary's Patience. This world being a place of merit, is rightly called a valley of tears; for we are all placed in it to suffer, that we, by patience, gain our own souls unto life eternal, as our Lord himself says, "In your patience you shall possess your souls" (Luke 21:19). God gave us the Blessed Virgin Mary as a model of all virtues but more especially as an example of patience. Saint Francis de Sales, among other things, remarks, that it was precisely for this reason that at the marriage feast of Cana Jesus Christ gave the Blessed Virgin an answer, by which he seemed to value her prayers but little: "Woman, what is that to you and me?" (John 2:4). And he did this that he might give us the example of the patience of his most holy Mother. But what need have we to seek for instances of this virtue? Mary's whole life was a continual exercise of her patience.

The Glories of Mary, Part 4 (Grimm, 7–8:581–82)

Prayers to Obtain the Seven Gifts of the Holy Spirit

Formula

Holy Spirit, Divine Consoler! I adore you as my true God, just as I adore God the Father and God the Son. I bless you by uniting myself to the blessings that you receive from the angels and seraphs. I offer you my whole heart, and I render you heartfelt thanks for all the benefits that you have bestowed and continue to bestow on the world. You who are the author of all supernatural gifts, and who enriched with immense favors the soul of the Blessed Virgin Mary, the Mother of God, I beseech you to visit me with your grace and your love and to grant me (go to *Conclusion*)

Conclusion

1. …the Gift of Fear, so that it may prevent me from falling any more into my past infidelities, for which I now ask you a thousand times to forgive me.

2. …the Gift of Piety, so that I may serve you in the future with greater fervor, follow your holy inspirations with greater promptness, and observe your holy precepts with greater exactness.

3. …the Gift of Knowledge, so that I may be able to know well the things of God, and that, enlightened by your holy instructions, I may steadily walk in the way of my eternal salvation.

4. …the Gift of Fortitude, so that I may be able to overcome with courage all the attacks of the devil and escape all the dangers of the world that stand in the way of my eternal salvation.

5. …the Gift of Counsel, so that I may be able to choose what is most suitable to my spiritual advancement and discover all the snares and artifices of the evil spirit who tempts me.

6. ...the Gift of Understanding, so I may be able to understand the divine mysteries and by the contemplation of heavenly things detach my thoughts and affections from all the vanities of this miserable world.

7. ... the Gift of Wisdom, so that I may be able to direct all my actions by referring them to God as my last end, so that by loving and serving you in this life, I may have the happiness of eternally possessing you in the next.

Humble Supplication
Holy Spirit, Divine Paraclete, Father of the poor, consoler of the afflicted, light of hearts, sanctifier of souls! Behold me prostrate in your presence; I adore you with the most profound submission, and I repeat a thousand times with the seraphs who are before your throne: Holy, Holy, Holy! I firmly believe that you are eternal, consubstantial with the Father and the Son. I hope that by your goodness you will sanctify and save my soul. I love you, O God of love! I love you with all my heart, because you are infinite goodness and alone merit all love. Since, I have been insensible to your holy inspiration and so ungrateful as to offend you by my many sins, I ask you a thousand pardons for them. I supremely regret having ever displeased you, O Sovereign Good! Cold as it is, I offer you my heart, and I ask you to let a ray of your light and a spark of your fire enter there to melt the hardened ice of my iniquities. You who have filled the soul of Mary with immense graces and inflamed the hearts of the apostles with a holy zeal, set my heart on fire with your love. You are a Divine Spirit; fortify me against evil spirits. You are a Fire; enkindle in me the fire of your love. You are a Light; enlighten me so that I may know eternal things. You are a Dove; give me great purity of heart. You are a Breath that is full of sweetness; dissipate the storms that my passions raise up against me. You are a Tongue; teach me the manner of praising you without ceasing. You are a Cloud; cover me with the shadow of your protection. And if, finally, you are the author of all heavenly gifts, ah, I beseech you to grant them to me. Vivify me by your grace, sanctify me by your charity, govern me by your wisdom, adopt me by your bounty as your child, and save me by your infinite mercy, so that I may never cease to bless you, to praise you, to love you, first during my life on this earth, and afterwards for all eternity. Amen.

Pious Exercise to Obtain the Seven Gifts of the Holy Spirit (Grimm, 6: 498–503).

APPENDIX B

Internet Resources on the Moral Life

Note: The following websites are a sampling of the resources available on the Internet concerning the moral life of both the major and minor religious traditions in the world today. The list is offered as a starting point for those interested in familiarizing themselves with their own tradition or learning more about another. For the *Catechism of the Catholic Church*, a single website is given with the relevant topics and paragraphs identified below it.

I. The Bible, Open Bible
www.openbible.info/topics/
Virtue, www.openbible.info/topics/virtue
Faith, www.openbible.info/topics/faith
Hope, www.openbible.info/topics/hope
Charity, www.openbible.info/topics/charity
Prudence, www.openbible.info/topics/prudence
Justice, www.openbible.info/topics/justice
Courage, www.openbible.info/topics/courage
Temperance, www.openbible.info/topics/moderation
Gifts of the Spirit, www.openbible.info/topics/gifts_of_the_holy_spirit
Wisdom, www.openbible.info/topics/wisdom
Understanding, www.openbible.info/topics/understanding
Counsel, www.openbible.info/topics/counsel
Knowledge, www.openbible.info/topics/knowledge
Fortitude, www.openbible.info/topics/fortitude
Piety, www.openbible.info/topics/devotion_to_god
Fear of the Lord, www.openbible.info/topics/fear_of_the_lord
Fruits of the Spirit, www.openbible.info/topics/fruit_of_the_spirit
Love, www.openbible.info/topics/love

Joy, www.openbible.info/topics/joy
Peace, www.openbible.info/topics/peace
Patience, www.openbible.info/topics/patience
Kindness, www.openbible.info/topics/kindness
Generosity, www.openbible.info/topics/generosity
Faithfulness, www.openbible.info/topics/faithfulness
Gentleness, www.openbible.info/topics/gentleness
Self-Control, www.openbible.info/topics/self-control
Beatitudes, www.openbible.info/topics/beatitudes
Ten Commandments, www.openbible.info/topics/ten_commandments

Seven Capital Sins
Pride, www.openbible.info/topics/pride
Avarice, www.openbible.info/topics/avarice
Envy, www.openbible.info/topics/envy
Wrath, www.openbible.info/topics/wrath
Lust, www.openbible.info/topics/lust
Gluttony, www.openbible.info/topics/gluttony
Sloth, www.openbible.info/topics/sloth

II. Catechism of the Catholic Church: Part Three: Life In Christ
www.vatican.va/archive/ENG0015/__P5D.HTM

Section One: Man's Vocation: Life in the Spirit, no. 1699
Chapter One: The Dignity of the Human Person, no. 1700
    Man: The Image of God, nos. 1701-15
    Our Vocation to Beatitude, nos. 1716-29
    Man's Freedom, nos. 1730-48
    The Morality of Human Acts, nos. 1749-61
    The Morality of the Passions, nos. 1762-75
    Moral Conscience, nos. 1776-1802
    The Virtues and Gifts of the Spirit, nos. 1803-45
    Sin, nos. 1846-76
Chapter Two: The Human Communion, no. 1877
    The Person and Society, nos. 1878-96
    Participation in Social Life, nos. 1897-1927
    Social Justice, nos. 1928-48
Chapter Three: God's Salvation: Law and Grace, no. 1949
    The Moral Law, nos. 1950-86

Grace and Justification, nos. 1987-2029

The Church, Mother and Teacher, nos. 2030-51

Section Two: The Ten Commandments nos. 2052-82

Chapter One: "You Shall Love the Lord Your God With All Your Heart, and With all Your Soul, and All Your Mind," nos. 2083

Article One: The First Commandment, nos. 2084-2141

Article Two: The Second Commandment, nos. 2142-67

Article Three: The Third Commandment, nos. 2168-95

Chapter Two: "You Shall Love Your Neighbor As Yourself," no. 2196

Article Four: The Fourth Commandment, nos. 2197-2257

Article Five: The Fifth Commandment, nos. 2258-2330

Article Six: The Sixth Commandment, nos. 2331-2400

Article Seven: The Seventh Commandment, nos. 2401-63

Article Eight: The Eighth Commandment, nos. 2464-2513

Article Nine: The Ninth Commandment, nos. 2514-33

Article Ten: The Tenth Commandment, nos. 2534-57

III. Recent Papal Documents on the Moral Life

Benedict XVI

Caritas in Veritate (Papal Encyclical, June 29, 2009)
w2.vatican.va/content/benedict-xvi/en/encyclicals/documents/hf_ben-xvi_enc_20090629_caritas-in-veritate.html

Deus Caritas Est (Papal Encyclical December 25, 2005)
w2.vatican.va/content/benedict-xvi/en/encyclicals/documents/hf_ben-xvi_enc_20051225_deus-caritas-est.html

Spe salvi (Papal Encyclical, November 30, 2007)
w2.vatican.va/content/benedict-xvi/en/encyclicals/documents/hf_ben-xvi_enc_20071130_spe-salvi.html

Francis

Lumen fidei (Papal Encyclical, June 29, 2013)
w2.vatican.va/content/francesco/en/encyclicals/documents/papa-francesco_20130629_enciclica-lumen-fidei.html

John Paul II
Evangelium vitae (Papal Encyclical, March 25, 1995)
w2.vatican.va/content/john-paul-ii/en/encyclicals/documents/hf_jp-ii_
    enc_25031995_evangelium-vitae.html

Veritatis splendor (Papal Encyclical, August 3, 1993)
w2.vatican.va/content/john-paul-ii/en/encyclicals/documents/hf_jp-ii_
    enc_06081993_veritatis-splendor.html

IV. Examination of Conscience for Catholics

Using the Virtues and Vices,
Catholic Mom
www.catholicmom.com/2015/10/28/what-does-heroic-virtue-look-like-a-new-
    examination-of-conscience/

Eternal Revolution
www.eternalrevolution.com/virtue-vice-examination-conscience/

For Adults,
Fatima.org
www.fatima.org/essentials/requests/examconc.asp

For Students,
Focus
www.focusequip.org/assets/pdf/examination-of-conscience.pdf

For Children,
John Paul II Center
www.johnpaul2center.org/JohnPaulIICenter/LayFormation/AdultFormation/
    SeasonofMercyFaithFormationRes/10Commandments_Child_EC.pdf

V. Making a Good Confession
Good Confession.org
https://goodconfession.com/about-us/

Examination of Conscience Based on the Theological Virtues
https://www.ewtn.com/library/SPIRIT/EXAMCONS.TXT

VI. Non-Catholic Christian Teachings

www.patheos.com

Eastern Orthodoxy
www.patheos.com/library/eastern-orthodoxy

Protestantism
www.patheos.com/library/protestantism

Anglican/Episcopalian
www.patheos.com/library/anglican

Baptist
www.patheos.com/library/baptist

Holiness and Pentecostal
www.patheos.com/library/pentecostal

Lutheran
www.patheos.com/library/lutheran

Methodist
www.patheos.com/library/methodist

Presbyterian and Reformed
www.patheos.com/library/presbyterian

VII. Non-Christian Religions

Internet Sacred Archive
www.sacred-texts.com/trad.htm

Baha'i
www.patheos.com/library/bahai

Buddhism
Buddhist Ethics
www.buddhanet.net/e-learning/budethics.htm

The Buddhist Society
www.thebuddhistsociety.org/page/fundamental-teachings

www.patheos.com/library/buddhism

Confucianism
www.patheos.com/library/confucianism

Islam
Islamic Information Portal
islam.ru/en/content/story/36-islamic-everyday-virtues

www.patheos.com/library/islam

Shi'a Islam
www.patheos.com/library/shia-islam

Sunni Islam
www.patheos.com/library/sunni-islam

Hinduism
The Heart of Hinduism
www.iskconeducationalservices.org/HoH/index.htm

www.patheos.com/library/hinduism

Judaism
Torah.org
torah.org/series/jewish-values/

www.patheos.com/library/judaism

Mormonism
www.patheos.com/library/mormonism

New Age
www.patheos.com/library/new-age

Sikhism
www.patheos.com/library/sikhism

Taoism
Taoist Ethics
www.taoism.net/articles/mason/ethics.htm

www.robwaxman.com/id3.html

www.patheos.com/library/taoism

Zen
www.patheos.com/library/zen

Notes

PREFACE

1. John Paul II, *Spiritus Domini*, Apostolic Letter for the Bicentenary of the Death of St. Alphonsus de Liguori (August 17, 1987), https://www.ewtn.com/library/papaldoc/jp2sprdo.htm.
2. Benedict XVI, Papal Audience (March 20, 2011), http://w2.vatican.va/content/benedict-xvi/en/audiences/2011/documents/hf_ben-xvi_aud_20110330.html.

INTRODUCTION

1. For a complete chronological listing of Alphonsus' works, see Frederick M. Jones, *Alphonsus de Liguori: The Saint of Bourbon Naples, 1696-1787* (Liguori, Mo.: Liguori Publications, 1999), 491-94.
2. Alphonsus de Liguori, *Del gran mezzo della preghiera* (*Prayer, The Great Means of Salvation*), part 1, chapter 1 in *Opere ascetiche*, Editio Critica, 11 volumes [intro., 1-2, 4-7, 9-10, 14-15] (Rome: Sant'Alfonso, 1933-): 2.32. Unless otherwise stated, all references to Alphonsus' ascetical works come from this critical edition [Hereafter referred to as "*Opere ascetiche*"]. Unless otherwise stated, all English translations of Alphonsus' writings come from *The Complete Works of Alphonsus de Liguori*, ed. Eugene Grimm, 22 vols. (New York: Redemptorist Fathers, 1886-94; reprint ed. 1926-27) [Hereafter referred to as "Grimm"]. For most citations of Alphonsus' works, the corresponding English title follows in parentheses. The present quotation comes from Grimm, 3:49.
3. See, for example, the review of Louis Bouyer's *Introduction à la vie spirituelle* (Paris: Desclée, 1960) by Jean Daniélou, "A propos d'une introduction à la vie spirituelle," *Études* 94 (1961): 170-74 and the response by Louis Bouyer (ibid., 411-15). For more references to the debate over whether there is only one Christian spirituality or many, see Walter H. Principe, "Toward Defining Spirituality," *Studies in Religion/Sciences religieuses* 12 (1983): 127, esp. no. 3.

CHAPTER ONE: SPIRITUAL DIRECTION

1. Dennis Billy, *What is Spiritual Direction?* (Liguori, MO: Liguori Publications, 2009).

CHAPTER TWO: RELATIONSHIPS

1. John of the Cross, *Sayings of Light and Love*, no. 8 in *The Collected Works of St. John of the Cross*, trans. Kieran Kavanaugh ad Otilio Rodriguez (Garden City, NY: Doubleday, 1964), 667.
2. The understanding of spiritual direction as a helping relationship designed to help another become herself in the faith comes from Jean LaPlace, *The Direction of Conscience*, trans. John C. Guiness (New York: Herder and Herder, 1967), 26.
3. For the marks of friendship and their pertinence for one's relationship with God, See Paul J. Wadell, *Friendship and the Moral Life* (Notre Dame, IN: University of Notre Dame Press, 1989), 130-41.
4. See Athanasius of Alexandria, *De incarnatione*, 54.3. Cited in *Catechism of the Catholic Church*, no. 460.
5. John R. Sheets, "Spiritual Direction in the Church," *Review for Religious*, 46 (1987): 506.
6. Ibid.
7. Ibid.
8. For how to deal with disturbances in the relationship between director and the person seeking guidance, see William A. Barry and William J. Connolly, *The Practice of Spiritual Direction* (Minneapolis, MN: The Seabury Press), 155-74.

CHAPTER THREE: LISTENING

1. Francis de Sales, *Introduction to the Devout Life*, 2.12, trans. John K. Ryan (Garden City, NY: Doubleday, 1966), 97.
2. For more on fostering a contemplative attitude toward life, see Barry and Connolly, *The Practice of Spiritual Direction*, 46-64.
3. See Spiritual Directors International, http://www.sdiworld.org.
4. For more on the role of listening in the ministry of spiritual direction, see Margaret Guenther, *Holy Listening: The Art of Spiritual Direction* (Cambridge/Boston, MA: Cowley Publications, 1992). See also Teresa Di Biase, "Listening with the Ear of the Heart: Benedictine Values and Spiritual Direction," *Presence* 15 (no. 4, 2009): 15-19.

CHAPTER FOUR: PRAYER

1. Maximus the Confessor, *Various Texts on Theology, the Divine Economy, and Virtue and Vice*, 4.90 in *The Philokalia*, trans. G. E. H. Palmer, Philip Sherrard, and Kallistos Ware (London: Faber and Faber, 1981), 2.257.
2. Evagrius Ponticus, *On Prayer: One Hundred and Fifty-Three Texts*, no. 61 in *The Philokalia*, 1.62.
3. Irenaeus of Lyons, *Adversus haereses* 4.20.7 in *The Ante-Nicene Fathers*, ed. Alexander Roberts and James Donaldson, volume 1 (New York: Charles Scribner's Sons, 1925), 490. Cited in *Catechism of the Catholic Church*, no. 294.
4. Alphonsus de Liguori, *Modo di conversare continuamente ed alla familiare con Dio* (*The Way to Converse Always and Familiarly with God*), no. 5 (*Opere ascetiche* 1.316; Grimm, 2.395).

5. Augustine of Hippo, *The City of God*, 19.13, in *The Nicene and Post-Nicene Fathers*, ed. Philip Schaff, volume 2 (New York: Charles Scribner's Sons, 1903), 409-10.
6. See the Glossary in *The Philokalia: The Complete Text*, 2.389.
7. See Anselm of Canterbury, *The Proslogion*, chapter 1; *Biblia sacra vulgata*, Is 7:9; Augustine of Hippo, *On the Trinity*, 8.5.8.
8. See Thomas Aquinas, *Summa Theologiae*, I-II, q. 68, a. 8; II-II, q. 45.
9. Alphonsus de Liguori, *Del gran mezzo della preghiera (Prayer, The Great Means of Salvation)* part 1, chapter 1 in *Opere ascetiche* 2.13; Grimm 3:23).

PART TWO: AN ALPHONSIAN APPROACH TO SPIRITUAL DIRECTION

1. Dennis Billy, *With Open Heart: Spiritual Direction in the Alphonsian Tradition* (Liguori, MO: Liguori Publications, 2003).

CHAPTER FIVE: THE SPIRITUAL LEGACY OF ST. ALPHONSUS DE LIGUORI

1. Liguori, *Pratica di amar Gesù Cristo*, chapter 1, no. 18 (*Opere ascetiche* 1.10; Grimm, 6:272).
2. For a treatment of the spiritual landscape of eighteenth-century Naples, see Giuseppe Orlandi, "Il regno di Napoli nel settecento," in *Storia della Congregazione del Santissimo Redentore*, volume 1, *Le origini (1732-1793)*, ed. Francesco Chiovaro (Rome: Edizioni Rogate, 1993), 96-117.
3. For objections to the use of the confessional as a *locus* of spiritual direction on a regular basis, see, Kenneth Leech, *Soul Friend: The Practice of Christian Spirituality* (San Francisco: Harper & Row, 1977), 224-25.
4. See, for example, Leech, *Soul Friend*, 193; Kathleen Fischer, *Women at the Well: Feminist Perspectives on Spiritual Direction* (New York/Mahwah, NJ: Paulist Press, 1988), 3.
5. A look at a recent directory of Spiritual Directors International shows a strong ecumenical dimension and a large lay component in its membership. See *SDI Membership Directory, September 2000* (San Francisco, CA: Spiritual Directors International, 2000). For a brief history of the 4,650 member organization, see Carol Ludwig, "A Brief History of Spiritual Directors International: Part I," *Presence* 8 (no. 1, 2002): 8-18; Idem, "A Brief History of Spiritual Direction, Part II," *Presence* 8 (no. 2, 2002): 21-28.
6. Alphonsus' development of the *Capelle Serotine* in Naples and his emphasis on the *Esercizio della Vita Devota* as an organic part of the structure of the parish mission are but two of his more creative pastoral innovations. See Jones, *Alphonsus de Liguori*, 62-5, 253-54. See also Théodule Rey-Mermet, "Il Fondatore," in *Storia della Congregazione del Santissimo Redentore*, volume 1, pp. 124-26; Giuseppe Orlandi, "Attività apostoliche, Sezione prima- La missione," in *Storia della Congregazione del Santissimo Redentore*, volume 1, p. 365.
7. For a summary of Alphonsian spirituality with special emphasis on its relationship to his moral theology, see Marciano Vidal, *Moral y espiritualidad: De la separaciòn a la convergencia*, Cuadernos PS 1 (Madrid: Editorial, 1997), 83-103.
8. For the basis of Alphonsus' popular pastoral orientation, see Sabatino Majorano, "Il popolo chiave pastorale di s. Alfonso," *Spicilegium historicum CSSR* 45 (1997): 71-89.

9. For the early missions of the Congregation, see Giusepe Orlandi, "Attività apostoliche," 325-99. For the pastoral care given in the environs of their earliest permanent establishments, see Fabricano Ferrero, "L'apostolato domestico," in *Storia della Congregazione del Santissimo Redentore*, volume 1, pp. 400-21.

10. See introduction, n. 3.

11. For the various levels of spirituality (i.e., experiential, doctrinal, analytical), see Principe, "Toward Defining Spirituality," 135-37; *The New Catholic Dictionary of Spirituality*, s. v. "Spirituality, Christian," by Walter Principe. For an application of these levels to Alphonsus, see Dennis J. Billy, *Plentiful Redemption: An Introduction to Alphonsian Spirituality* (Liguori, Mo.: Liguori Publications, 2001), 98-101.

12. Liguori, *Del gran mezzo della preghiera (Prayer, the Great Means of Salvation)*, part 1, chapter 1 (*Opere ascetiche* 2:32; Grimm, 3:49).

13. See Ibid., intro. (*Opere ascetiche* 2:7-9; Grimm 3:19-22).

14. See Alphonsus de Liguori, *La vera sposa di Gesù Cristo (The True Spouse of Jesus Christ)*, chapter 15, section 1, nos. 1-5 (*Opere ascetiche* 15:84-89; Grimm, 10/11:441-45). It bears noting that Alphonsus sometimes ditinguishes meditation from mental prayer. At such times, he associates the former with thoughtful reflection and the latter with raising those reflections, along with one's needs and heartfelt affections to God.

15. See Théodule Rey-Mermet, *Le saint de siècle des lumières: Alfonso de Liguori* (Paris: Nouvelle Cité, 1982), 401-2; Jones, *Alphonsus de Liguori*, 254.

16. Liguori, *Pratica di amar Gesù Cristo*, chapter 17, section 1, no. 15 (*Opere ascetiche* 1.219; Grimm, 6:456).

17. Liguori, *Del gran mezzo della preghiera (Prayer, The Great Means of Salvation)*, part 2, chapter 4 (*Opere ascetiche* 2:171; Grimm, 3:240).

18. See, for example, Pope Pius XI, "Allocuzione del 20 Settembre 1934," in *Annuarium Apostolatus Orationis* (Rome, 1935), 73. See also *Dizionario di Mistica* (Rome: Libreria Editrice Vaticana, 1998), s. v. "Alfonso Maria de Liguori (santo)" by G. Velocci.

19. For a variety of definitions of spiritual direction, see Dennis J. Billy, "The Relations of Spiritual Direction," *Studia moralia* 36 (1998): 67 no. 1.

20. Marciano Vidal describes this union between the ethical and the spiritual in Alphonsus as "a spirituality centered on the practice of love." See Vidal, *Moral y espiritualidad*, 96.

21. For a general exposition of Alphonsus' approach to spiritual direction, see William A. Sutton, "An Exposition of St. Alphonsus Liguori's Doctrine on Spiritual Direction" (S.T.D. diss., The Pontifical University of St. Thomas, 1978). See also Emilio Lage, "S. Alfonso e la direzione spirituale," *Spicilegium historicum CSSR* 48 (2000): 9-48.

22. For spiritual direction in Alphonsus' correspondence, see Sean Wales, "The Ministry of Spiritual Direction: Saint Alphonsus, the Spiritual Director as Seen though His Letters," in *Reflections on the Spirit of Saint Alphonsus*, ed. M. O'Shea (Monroe, Mich.: IHM Publications, 1987), 93-107.

23. See Lage, "S. Alfonso e la direzione spirituale," 22-25.

24. See Alphonsus de Liguori, *Praxis confessarii ad bene excipiendas confessiones*, chapter 1, sects. 1-4, nos. 2-20 in *Theologia moralis*, volume 4 (Rome: Typis Polyglottis Vaticanis, 1912; reprint 1953), 528.

25. Lage, "S. Alfonso e la direzione spirituale," 14. For a general treatment of Alphonsus' moral teaching, see Théodule Rey-Mermet, *Moral Choices: The Moral Theology of Saint Alphonsus Liguori*, trans. Paul Laverdure (Liguori, MO: Liguori Publications, 1998).
26. Joseph Oppitz, ed., *Alphonsus Liguori: The Redeeming Love of Christ* (Hyde Park, NY: New City Press, 1992), 28.

CHAPTER SIX: INTERPRETING ST. ALPHONSUS TODAY

1. Liguori, *Modo di conversare continuamente ed alla familiare con Dio* (*The Way to Converse Always and Familiarly with God*), no. 6 (*Opere ascetiche* 1.316; Grimm, 2.395).
2. For the spiritual influences on St. Alphonsus and his use of them, see Joseph Oppitz, *Alphonsian History and Spirituality: A Study of the Spirit of the Founder, Saint Alphonsus M. Liguori and of the Missionary Institute, The Congregation of the Most Holy Redeemer* (Suffield, CT: *ad usum privatum*, 1978; 2d printing), 26-32.
3. For the close relationship between spiritual direction and sacramental reconciliation in Alphonsus' thought, see Lage, "S. Alfonso e la direzione spirituale," 21-30.
4. One Redemptorist author puts it this way: "Of course, if one is looking for answers to modern problems, one will not find them in St. Alphonsus: he had to struggle to find answers for the problems of his day and he expects us to do the same in our day." See Carl Hoegerl, "Preface," in *Heart Calls to Heart: An Alphonsian Anthology*, ed., Carl Hoegerl (Rome: Collegio Sant'Alfonso, 1981), xvii.
5. Liguori, *Del gran mezzo della preghiera* (*Prayer, The Great Means of Salvation*), part 2, chapter 3 (*Opere ascetiche* 2.143-44; Grimm 3:201).
6. Ibid., part 1, chapter 1 (*Opere ascetiche* 2.32; Grimm, 3:49).
7. Liguori, *Modo di conversare continuamente ed alla familiare con Dio* (*The Way to Converse Always and Familiarly with God*), no. 1 (*Opere ascetiche* 1.313; Grimm, 2.391).
8. See Liguori, *La vera sposa di Gesù Cristo* (*The True Spouse of Jesus Christ*), chapter 15, section 1, no. 6 (*Opere ascetiche* 15:90-91; Grimm, 10/11:446-47); Idem, *Necessità dell'orazione mentale* (*Opere ascetiche* 2:209-21; no English translation); Idem, *Dell'amore divino e dei mezzi per acquistarlo*, no. 20 (*Opere ascetiche* 1:278-79; Grimm, 2:327).
9. For an expanded treatment of the characteristics of Alphonsian prayer, see Billy, *Plentiful Redemption*, 3-20.
10. In explaining his teaching on mental prayer, Alphonsus states: "...as for mental prayer, neither I nor any of our Congregation have ever said that it is necessary for salvation. We have claimed two things: First, prayer of petition is a necessary means (and this is nothing new since very reliable theologians have taught it before us) because almost all help we need for salvation is given us through prayer; and second, mental prayer is necessary but we expressly underlined this point—it is a moral necessity, since without meditation on the eternal truths it is morally impossible, that is, extremely difficult, for a person to persevere for any length of time in grace..." See *Adnotationes in Busembaum* (1748), col. 1029-32. The English translation comes from Théodule Rey-Mermet, *St. Alphonsus Liguori: Tireless Worker for the Poor and Most Abandoned*, 2d ed., trans. Jehanne-Marie Marchesi (Brooklyn, N.Y.: New City Press, 1989), 430. See also Liguori, *Praxis confessarii ad bene excipiendas confessiones*, chapter 9, section 1, no. 122 [Theologia moralis, ed. L. Gaudé (1905-12): 4:596].

11. For a presentation of these methods of mental prayer, see Giacomo Lercaro, *Metodi di orazione mentale* 2d ed. (Genoa/Milan: Bevilaqua & Solari/ Editrice Massimo, 1957), esp. 5, 91, 120, 146, 171, 216.
12. See Jordan Aumann, *Spiritual Theology* (London: Sheed and Ward, 1980; seventh impression, 1993), 322.
13. The more prominent accounts appear in Alphonsus de Liguori, *Homo apostolicus (The Apostolic Man)*, app. 4, section 3 (*Opere morali* 3:648-52 [Naples, 1871]); *Praxis confessarii (The Practice of the Confessor)*, chapter 9, section 1, nos. 122-25 (*Theologia moralis* 4:596-98); Idem, *Pratica del confessore (The Practice of the Confessor)*, chapter 9, section 1, nos. 115-18 (*Opere morali italiane* 1:790-91[Naples, 1871]); Idem, *Selva di materie predicabile ed istruttive (On the Dignity and Duties of the Priest or Selva)*, part 2, inst. 5 (*Opere ascetiche* 3:102-7 [Naples, 1871]; Grimm, 12:289-304); Idem, *La vera sposa di Gesu Cristo (The True Spouse of Jesus Christ)*, chapter 15, section 2, nos. 1-13 (*Opere ascetiche* 15:104-15; Grimm 10/11:457-65); Idem, *Regolamento di vita di un Cristiano (A Christian's Rule of Life)*, chapter 2, section 2 (*Opere ascetiche* 10:282-84; Grimm, 1:415-18).
14. Lercaro, *Metodi di orazione mentale*, 110.
15. See, for example, Liguori, *La vera sposa di Gesù Cristo (The True Spouse of Jesus Christ)*, chapter 15, section 2, no. 6 (*Opere ascetiche* 15:104; Grimm, 10/11:457); Idem, *Regolamento di vita di un cristiano (A Christian's Rule of Life)*, chapter 2, section 2 (*Opere ascetiche* 10:282; Grimm, 1:415). N.B.: Although "il modo" can be legitimately be translated into English as "method," the words "manner" or "way" are more primary meanings and come closer to the general spirit of Alphonsus' approach to mental prayer.
16. For the anthropological dimensions embraced by Alphonsus' approach to mental prayer, see Billy, *Plentiful Redemption*, 31-32.
17. See Lercaro, *Metodi di orazione mentale*, 111.
18. Alphonsus de Liguori, *Riflessioni divote (Pious Refections)*, section 15 (This work is not in the critical edition of the *Opere ascetiche*). See the earlier *Opere ascetiche* (Turin: Marietti, 1845-47) 2:273; Grimm, 2:219).
19. See Liguori, *La vera sposa di Gesù Cristo (The True Spouse of Jesus Christ)*, chapter 15, section 2, nos. 6-13 (*Opere ascetiche* 15:104-15; Grimm, 10/11:457-65); Idem, *Regolamento di vita di un cristiano (A Christian's Rule of Life)*, chapter 2, section 2 (*Opere ascetiche* 10:282-84; Grimm, 1:415-18).
20. See Alphonsus de Liguori, *Dell'amore divino e dei mezzi per acquistarlo (On the Means to Acquire the Love of God)*, no. 19 (*Opere ascetiche* 1:277-78; Grimm, 2:325-26).
21. Liguori, *La vera sposa di Gesù Cristo (The True Spouse of Jesus Christ)*, chapter 15, section 2, no. 11 (*Opere ascetiche* 15:111-12; Grimm, 10/11:462-63); Idem, *Regolamento di vita di un cristiano (A Christian's Rule of Life)*, chapter 2, section 2 (*Opere ascetiche* 10:284; Grimm, 1:417-18).
22. For the relevance of Alphonsus' approach to mental prayer for today, see Billy, *Plentiful Redemption*, 21-37.

Notes

CHAPTER SEVEN: AN ALPHONSIAN MODEL OF SPIRITUAL DIRECTION

1. Alphonsus de Liguori, *Mental Prayer and the Exercises of a Retreat*, 1.2 (Grimm, 3:258).
2. This insight was first developed in Dennis J. Billy, "A Redemptorist Model of Spiritual Direction," *Spiritus Patris* 28 (no. 1, 2002): 11-14. For a description of a typical session of direction based on this approach, see Idem, "From Silence to Silence: The Session of Spiritual Direction," *Presence* 8 (no. 2, 2002): 38-43.
3. For Alphonsus' preparatory acts of faith, humility and contrition, and petition for light, see Liguori, *La vera sposa di Gesù Cristo (The True Spouse of Jesus Christ)*, chapter 15, section 2, no. 6 (*Opere ascetiche* 15:104-5; Grimm, 10/11:457-58); Idem, *Regolamento di vita di un cristiano*, chapter 2, section 2 (*Opere ascetiche* 10:282-83; Grimm, 1:415-16).
4. See *Catechism of the Catholic Church*, no. 2855.
5. See chapter three for the steps of this process. See also Dennis J. Billy, "Spiritual Direction and the Art of Active Listening," *Seminary Journal* 19 (no. 1, 2013): 22-26.
6. See Liguori, *La vera sposa di Gesù Cristo (The True Spouse of Jesus Christ)*, chapter 15, section 2, nos. 7-8 (*Opere ascetiche* 15:105-8; Grimm, 10/11:458-59); Idem, *Regolamento di vita di un cristiano (A Christian's Rule of Life)*, chapter 2, section 2 (*Opere ascetiche* 10:283; Grimm, 1:416-17).
7. Ibid., chapter 15, section 2, no. 9 (*Opere ascetiche* 15:108-10; Grimm, 10/11:460-61); Idem, chapter 2, section 2 (*Opere ascetiche* 10:283; Grimm, 1:417).
8. Ibid., chapter 15, section 2, no. 10 (*Opere ascetiche* 15:110-11; Grimm, 10/11:461-62); Idem, chapter 2, section 2 (*Opere ascetiche* 10:283-84; Grimm, 1:417).
9. Ibid., chapter 15, section 2, no. 11 (*Opere ascetiche* 15:111-12; Grimm, 10/11:462); Idem, chapter 2, section 2 (*Opere ascetiche* 10:284; Grimm, 1:417-18).
10. Ibid., chapter 15, section 2, nos. 12-13 (*Opere ascetiche* 15:112-15; Grimm, 10/11:463-65); Idem, chapter 2, section 2 (*Opere ascetiche* 10:284; Grimm, 1:418).
11. According to Jean LaPlace, spiritual direction is "...the help one person gives another to enable him to become himself in his faith." See *The Direction of Conscience*, 26. For a discussion of what such a process means in relation to the fields of spirituality and morality, see Dennis J. Billy, "Growing in the Virtues and the Gifts: Spiritual Direction as a Practical Theological Locus for the Convergence of Spirituality and Morality," *Studia moralia* 39 (2001): 433-59.
12. For the primacy of the personal relationship between the directee and God in spiritual direction, see Billy, "The Relations of Spiritual Direction," 68-72.

CHAPTER EIGHT: THE QUALITIES OF AN ALPHONSIAN DIRECTOR

1. Liguori, *Pratica di amar Gesù Cristo*, chapter 4, no. 12 (*Opere ascetiche* 1.38-39; Grimm, 6:301).
2. For a helpful guide for supervision, see Maureen Conroy, *Looking into the Well: Supervision of Spiritual Directors* (Chicago: Loyola University Press, 1995).
3. For a classic work on the contemporary ministry of spiritual direction, see Barry and Connolly, *The Practice of Spiritual Direction*. For some general treatments of the theory and practice of spiritual direction, see Luis M. Mendizábal, *Direccion spiritual: teoría y práctica* (Madrid: Biblioteca de Autores Cristianos, 1982); Raimondo Frattallone, *Direzione spirituale: Un cammino verso la pienezza della vita in Cristo* (Rome: LAS, 2006). For some excellent anthologies on spiritual direction, see Lavinia Byrne, ed., *Traditions of Spiritual Guidance* (Collegeville, MN: The Liturgical Press, 1990); Kevin C. Culligan, ed., *Spiritual Direction: Contemporary Readings* (Locust Valley, NY: Living Flame Press1983); David L. Fleming, ed., *The Christian Ministry of Spiritual Direction* (St. Louis, MO: Review for Religious, 1988). For some particular approaches to spiritual direction, see, Billy, *With Open Heart: Spiritual Direction in the Alphonsian Tradition*; Bennet Kelley, *Spiritual Direction according to St. Paul of the Cross* (New York: Alba House, 1993); Benedict Ashley, *Spiritual Direction in the Dominican Tradition* (New York: Paulist Press, 1995); William A. Barry, *Spiritual Direction and the Encounter with God* (New York: Paulist Press, 1992). Many of these books conclude with comprehensive bibliographies on direction.
4. Associations such as Spiritual Directors International can be helpful in developing these contacts as well as putting directors in touch with other directors in the locality.
5. See, for example, Dennis J. Billy, "Spiritual Direction as 'Faith Seeking Understanding,'" *Seminary Journal* 19 (no. 1, 2013): 27-32.

CHAPTER NINE: THE MORAL DIMENSIONS OF PRAYER

1. *Catechism of the Catholic Church*, nos. 1071-73, 2700-24.
2. Dennis J. Billy, *Evangelical Kernels: A Theological Spirituality of the Religious Life*. Staten Island, NY: Alba House, 1993), 170-78.
3. Irenaeus of Lyon, *Against the Heresies*, 4.20.7.
4. Augustine of Hippo, Sermon 22.7.
5. Pope Pius XI, "Allocuzione de 20 Settembre 1934" in *Annuarium Apostolatus Orationis* (Rome: Libreria Editrice Vaticana, 1935), 73.
6. Jones, *Alphonsus de Liguori*, 491-94.
7. Liguori, *Il gran mezzo della preghiera* (*Prayer, The Great Means of Salvation*), part 1, chapter 1 (*Opere ascetiche* 2:32; Grimm 3:49).
8. Servais Pinckaers, *The Sources of Christian Ethics*, trans. Sr. Mary Thomas Noble (Edinburgh: T&T Clark, 1995), 240-79.
9. Thomas D. McGonigle, "The Three Ways" in *The New Dictionary of Catholic Spirituality*, ed. Michael Downey (Collegeville, MN: The Liturgical Press, 1993), 963-95.
10. Pseudo-Dionysius, *The Divine Names*, 4.8-9, in *Pseudo-Dionysius: The Complete Works*, trans. Colm Luibheid (New York: Paulist Press, 1987), 78.
11. Pope John Paul II, *Veritatis splendor* (Vatican City: Libreria Editrice Vaticana, 1993), no. 35.

12. Thomas Aquinas, *Summa Theologiae*, I, q., 79, a. 12.
13. Ibid., I-II, q., 94, aa. 1-4.
14. William of St. Thierry, *The Golden Epistle*, trans. Theodore Berkeley (Kalamazoo, MI: Cistercian Publications, 1980), 25.
15. Liguori, *Del gran mezzo della preghiera* (*Prayer, The Great Means of Salvation*), part 2, chapter 4 (*Opere ascetiche* 2:145; Grimm 3:201).
16. Alphonsus de Liguori, *Breve trattato della necessita della preghiera, della sua efficacia, e delle condizioni con cui deve essere fatta* (*A Short Treatise on the Necessity of Prayer, Its Efficacy, and the Conditions Requisite for Its Due Performance*) (*Opere ascetiche* 2:192-93; Grimm 2: 445.
17. Pope Benedict XVI, *Deus caritas est* (Vatican City: Libreria Editrice Vaticana, 2005), no. 28.
18. Pope Francis, *Lumen fidei* (Vatican City: Libreria Editrice Vaticana, 2013), no. 4.
19. Henri de Lubac *Exégèse médiéval: les quatre sens de l'Écriture* volume 2. Aubier: Editions Montaigne n 1959), 643-56.
20. Pontifical Biblical Commission, *The Interpretation of the Bible in the Church* (Vatican City: Libreria Editrice Vaticana, 1993), 77-84.
21. Evagrius Ponticus, *Chapters on Prayer*, trans. John Eudes Bamberger (Kalamazoo, MI: Cistercian Publications, 1978), 65.
22. International Theological Commission, *In Search of a Universal Ethic: A New Look at the Natural Law* (Vatican City: Libreria Editrice Vaticana, 2009), no. 109.

CHAPTER TEN: THE SPIRITUAL JOURNEY

1. See, for example, Reginald Garrigou-LaGrange, *The Three Ages of the Interior Life*, trans. M. Timothea Doyle, 2 vols (London: Catholic Way Publishing, 2013).
2. Clement of Alexandria, *Stromata*, 6.12.
3. John Cassian, *Conferences*, 11.6-8.
4. Augustine of Hippo, *On Nature and Grace*, 70.84.
5. Bernard of Clairvaux, *Epistle*, 11.8.
6. William of St. Thierry, *The Golden Epistle*, 140.
7. Aelred of Rievaulx, *Spiritual Friendship*, 2.24.
8. Bonaventure of Bagnoregio, *The Triple Way*, Prol.
9. Thomas Aquinas, *Summa Theologiae*, 2a2ae, q. 24, a. 9.
10. Pseudo-Dionysius, *The Divine Names*, chapter 4.
11. See, for example, Thomas D. McGonigle, "The Three Ways" in *The New Dictionary of Catholic Spirituality*, ed. Michael Downey (Collegeville, MN: Michael Glazier, 1993), 963-65.

CHAPTER ELEVEN: THE WAY OF VIRTUE

1. Aristotle, *Nichomachean Ethics*, Bk 1.
2. Thomas Aquinas, *Summa Theologiae*, I-II, q. 2, aa. 1-8
3. The phrase, *visio Dei*, can be taken to contain with an objective or possessive genitive.

The former would pertain to God's objective vision of reality (i.e., God's vision), while the former would pertain to our vision of God (i.e., the beatific vision).

4. Aquinas, *Summa Theologiae*, III, q. 4, a. 1, as 2m.
5. Athanasius of Alexandria, *De incarnatione*, 54.3. *Catechism of the Catholic Church*, no. 460.
6. Irenaeus of Lyons, *Adversus haereses*, 4.20.7.
7. Josef Pieper, *Faith, Hope, Love*, trans. Richard and Clara Winston, Mary Frances McCarhy (San Francisco: Ignatius Press, 1997), 29
8. Ibid., 91.
9. Ibid., 224.
10. Aquinas, *Summa Theologiae*, I-II, q. 62, a. 1, resp.
11. Josef Pieper, *Faith, Hope, Love*, 103.
12. Josef Pieper, *A Brief Reader on the Virtues of the Human Heart*, trans. Paul C. Duggan (San Francisco: Ignatius Press, 1991), 10-11.
13. See Thomas Aquinas, *Summa Theologiae*, II-II, q. 23, a. 8, resp.
14. For a brief summary of Alphonsus' commentary on 1 Corinthians 13, see Appendix A under "The Daughters of Charity."
15. Alphonsus de Liguori, *The Practice of the Love of Jesus Christ*, trans. Peter Heinegg (Liguori, MO: Liguori Publications, 1997), 38-39. See also Idem, Liguori, *Pratica di amar Gesù Cristo*, chapter 4, no. 11 (*Opere ascetiche* 1.38; Grimm, 6:299-300).
16. Oppitz, ed., *Alphonsus Liguori*, 27-28.
17. See Servais Pinckaers, *The Sources of Christian Ethics*, trans. Mary Thomas Noble (Edinburgh: T&T Clark, 1995),375.
18. Aquinas, *Summa Theologiae*, I, q. 5, a. 4; Pseudo-Dionysius, *De divinis nominibus*, chapter 4.

CHAPTER TWELVE: THE GIFTS OF THE SPIRIT

1. See William Johnston, *Mystical Theology*, 9.
2. See *Catechism of the Catholic Church*, nos. 1266, 1299, 1830-31.
3. Ibid., nos. 1266, 1303.
4. For the importance of the gifts and their relation to moral action, see Charles E. Bouchard, "Recovering the Gifts of the Holy Spirit in Moral Theology," *Theological Studies* 63 (2002): 539-58. For a helpful presentation of the gifts and an extended bibliography, see Paul Wadell, *Friends of God: Virtues and Gifts in Aquinas* (New York: Peter Lang, 1981).
5. See Thomas Aquinas, *Summa Theologiae*, I-II, q. 68, a. 4, resp.
6. See François Jamart, *Complete Spiritual Doctrine of St. Thérèse of Lisieux*, trans. Walter van de Putte (Staten Island: Alba House, 1961), 1-22.

CHAPTER THIRTEEN: ATTENDING TO THE VIRTUES AND GIFTS IN SPIRITUAL DIRECTION

1. "Forma nihil aliud est quam actus materiae." See Aquinas, *Summa Theologiae*, I. q. 105, a. 1 resp. See also Mondin, *Dizionario enciclopedico del pensiero di San Tommaso d'Aquino*, s.v. "Forma."
2. See Principe, "Toward Defining Spirituality,"135-36; *The New Dictionary of Catholic Spirituality*, s. v. "Spirituality, Christian," by Walter Principe.

Notes

3. For Aquinas' general treatment of the virtues, see *Summa Theologiae*, I-II, qq. 55-67. For his treatment of particular virtues, see *Summa Theologiae*, II-II, qq. 1-9, 17-19, 23-33, 47-51, 57-58, 60-62, 79-91, 101-04, 106, 108-09, 114, 117, 120-24, 128-29, 134, 136-37, 139-41, 13-47, 149, 151-52, 155, 157, 160-1, 168. For the virtues in Thomistic thought, see Aumann, *Spiritual Theology*, 247-315; Cessario, *The Moral Virtues and Theological Ethics*, 72-125; Porter, *The Recovery of Virtue*, esp. 100-171. For recent developments in the area of virtue ethics, see John W. Crossin, *What Are They Saying about Virtue?* (New York/Mahwah, NJ: Paulist Press, 1985), esp. 13-35; James F. Keenan, "Virtue Ethics: Making a Case as It Comes of Age," *Thought* 67 (1992):115-27; Idem, "Proposing Cardinal Virtues," *Theological Studies* 56 (1995): 709-29; Joseph J. Kotva, Jr. *The Christian Case for Virtue Ethics* (Washington, DC: Georgetown University Press, 1996), esp. 48-68.

4. For Aquinas' general treatment of the vices, see *Summa Theologiae*, I-II, qq. 71-89. For his treatment of particular vices, see *Summa Theologiae,* II-II, qq. 10-15, 20-21, 34-43, 53-56, 59, 63-78, 92-100, 105, 107, 110-13, 115-16, 118-19, 125-27, 130-33, 135, 138, 142, 148, 150, 153-54, 156, 158-59, 162-67, 169. Treatments of the vices can also be found in traditional Thomistic manuals such as John A. McHugh and Charles J. Callan, revised and enlarged by Edward P. Farrell, *Moral Theology: A Complete Course Based on St. Thomas Aquinas and the Best Modern Authorities*, 2 vols. (New York/London: Joseph F. Wagner/Herder, 1958). See also the particular entries in Mondin, *Dizionario enciclopedico del pensiero di San Tommaso d'Aquino*. For the insights of psychology into spiritual direction, see Eugene Geromel, "Depth Psychology and Spiritual Direction," *Review for Religious* 36 (1977): 753-63; Robert Rossi, "Staging, Typing, and Spiritual Direction," *Review for Religious* 42 (1983): 614-19; C. Kevin Gillespie, "Listening for Grace: Self-Psychology and Spiritual Direction," in *Handbook of Spirituality for Ministers*, 347-64. Spiritual directors in need of a grounding in sound psychological theory can turn to Franco Imoda, *Human Development: Psychology and Mystery*, trans. Eugene Dryer (Leuven: Peeters, 1998).

5. For the role of listening and teaching in spiritual direction, see Margaret Guenter, *Holy Listening: The Art of Spiritual Direction* (Cambridge/Boston, MA: Cowley Publications, 1992),42-80. For its fundamental elements, see Shaun McCarty, "Basics in Spiritual Direction," in *Handbook of Spirituality for Ministers*, 56-76.

6. A comprehensive treatment of the virtues for spiritual directors is found in Aumann, *Spiritual Theology*, 247-315. For a virtues approach in a recent moral theology manual, see Benedict M. Ashley, *Living the Truth in Love: A Biblical Introduction to Moral Theology* (Staten Island, NY: Alba House, 1996). See also Josef Pieper, *Faith. Hope Love* (San Francisco: Ignatius Press, 1997; Idem, *The Four Cardinal Virtues*, trans. Richard and Clara Winston, Lawrence E. Lynch, Daniel F. Coogan (Notre Dame, IN: University of Notre Dame Press, 1966). See also Bernard Häring, *The Virtues of an Authentic Life: A Celebration of Spiritual Maturity* (Liguori, MO: Liguori, 1997); James F. Keenan, *Virtues for Ordinary Christians* (Kansas City, MO: Sheed and Ward, 1996); James F. Keenan and Joseph Kotva, eds., *Practice What You Preach:Virtues, Ethics and Power in the Lives of Pastoral Ministers and Their Congregations* (Kansas City, MO: Sheed and Ward, 1999); John W. Crossin, *Walking in Virtue: Moral Decisions and Spiritual Growth in Daily Life* (New York/Mahwah, NJ: Paulist Press, 1998).

7. "If story is the necessary genre for understanding human experience, then all spiritual direction must be based not in abstract principles or doctrines but in knowing how to understand stories." See *The New Dictionary of Catholic Spirituality*, s. v. Story," by Terrence W. Tilley. For the importance of narrative in theological reflection, see Anthony F. Krisak, "Theological Reflection: Unfolding the Mystery," in *Handbook of Spirituality for Ministers*, 308-29, esp. 317-25.

8. For a brief treatment of the senses of Scripture, see Robert M. Grant and David Tracy, *A Short History of the Interpretation of the Bible*, 2d ed (Philadelphia: Fortress Press, 1984), 59, 85-86; Karlfreid Froehlich, ed., *Biblical Interpretation in the Early Church* (Philadelphia: Fortress, 1984), 28-29. The authoritative work on the subject is Henri de Lubac, *Exégèse médiévale: les quatre sens de l'Ecriture*, 2 vols. (Aubier: Editions Montaigne, 1959). For the use of Scripture in prayer, see Hilary Ottensmeyer, "Using Scripture in Prayer," *Review for Religious* 45 (1986): 380-85. For the correlations between Scripture and virtue ethics, see Spohn, *Go and Do Likewise*, 12-16, 28-30.

9. See Aquinas, *Summa Theologiae*, I, q. 38, aa. 1-2; I-II, q. 68, aa. 1-8. See also Barry R. Strong, "The Closest Divine Person," in *Handbook of Spirituality for Ministers*," 291-307; Herbert Alfonso, "Docility to the Spirit: Discerning the Extraordinary in the Ordinary," in Billy and Orsuto, eds., *Spirituality and Morality*, 112-26; *Dizionario di mistica*, s. v. "Doni dello Spirito Santo," by A. M. Triacca; *The New Dictionary of Catholic Spirituality*, s. v "Gratitude," by Benjamin Baynham.

10. For Aquinas' treatment of prayer, see *Summa Theologiae*, II-II, q. 83. For the theological spirituality of prayer, see Billy, *Evangelical Kernels*, 167-84. For a systematic presentation of prayer in the Thomistic tradition, see Fabio Giardini, *Pray without Ceasing: Toward a Systematic Psychotheology of Christian Prayerlife* (Leominster, Herefordshire/Rome: Gracewing/Millennium, 1998) esp. 15-37. For a more popular presentation, see Simon Tugwell, *Prayer*, 2 vols. (Dublin: Veritas Publications, 1974).

11. For the union of prayer and resolution, see John Govan, "The Examen: A Tool for Holistic Growth," *Review for Religious* 45 (1986): 394-401; Joan L. Roccasalvo, "The Daily Examen," *Review for Religious*, 45 (1986): 278-83. For specific practices linking spirituality and virtue, see Spohn, *Go and Do Likewise*, 42-49. For the need of a practice-oriented spirituality in American culture, see Robert Wuthnow, *After Heaven: Spirituality in America Since the 1950s* (Berkeley/Los Angeles/London: University of California Press, 1998): 168-98.

12. Aumann lists nine essential aids to spiritual growth: the presence of God, examination of conscience, the desire of perfection, conformity to God's will, fidelity to grace, a plan of life, spiritual reading, holy friendships, and spiritual direction. See *Spiritual Theology*, 358-98.

13. Despite the difficulties in the historical transmission and diffusion of Aquinas' teaching on the virtues, the Dominican tradition has still provided a prominent locus for its implementation in the spiritual direction process. For a historical exposition of the Dominican approach to spiritual direction, see Benedict M. Ashley, *Spiritual Direction in the Dominican Tradition* (New York/Mahwah,NJ: Paulist Press, 199), esp. 118-32. See also, Idem, "St. Catherine of Siena's Principles of Spiritual Direction," in Kevin G. Culligan, ed., *Spiritual Direction: Contemporary Readings*," 188-95; Aumann, *Spiritual Theology*, 247-315.

CHAPTER FOURTEEN: AN OPEN VIEW OF SPIRITUALITY

1. Walter Principe, "Toward Defining Spirituality," 136.
2. Ronald Rolheiser, *The Holy Longing: The Search for a Christian Spirituality* (New York: Doubleday, 1999), 11.
3. Principe, "Toward Defining Spirituality," 135.
4. Principe, "Toward Defining Spirituality," 136.
5. Ibid.
6. See Sandra M. Schneiders, "Spirituality in the Academy, *Theological Studies* 50 (1989): 692.
7. Pat Collins, *Intimacy and the Hungers of the Heart* (Dublin: The Columba Press, 1991), 6.

CHAPTER FIFTEEN: NATURAL LAW AND INTERSPIRITUALITY

1. International Theological Commission, *In Search of a Universal Ethic: A New Look at the Natural Law* (2009), http://www.vatican.va/roman_curia/congregations/cfaith/cti_documents/rc_con_cfaith_doc_20090520_legge-naturale_en.html. For responses to the document, see John Berkman and William C. Morrison III, eds., *Searching for a Universal Ethic: Mutidisciplinary, Ecumenical, and Interfaith Responses to the Catholic Natural Law Tradition* (Grand Rapids, MI: William B. Eerdmans, 2014).
2. Ibid., no. 115.
3. Ibid., 116.
4. United Nations, *Declaration of Human Rights* (1948), http://www.un.org/en/universal-declaration-human-rights/.
5. International Theological Commission, *In Search of a Universal Ethic*, no. 5.
6. For a discussion of recent natural law theories, see Kai-man Kwan, "Reflections on Contemporary Natural Law Theories and their Relevance," *China Graduate School of Theology Journal* 53/7 (2012): 197-224. See also Robert P. George, "Natural Law," *Harvard Journal of Law & Pubs Policy* 31 (2008): 171-96.
7. See Oppitz, ed., *Alphonsus Liguori*, 16.
8. See Aquinas, *Summa Theologiae*, I-II, q. 94, a. 3, resp. See also International Theological Commission, *In Search of a Universal Ethic*, nos. 48-50.
9. International Theological Commission, *In Search of a Universal Ethic*, no. 46.
10. Ibid., no. 88.
11. Ibid., no. 5.
12. Human Rights Research Center, *Declaration of Human Rights* (1948), Abbreviated Version, ed. Nancy Flowers, http://hrlibrary.umn.edu/edumat/hreduseries/hereandnow/Part-5/8_udhr-abbr.htm.
13. Thomas Keating, "Guidelines for Interreligious Understanding: Points of Agreement or Similarity," in Joel Beversluis, ed., *Sourcebook for Earth's Community of Religions* (Grand Rapids, MI: CoNexus Press, 1995), 148; Idem, "Guidelines for Interreligious Understanding," in *Speaking of Silence: Christians and Buddhists on the Contemplative Way*, ed. Susan Walker (New York: Paulist Press, 1987), 126-29.
14. Wayne Teasdale, *The Mystic Heart: Discovering a Universal Spirituality in the World's Re-*

ligions Novato, CA: New World Library, 2001).

15. Ibid., 268.
16. Ibid., 236-42.

CHAPTER SIXTEEN: EMBRACING ONE'S TRADITION

1. Jaroslav Pelikan, *The Vindication of Tradition* (New Haven/London: Yale University Press, 1984), 81-82.
2. Paul Tillich, *Dynamics of Faith* (New York: Harper & Row, 1957), 1.
3. N. Max Wildiers, *The Theologian and His Universe*, (New York: The Seabury Press, 1982), 1.
4. Geoffrey Wainwright, "Types of Spirituality" in *The Study of Spirituality*, eds. Chesyln Jones, Geoffrey Wainwright, Edward Yarnold (London: SPCK, 1986, 1992), 592-605; H. Richard Niebuhr, *Christ and Culture* (New York: Harper & Row, 1951).
5. Pelikan, *The Vindication of Tradition*, 65.
6. *A Latin Dictionary*, eds. Lewis and Short (Oxford: Clarendon Press, 1879), s.v. "trado."
7. See International Theological Commission, *In Search of a Universal Ethic*, nos. 22-23.
8. *Torah.org*, http://torah.org/series/jewish-values/.
9. See International Theological Commission, *In Search of a Universal* Ethic, no. 8. See also Remi Brague, *The Law of God: The Philosophical History of an Idea* (Chicago/London: The University of Chicago Press, 2008), 254.
10. Howard Kainz, "The Two Religions of Islam," *The Catholic Thing* (December 9, 2017), https://www.thecatholicthing.org/2017/12/09/the-two-religions-of-the-koran/.
11. See International Theological Commission, *In Search of a Universal Ethic*, no. 17.
12. *Islamic Information Portal*, http://islam.ru/en/content/story/36-islamic-everyday-virtues.
13. See Livia Kohn, *Cosmos & Community: The Ethical Dimensions of Daoism* (Cambridge, MA: Three Pines Press, 2004), 184.
14. See International Theological Commission, *In Search of a Universal Ethic*, no. 15.
15. Taoist Ethics, http://www.taoism.net/articles/mason/ethics.htm. See also, *Taoist Ethics*, http://www.taoism.net/articles/mason/ethics.htm.
16. International Theological Commission, *In Search of a Universal Ethic*, no. 13.
17. *The Heart of Hinduism*, https://iskconeducationalservices.org/HoH/index.htm.
18. International Theological Commission, *In Search of a Universal Ethic*, no. 14.
19. *The Buddhist Society*, http://www.thebuddhistsociety.org/page/fundamental-teachings.
20. *Buddhist Ethics*, http://www.buddhanet.net/e-learning/budethics.htm.
21. International Theological Commission, *In Search of a Universal Ethic*, no. 12.
22. Ibid., nos. 12-35
23. C. S. Lewis, *The Abolition of Man* (New York: Macmillan, 1947; 10th printing, 1973), 93-121.
24. Richard T. Kinnier, Jerry L. Kernes, and Therese M. Dautheribes, "A Short List of Universal Moral Values," *Counseling and Values* 45 (2000): 1-16.
25. Sir John Templeton, *Discovering the Laws of Life* (New York: Continuum, 1995); Idem,

Worldwide Laws of Life: 200 Eternal Spiritual Principles (Philadelphia & London: Templeton Foundation Press, 1997); Idem, *Agape Love: A Tradition Found in Eight World Religions* (Philadelphia & London: Templeton Foundation Press, 1999); Idem, *Wisdom from World Religions: Pathways toward Heaven on Earth* (Philadelphia & London: Templeton Foundation Press, 2002).

26. *Internet Sacred Archive,* http://www.sacred-texts.com/trad.htm.

CHAPTER SEVENTEEN: A SUGGESTED TEMPLATE

1. Lewis, *The Abolition of Man,* 91.
2. See Jaroslav Pelikan's discussion of tradition in *The Vindication of Tradition,* 65.

CHAPTER EIGHTEEN: LIVING IN THE GAP

1. William Johnston, *Being in Love: A Practical Guide to Christian Prayer* (New York: Fordham University Press, 1999), 147.
2. The phrase "living in the gap" comes from Dennis J. Billy, *Living in the Gap: Religious Life and the Call to Communion* 2d ed (Hyde Park, NY: New City Press, 2014).
3. Servais Pinckaers, *The Sources of Christian Ethics,* trans. Sr. Mary Thomas Noble (Edinburgh: T&T Clark, 1995), 135-39.
4. For a brief discussion of emotivism, see C.S. Lewis, *The Abolition of Man,* 13-35. For a reference to the dictatorship of relativism, see Josef Cardinal Ratzinger, *Homily, Mass "Pro Eligendo Romano Pontifice"* (April 18, 2005), http://www.vatican.va/gpII/documents/homily-pro-eligendo-pontifice_20050418_en.html.
5. See, for example, The International Theological Commission, *In Search of a Universal Ethic,* nos. 12-35; Lewis, The Abolition of Man, 95-121; Richard T. Kinnier, Jerry L. Kernes, and Therese M. Dautheribes. "A Short List of Universal Moral Values." *Counseling and Values* 45 (2000):1-16; Kent M. Keith, "The Universal Moral Code," http://www.universalmoralcode.com.

CONCLUSION

1. Pope John Paul II, *Veritatis splendor,* nos. 92-93.
2. Ibid., no. 92.

Suggested Readings

Part One: Moorings in Spiritual Direction

Barry, William A. *Spiritual Direction and the Encounter With God: A Theological Inquiry.* New York/Mahwah, NJ: Paulist Press, 1992.

Barry, William A. and William J. Connolly. *The Practice of Spiritual Direction.* Minneapolis, MN: The Seabury Press, 1982.

Billy, Dennis J. "From Silence to Silence: The Spiritual Direction Session," Presence 8 (no. 2, 2002): 38-43

_____. "Growing in the Virtues and the Gifts: Spiritual Direction as a Practical Theological Locus for the Convergence of Spirituality and Morality," *Studia moralia* 39 (2001): 433-59.

_____. "The Relations of Spiritual Direction," *Studia moralia* 36 (1998): 67-94.

_____. "Spiritual Direction and the Art of Active Listening," *Seminary Journal* 19 (no. 1, 2013): 22-26.

_____. "Spiritual Direction as 'Faith Seeking Understanding,'" *Seminary Journal* 19 (no. 1, 2013): 27-32.

_____. *What Is Spiritual Direction?* Liguori, MO: Liguori Publications, 2009.

Byrne, Lavinia, ed. *Traditions of Spiritual Guidance.* Collegeville, MN: The Liturgical Press, 1990.

Conroy, Maureen. *The Discerning Heart: Discovering a Personal God.* Chicago: Loyola Press, 1993.

_____. *Looking Into the Well: Supervision of Spiritual Directors.* Chicago: Loyola University Press, 1995.

Culligan, Kevin G. Spiritual Direction: Contemporary Readings. Locust Valley, NY: Living Flame Press, 1983.

Fleming, David L., ed. *The Christian Ministry of Spiritual Direction. The Best of the Review* 3. St. Louis, MO: Review for Religious, 1988.

Frattallone, Raimondo. *Direzione spirituale: Un cammino verso la pienezza della vita in Cristo.* Rome: LAS, 2006.

Gratton, Carolyn. *The Art of Spiritual Guidance.* New York: Crossroad, 2004.

Guenther, Margaret. *Holy Listening: The Art of Spiritual Direction.* Cambridge, MA: Cowley Publications, 1992.

Kaam, Adrian van. *The Dynamics of Spiritual Self Direction.* Denville, NJ: Dimension Books, 1976.

Mendizábal, Luis M. *Direccion spiritual: teoría y práctica.* Madrid: Biblioteca de Autores Cristianos, 1982.

Muto, Susan, and Adrian van Kaam. *Divine Guidance: Seeking to Find and Follow the Will of God.* Middlegreen Slough, UK: St. Pauls, 1994.

Part Two: An Alphonsian Approach to Spiritual Direction

Billy, Dennis J. "An Alphonsian Model of Spiritual Direction," Studia moralia 41 (2003): 47-72.

_____. "Fifteen Qualities of a Spiritual Director," Pastoral Life 39 (no. 10, 1990): 2-9.

_____. *Plentiful Redemption: An Introduction to Alphonsian Spirituality.* Liguori, MO: Liguori Publications, 2001.

_____. *Simple, Heartfelt Words: Preaching in the Alphonsian Tradition.* Liguori, MO: Liguori Publications, 2006.

_____. *With Open Heart: Spiritual Direction in the Alphonsian Tradition.* Liguori, MO: Liguori Publications, 2003.

Grimm, Eugene, ed. *The Complete Works of Alphonsus de Liguori.* 22 vols. New York: Redemptorist Fathers, 1886-94; reprint ed. 1926-27.

Hoegerl, Carl, ed. *Heart Calls to Heart: An Alphonsian Anthology.* Rome: Collegio Sant'Alfonso, 1981.

Jones, Frederick M. *Alphonsus de Liguori: The Saint of Bourbon Naples, 1696-1787.* Liguori, MO.: Liguori Publications, 1999.

_____, ed. *Alphonsus de Liguori: Selected Writings. The Classics of Western Spirituality.* New York/Mahwah, NJ: Paulist Press, 1999.

Liguori, Alphonsus de. *Talking with God: Four Treatises on the Interior Life from St. Alphonsus Liguori.* Mesa, AZ: Scriptoria Books, 2011.

_____. *The Glories of Mary. A New Translation from the Italian.* Liguori, MO: Liguori Publications, 2000.

_____. *Guide for Confessors.* From the *Praxis Confessarii.* Edited by Richard Schiblin. Esopus, NY: Matthew. St. Alphonsus, 1978.

_____. *Opere ascetiche,* Editio Critica, 11 volumes, Rome: Sant'Alfonso, 1933-.

_____. *The Practice of the Love of Jesus Christ.* Translated by Peter Heinegg. Liguori, MO: Liguori Publications, 1997.

_____. *Theologia Moralis. Moral Theology.* Translated by Ryan Grant. Vol. 1, Bks. 1-3. Post Falls ID: Mediatrix Press, 2017.

———, *Visits to the Most Holy Sacrament and to Most Holy Mary*. Notre Dame, IN: Ave Maria Press, 2007.

Muckerman, Norman J. *From the Heart of St. Alphonsus: Favorite Devotions from the Doctor of Prayer*. Liguori, MO: Liguori Publications, 2002.

Oppitz, Joseph W. *Alphonsian History and Spirituality: A Study of the Spirit of the Founder, Saint Alphonsus M. Liguori and of the Missionary Institute, The Congregation of the Most Holy Redeemer*. Rome: Sant'Alfonso, 1978.

———, ed. *Alphonsus Liguori: The Redeeming Love of Christ—Selected Writings*. Hyde Park, NY: New City Press, 1992.

Rey-Mermet, Théodule. *Moral Choices: The Moral Theology of Saint Alphonsus Liguori*. Traslated by Paul Laverdure. Liguori, MO: Liguori Publications, 1998.

———. *St. Alphonsus Liguori: Tireless Worker for the Most Abandoned*. Translated by Jehanne-Marie Marchesi. Brooklyn, NY: New City Press, 1987.

Swanston, Hamish F. G. *Celebrating Eternity Now: A Study in the Theology of St. Alphonsus de Liguori*. Liguori, MO: Liguori Publications, 1995.

Wales, Sean and Dennis Billy, eds. *Lexicon of Redemptorist Spirituality*. Rome: The General Secretariat for Redemptorist Spirituality, 2011.

Part Three: Spiritual Direction and the Moral Life

Aquinas, Thomas. *Summa Theologiae*, I-II, qq. 62, 68-70; II-II, qq. 1-46. Internet: http://www.newadvent.org/summa/.

Ashley, Benedict M. *Living the Truth in Love: A Biblical Introduction to Moral Theology*. New York: Alba House, 1996.

———. *Theology of the Bodies: Humanist and Christian*. Braintree, MA: The Pope John Center, 1985.

Billy, Dennis J. "The Silent Reader: Prayer as the Source of the Moral Life." *Studia moralia* 56 (2018):103-21.

Billy, Dennis J. and Donna Orsuto, eds. *Spirituality and Morality: Integrating Prayer and Action*. New York/Mahwah, NJ: Paulist Press, 1996.

Cameron, John Peter. *The Gifts of the Holy Spirit According to St. Thomas Aquinas*, New Haven, CT: Catholic Information Service, 2002.

Cessario, Romansanus. *The Moral Virtues and Theological Ethics*. Notre Dame, IN/London: University of Notre Dame Press, 1991.

———. *The Virtues or The Examined Life*. London/New York: Continuum, 2002.

Collins, Pat. *Intimacy and the Hungers of the Heart*. Dublin: The Columba Press, 1991.

Crossin, John W. *Walking in Virtue: Moral Decisions and Spiritual Growth in Daily Life*. New York/Mahwah, NJ: Paulist Press, 1998.

Curran, Charles E. and Lisa A. Fullam. *Virtue. Readings in Moral Theology No. 16*. New York/Mahwah, NJ: Paulist Press, 2011.

Donovan, Jean. *The Seven Virtues: An Introduction to Catholic Life*. New York: Crossroad, 2007.

Garrigou-Lagrange, Reginald. *The Three Ages of the Interior Life*. Transated by M. Timothea Doyle. 2 vols. London, UK: Catholic Way Publishing, 2013.

Groeschel, Benedict. *The Virtue-Driven Life*. Huntington, IN: Our Sunday Visitor, 2006.

Gula, Richard M. *The Call to Holiness: Embracing a Fully Christian Life*. New York/Mahwah, NJ: Paulist Press, 2003.

_____. *The Good Life: Where Morality and Spirituality Converge*. New York/Mahwah, NJ: Paulist Press, 1999.

Harak, G. Simon. *Virtuous Passions: The Formation of Christian Character*. New York/Mahwah, NJ: Paulist Press, 1993.

Kotva, Joseph J, Jr. *The Christian Case for Virtue Ethics*. Washington, D.C.: Georgetown University Press, 1996.

MacIntyre, Alasdair. *After Virtue: A Study in Moral Theory*. 2d ed. London: Duckworth, 1985.

Mattison, William C., III. *Introducing Moral Theology: True Happiness and the Virtues*. Grand Rapids, MI: Brazos Press, 2008.

Nault, Joan-Charles. *The Noonday Devil: Acedia, the Unnamed Evil of Our Times*. Translated by Michael J. Miller. San Francisco: Ignatius Press, 2013.

O'Keefe, Mark. *Becoming Good, Becoming Holy: On the Relationship between Christian Ethics and Spirituality*. New York/Mahwah, NJ: Paulist Press, 1995.

O'Shaughnessy, Mary Michael. *Feelings and Emotions in Christian Living*. Staten Island, NY: Alba House, 1988.

Pieper, Josef. *A Brief Reader on the Virtues of the Human Heart*. Translated by Paul C. Duggan. San Francisco: Ignatius Press, 1991.

_____. *Faith, Hope, Love*. Translated by Richard and Cara Winston, and Sr. Mary Frances McCarthy. San Francisco: Ignatius Press, 1997 reprint.

Pinckaers, Servais. *The Sources of Christian Ethics*. Washington, DC: The Catholic University of America Press, 1995.

Pontifical Biblical Commission. *The Bible and Morality: Biblical Roots of Christian Conduct* (2008). Internet: http://www.vatican.va/roman_curia/congregations/cfaith/pcb_documents/rc_con_cfaith_doc_20080511_bibbia-e-morale_en.html.

Porter, Jean. *The Recovery of Virtue: The Relevance of Aquinas for Christian Ethics*. Louisville, KY: Westminster: John Knox Press, 1990.

Ratzinger, Josef (Pope Benedict XVI). *The Yes of Jesus Christ: Spiritual Exercises in Faith, Hope, and Love*. Translated by Robert Nowell. New York: Crossroad, 2014.

Rausch, Thomas P. *Faith, Hope, and Charity: Benedict XVI on the Theological Virtues.* Mauwah, NJ: Paulist Press, 2015.

Russell, Daniel C., ed. *The Cambridge Companion to Virtue Ethics.* Cambridge, England: Cambridge University Press, 2013.

Shelton, Charles M. *Morality of the Heart: A Psychology for the Christian Moral Life.* New York: Crossroad, 1990.

Vacek, Edward Collins. *Love, Human and Divine: The Heart of Christian Ethics.* Washington, DC: Georgetown University Press, 1994.

Vost, Kevin. *The Seven Deadly Sins: A Thomistic Guide to Vanquishing Vice and Sin.* Manchester, NH: Sophia Institute Press, 2015.

Wadell, Paul J. *Friends of God: Virtues and Gifts in Aquinas.* New York: Peter Lang, 1981.

———. *The Primacy of Love: An Introduction to the Ethics of Thomas Aquinas.* New York/Mahwah, NJ: Paulist Press, 1992.

Part Four: Dialoguing with Other Traditions

Berkman John and William C. Mattison III, eds. *Searching for a Universal Ethic: Multidisciplinary, Ecumenical, and Interfaith Responses to the Catholic Natural Law Tradition.* Grand Rapids, MI/Cambridge, UK: William B. Eerdmans, 2014.

Brague, Remi. *The Law of God: The Philosophical History of an Idea.* Chicago/London: The University of Chicago Press, 2008.

Happold, F. C. *Mysticism: A Study and an Anthology.* New York: Penguin Books, 1963.

Human Rights Research Center. *Declaration of Human Rights* (1948), Abbreviated Version, ed. Nancy Flowers. Internet: http://hrlibrary.umn.edu/edumat/hreduseries/hereandnow/Part-5/8_udhr-abbr.htm.

International Theological Commission. *The Search of a Universal Ethic: A New Look at the Natural* Law (2009). Internet: http://www.vatican.va/roman_curia/congregations/cfaith/cti_documents/rc_con_cfaith_doc_20090520_legge-naturale_en.html.

Johnston, William. *Arise, My Love…Mysticism for a New Era.* Maryknoll, NY: Orbis Books, 2000.

———. *Being in Love: A Practical Guide to Christian Prayer.* New York: Fordham University Press, 1999.

———. *Mystical Theology: The Science of Love.* London: HarperCollins, 1995.

———. *The Mystical Way.* London: HarperCollins, 1993.

Keating, Thomas. "Guidelines for Interreligious Understanding: Points of Agreement or Similarity." In *Sourcebook for Earth's Community of Religions.* Edited by Joel Beversluis. Grand Rapids, MI: CoNexus Press, 1995.

———. "Guidelines for Interreligious Understanding." Chapter in *Speaking of Silence: Christians and Buddhists on the Contemplative Way.* Edited by Susan Walker (New York: Paulist Press, 1987).

Keith, Kent M. "The Universal Moral Code." (2017). Internet: http://www.universalmoralcode.com.

Kinnier, Richard T., Jerry L. Kernes, and Therese M. Dautheribes. "A Short List of Universal Moral Values." *Counseling and Values* 45 (2000): 1-16.

Lewis, C.S. *The Abolition of Man*. New York: Macmillan, 1947.

Niebuhr, H. Richard. *Christ and Culture*. New York: Harper & Row, 1951.

Nusseibeh, Sari. *The Story of Reason in Islam*. Redwood City, CA: Stanford University Press, 2016.

Pelikan, Jaroslav. *The Vindication of Tradition*. New Haven/London: Yale University Press, 1984.

Principe, Walter. "Toward Defining Spirituality." *Studies in Religion/Sciences religieuses* 12 (1983): 127-41.

Rolheiser, Ronald. *The Holy Longing: The Search for a Christian Spirituality*. New York: Doubleday, 1999.

Teasdale, Wayne. *The Mystic Heart: Discovering a Universal Spirituality in the World's Religion*. Novata, CA: New World Library, 1999.

Templeton, Sir John, *Agape Love: A Tradition Found in Eight World Religions*. Philadelphia & London: Templeton Foundation Press, 1999.

———. *Discovering the Laws of Life*. New York: Continuum, 1995.

———. *Wisdom From World Religions: Pathways Toward Heaven on Earth*. Philadelphia & London: Templeton Foundation Press, 2002.

———. *Worldwide Laws of Life: 200 Eternal Spiritual Principles*. Philadelphia & London: Templeton Foundation Press, 1997.

Underhill, Evelyn. *Mysticism: A Study on the Nature and Development of Man's Spiritual Consciousness*. New York: New American Library, 1955.

United Nations. *Declaration of Human Rights*. (1948). Internet: http://www.un.org/en/universal-declaration-human-rights/.

Wainwright, Geoffrey. "Types of Spirituality." Chapter in *The Study of Spirituality*. Edited by Chesyln Jones, Geoffrey Wainwright, Edward Yarnold. London: SPCK, 1986, 1992. 592-605.

Woods, Richard, ed. *Understanding Mysticism: Its Meaning, Its Methodology, Interpretation in Word Religions, Psychological Evaluations, Philosophical and Theological Appraisals*. Garden City, NY: Image Books, 1980.

About the Author

Dennis J. Billy, CSsR, is professor emeritus of the history of moral theology and Christian spirituality at the Alphonsian Academy of Rome's Pontifical Lateran University, and currently serves as the Karl Rahner Professor of Catholic Theology at the Graduate Theological Foundation in Mishawaka, Indiana. An American Redemptorist of the Baltimore Province, Fr. Billy has advanced degrees from Harvard University, the Pontifical University of St. Thomas (Angelicum), and the Graduate Theological Foundation. The author of numerous books and articles on a variety of religious topics, he is also very active in his order's retreat apostolate and in the ministry of spiritual direction.

www.ingramcontent.com/pod-product-compliance
Lightning Source LLC
Chambersburg PA
CBHW031725230426
43669CB00007B/243